Hong Kong's Second Return to China

Jennifer Eagleton

Hong Kong's Second Return to China

A Critical Discourse Study of the National Security Law and its Aftermath

palgrave
macmillan

Jennifer Eagleton
University of Hong Kong
Hong Kong, Hong Kong

ISBN 978-3-031-84586-4 ISBN 978-3-031-84587-1 (eBook)
https://doi.org/10.1007/978-3-031-84587-1

Cover illustration: Getty Images / CHUNYIP WONG

This Palgrave Macmillan imprint is published by the registered company Springer Nature Switzerland AG.
The registered company address is: Gewerbestrasse 11, 6330 Cham, Switzerland

To the people of Hong Kong, a place I have lived for over two decades, a place I have grown to love and cherish. 加油!

A List of Frequently Referred to Texts

These texts will be referred to in most chapters. They will be listed here instead of at the end of each chapter.

Joint Declaration of the Government of the United Kingdom of Great Britain and Northern Ireland and the Government of the People's Republic of China on the Question of Hong Kong – The three annexes and memoranda.

https://www.cmab.gov.hk/en/issues/joint3.htm

The Basic Law of the Hong Kong Special Administrative Region of the People's Republic of China

https://www.basiclaw.gov.hk/filemanager/content/en/files/basiclaw-text/basiclaw_full_text.pdf

The Law of the People's Republic of China on Safeguarding National Security in the Hong Kong Special Administrative Region (NSL) https://www.gld.gov.hk/egazette/pdf/20202448e/egn2020244872.pdf

Safeguarding National Security Ordinance (Article 23)

https://www.gld.gov.hk/egazette/pdf/20242812e/es1202428126.pdf

The International Covenant on Civil and Political Rights (ICCPR)

https://www.ohchr.org/sites/default/files/ccpr.pdf

The International Covenant on Economic, Social and Political Rights (ICESP)

https://www.ohchr.org/sites/default/files/cescr.pdf

Contents

About the Author

Jennifer Eagleton A Hong Kong resident since October 1997, Jennifer Eagleton is a close observer of Hong Kong society and politics. After degrees in Chinese, Asian studies, and applied linguistics, she received a PhD from Macquarie University in Sydney on the discourse of democratization in post-handover Hong Kong focusing on metaphor. Jennifer has worked on bilingual dictionaries at the Chinese University of Hong Kong, taught communication at Hong Kong University, and tutored in stylistics and discourse analysis at Hong Kong Metropolitan University. Apart from non-fiction writings on Hong Kong, Jennifer also has composed poems, reviews, and essays for Asian-focused publications such as *Verse & Voice, Cha: An Asian Literary Journal*, and *The Mekong Review*.

List of Figures

1

Introduction: The "Second Return"

Hong Kong's "first return" occurred on 1st July 1997 when Hong Kong officially became a part of China after over 150 years of British colonialisation. The "second return" occurred with the introduction of the National Security Law, in which many significant changes were made in the running of the Hong Kong Special Administrative Region of China (HKSAR). This book is a critical analytical discourse study of the aftermath of the introduction of the National Security Law, a discussion on the Law itself, on the social system, education, and other aspects of life in Hong Kong. The term "second return" was coined to indicate the massive change that the Chinese authorities thought Hong Kong needed. In this chapter there is a retelling of the history of the lead up to Hong Kong's "first return" as many of the themes and issues in this book are better and more completely understood by looking at the historical background of the region and its transition. This chapter will also detail the linguistic approach used to analyse and interpret texts used in the book and conclude with a brief rundown of other chapters of the book.

J. Eagleton, *Hong Kong's Second Return to China*,
https://doi.org/10.1007/978-3-031-84587-1_1

The Need for a "Second Return"

Zhang Xiaoming, deputy director of the Hong Kong and Macao Affairs Office of the State Council delivered a keynote address at a webinar on the thirtieth anniversary of the promulgation of the Basic Law on June 8, 2020 (Pepper 2020; Zhang 2020). Zhang was the first senior Mainland official to publicly acknowledge that the root cause of Hong Kong's unrest was political, rather than economic. In his view, Hong Kong's major problem was not the city's unaffordable housing or youth employment prospects, or social mobility, which had been a common refrain over the years. The main problem, he posited, was political, and concerned the basic question of *what kind of place Hong Kong should become*. Zhang's speech revolved around four questions:

(1) Why was "one-country, two-systems" established for Hong Kong in the first place?
(2) Why was the national government now taking the initiative to introduce a national security law for Hong Kong?
(3) Why was Beijing repeatedly insisting that "only a very few people" would be targeted by the new law?
(4) How could this initiative from the central government be viewed as a turn for the better?

The answer to the first question is that the "One-Country, Two-Systems" framework was adopted in the 1980s, and was about transferring sovereignty, maintaining prosperity, and amicably discussing with Britain how to maintain stability before the 1997 handover. The "One Country, Two Systems" principle under which Hong Kong is governed, arose out of an idea originally proposed by Deng Xiaoping, then paramount leader of the People's Republic of China (PRC), for the reunification of China during the 1970s, primarily with Taiwan in mind (to take into account the "historical realities" of vastly different political and social systems). Later, he extended the concept to Hong Kong when it was likely to be given back to China. He suggested that there would be only one China, but areas such as Hong Kong, Macau, and Taiwan could have their own capitalist economic and political systems, while the rest of

China would use the socialist system. Under this idea, these places could continue to have their own political system, legal, military, economic, and financial affairs, including commercial and cultural agreements with foreign countries, and would enjoy certain rights in foreign affairs as well as enjoy executive, legislative, and judicial power, continuing to take pleasure in "horseracing and dancing" all the while being an "inalienable part of China".

Secondly, why was the new law necessary? Zhang said that internal and external enemy forces had been stirring up trouble for a long period, thereby threatening national security. Things took a turn for the worse starting in June 2019 with the escalation of the anti-extradition law protests. There was violence, public transport disruptions, train stations vandalised, the airport was occupied, a man was set on fire, and even Molotov cocktails were thrown—all the manifestations of terrorism according to Zhang (Zhang 2020; see also Chap. 8 in Eagleton 2022). He did not mention the many peaceful protests that had also occurred over the period. He stated that some organisations and individuals were advocating Hong Kong independence and self-determination, desecrating the national flag, and defacing national symbols, attacking the Central Government's Hong Kong Liaison Office and Hong Kong's Legislative Council building (the latter incident took place on 1st July 2019).

According to Zhang, "foreign and Taiwan forces" also joined in, fanning the flames, encouraging the opposition and activists with funds and equipment, support, and protection. The United States passed a *Hong Kong Human Rights and Democracy Act* (US Gov. 2019) "directly institutionalizing and normalizing its intervention in Hong Kong in the form of domestic law. These activities not only seriously endangered Hong Kong's social stability, economic prosperity and public security, but also broke through the bottom line of 'one country, two systems'" (p. 9). These acts were considered against the original purpose of "One Country, Two Systems". If Hong Kong had dealt with the problem itself, that is institute Article 23 of Hong Kong's mini-constitution the Basic Law as required, Beijing would not have needed to intervene.

For the third question, Zhang was not clear about why Beijing felt the need to repeat that only "very few" people would be targeted by its new national security legislation, cryptically saying, "Reason is the light when you are confused and a sobering agent when you are impulsive. Only by thinking rationally can we avoid being confused by all kinds of specious and even confusing views, and not be incited by all kinds of alarmist remarks or even rumors" (理性是迷茫時的光亮，是衝動時的清醒劑。做到理性思考，才能不被各種似是而非甚至顛倒是非的觀點所迷惑，不被各種危言聳聽的言論甚至謠言所煽惑." (ibid., 13). He did not explain who among Hong Kong's political actors were likely to be targeted as secessionists, subversives, terrorists, or colluders under the new law. He did not mention that a record number of voters had turned out for 24 November's District Council election, nor did he mention that a record number of those voters favoured candidates who endorsed, without reservation, the protest movement (PORI 2019).

Zhang's fourth question was, in effect, how could anyone doubt that this new law would make things better: "Think dialectically. Why don't you regard this central government's move as a turning point for Hong Kong to bring order to things and get out of its predicament?" (第四，辯證思維，想一想為甚麼不把這次中央出手視為香港撥亂反正、走出困境的轉機?) (p. 17). According to Zhang, Hong Kong's pro-democracy opposition and its foreign backers were trying to turn Hong Kong into an independent or semi-independent political entity, to become an anti-China anti-communist bridgehead. That was why Beijing said Hong Kong had become a national security risk, aimed at changing the nature of Communist Party rule in China. This was laying waste to the Hong Kong project, producing too much politics and populism. National security was thus neglected, and national education resisted. Even examination questions for students were distorted.[1]

Zhang saw a larger purpose in the anti-China, anti-communist messaging from some quarters in Hong Kong. It was not just to create chaos in Hong Kong and subvert its political order. The real aim, he reiterated, was to overthrow China's Communist Party leadership and subvert its political system. People even openly published articles to this effect (likely referring to articles in the now defunct *Apple Daily*). Beyond such

[1] This last point referred to a recent controversy over the citywide secondary school graduation assessment examinations. Students were given a kind of trick question designed to test both their knowledge of Japan's aggression in China before and during World War II, as well as their ability to assess media accounts describing both positive and negative aspects of that period (Chan 2020).

concerns about the fate of China's communist revolution, Zhang, said Hongkongers should be able to walk the streets freely and travel on public transport and go shopping "without fear". Young people should not be "brainwashed" into breaking the law and everyone should be able to speak their minds in public without being attacked. For all this, there is a need for a "second return" (Italics added):

> .... based on a period of 50 years, the practice of "One Country, Two Systems" has entered the mid-term. As an unprecedented initiative, its success has been recorded in history. In particular, the smooth handover, smooth transition, unchanged system, high degree of autonomy, freedom and openness, and rapid recovery from the impact of the international financial crisis twice have exceeded many people's predictions. However, just like any new thing, in the process of exploring and advancing the practice of "One Country, Two Systems" it has also encountered some roadblocks, encountered some challenges, and revealed some problems, including the limitations of the top-level system design and the shortcomings of actual work. There is little worthy of our reflection and improvement. In particular, problems in governance and public support are so prominent that internationally renowned scholars such as Professor Zheng Yongnian from the Institute of East Asian Studies at the National University of Singapore have put forward a new proposition, that is, *Hong Kong needs a "second return"*. (Zhang 2020, 17)

In Zhang's words, the new National Security Law was something that would quickly resolve the issues he had raised. He also drew upon the metaphor of contagion. He likened Hong Kong's disorder to a political virus (italics added): "With this legislation, the practice of 'one country, two systems' in Hong Kong will be equipped with *anti-virus software*, and it will surely run safer, smoother, and longer!" (有了這部立法 '一國兩制'在香港的實踐就裝上了殺毒軟件，必定會運行得更安全、更順暢、更持久!)" (Zhang 2020, 23).

Looking back to the lead up to the "first return" will give us some idea about the present and also some speculation about the discourse of the HKSAR's future as Faulkner once said, "The past is never dead. In fact, it isn't even past" (Faulkner 1960, Act I Scene III) as how historically the "One Country, Two Systems" was formulated led to the issues inherent in the "first return".

Before the First Return

Historical "problems" were often cited or indirectly referred to in official documents relating to Hong Kong and its governance (italics added):

> The Government of the United Kingdom of Great Britain and Northern Ireland and the Government of the People's Republic of China have reviewed with satisfaction the friendly relations existing between the two Governments and peoples in recent years and agreed that a proper negotiated settlement of the question of Hong Kong, which is *left over from the past*, is conducive to the maintenance of the *prosperity and stability of Hong Kong* and to the further strengthening and development of the relations between the two countries on a new basis. (First paragraph of the Sino-British Joint Declaration, 1984)
>
> Hong Kong has been part of the territory of China since ancient times; it was occupied by Britain after the Opium War in 1840…Upholding national unity and *territorial integrity*, maintaining the *prosperity and stability* of Hong Kong, and taking account of its history and realities…. China's resumption of the exercise of sovereignty over Hong Kong, a Hong Kong Special Administrative Region will be established…
>
> (Preamble to the Basic Law (formally promulgated 4 April 1990 but came into effect 1 July 1997)

In these documents, issued decades apart, the "problem" and "history and its realities" referred to is the annexing of Hong Kong in the mid-1800s by Great Britain, long considered a "humiliation to the Chinese people". In fact, Hong Kong has been "written into Chinese national history as a sign of humiliation" (Callahan 2004, 212) at a time when China was neither stable nor prosperous but rather viewed as the "sick man of Asia" (東亞病夫). This subsequently gave rise to "a discourse of national humiliation", one that involves an active notion of history and recovery. For example, the film *The Opium War* (1997), one of the most expensive made by a Chinese studio, was released to coincide with the return of Hong Kong to China. The anguish over the Opium War is still vivid and has shaped the modern Chinese psyche (Lovell

2011). The concept of "national humiliation" has never really gone away even as the modern Chinese economy flourishes (Zhai 2010). This discourse of national humiliation forms a collective narrative model that becomes a template for later experience of all kinds—serving as a "root metaphor" of containment (Bruner 1990, 51), particularly in the case of foreign affairs. Such statements, written at the beginning of these texts, signal possible ways certain issues may be discursively and politically handled in the future, as regard to issues that possibly call into question China's sovereignty, prosperity, and stability. Therefore, the historical "baggage" of separation and sovereignty has always played a large part of the background to Hong Kong's socio-political situation since Hong Kong had its own "system" but is also part of "one country" being "sacred holy land on sacred Chinese soil" (香港這塊神聖的中國土地聖的中國土地) (Ta Kung Pao 2004).

Historical matters determine social change; the past influences the present and so the future. Foucault argued that studying history is a way of working out the present use of space and time, rather than simply seeing how the present has emerged from the past (Foucault 1972). The debate about Hong Kong's transition draws on a number of historical "sensitivities" such as *colonialism* (hegemonic usurpation of power over one state by another), communism (ownership by the state for the people as a whole), the *Confucian-Western dichotomy* (harmony/consensus in society vs. the pursuit of individualistic goals) and *capitalist-materialist culture* (competition/survival of the fittest) (Xu 1999). These sensitivities emerged at various stages of Hong Kong's "returns" as well as the aftermath of the introduction of the National Security law.

The Basic Law and its antecedent, the Joint Declaration can be seen as framers and central texts of any future discourse about Hong Kong's political system. Hong Kong was considered a "long-term lease" taken out by the British and its "handing back" the expiration of that lease. There was an actual lease, for 99 years on the area known as the New Territories which was negotiated between the United Kingdom and the Guangxu Emperor of China under the Second Convention of Peking

(1898). This lease was due to expire in 1997 and it was this expiration that concerned those who held land and property.

The Chinese Government had always taken the position that the whole of Hong Kong was Chinese territory; After China took Taiwan's seat at the United Nations in 1971, it requested the relevant UN Committee to remove Hong Kong from its decolonisation agenda as "Its position for many years was that the question of Hong Kong came into the category of unequal treaties left over from history; that it should be settled peacefully through negotiations when conditions were ripe" (paragraph 4, Draft Agreement, 1984). So, from this time onwards, the "question" of Hong Kong began to take purchase in people's minds, particularly in the late 1970s as the lease's expiration came nearer. When the need to "remove the uncertainty" about the 1997 deadline arose, discussions on Hong Kong's future began. Hong Kong then became a "borrowed place, borrowed time" (famously coined in the book title by Richard Hughes published in 1976).

Both Britain and China had "the common aim of maintaining the stability and prosperity of Hong Kong" (paragraph 8, Draft Agreement 1984), according to British Prime Minister Margaret Thatcher when she met Chairman Deng Xiaoping in Beijing on 24 September 1982 to open discussions. Communist China had benefited economically from free, capitalist, and prosperous Hong Kong as means for contact with the outside world, and as a source of finance and trade and wanted it remain this way (Shenzhen Special Economic Zone was established in August 1980 provided a partial challenge to this). For Britain's part, it wanted to maintain good trading links with China and leave on good terms with the Hong Kong public. Hong Kong's relinquishment was really an economic matter.

At the start of formal negotiations, Britain "explained in detail the systems prevailing in Hong Kong and the importance for these systems of the British administrative role and link" (paragraph 10, Draft Agreement 1984). It tried to make the case that Hong Kong was successful and prosperous because of its difference from China, the respective (and incompatible) systems co-existing because of its colonial status, and the presence of the British in running these systems. Following extensive discussion, however, it became clear that the continuation of British administration after 1997 was unacceptable to China in any form (that is, sovereignty in exchange for the right to rule. To the Chinese, this would be like colonialism by another name and would imply that China was unable to administer Hong Kong successfully by itself. For, as Deng Xiaoping said to Margaret Thatcher, this would make the "present Chinese government like the government of the late Qing dynasty and that the present Chinese leaders just like Li Hongzhang!" (a famous traitor) (Deng 1982).

However, if other "arrangements acceptable to the Hong Kong people" were found, Britain would acquiesce to China's demands for "full sovereignty". In other words, the colonial "buffer" would be removed. In its place Britain desired to replace this "buffer" with a legally binding promise that would largely keep in place its existing systems:

> …Examining with the Chinese how it might be possible to arrive at arrangements that would secure for Hong Kong a high degree of autonomy under Chinese sovereignty, and that would preserve the way of life in Hong Kong, together with the essentials of the present systems. (Wesley-Smith 1996, 106)

Such a metaphorical buffer ("a high degree of autonomy") would also suit the Chinese authorities. Talks then centred on Deng Xiaoping's principle of "One Country, Two Systems". Deng saw this principle as resolving the contradictions inherent in uniting such different places (Deng 2004). The application of this principle would allow the capitalist system to operate in Hong Kong but not contaminate the mainland's socialist system, provide an exemplar for reunification with Taiwan, and grant an economic "catch-up" period for China as it pursued marketisation under "socialism with Chinese characteristics" (Ibid.). Economics was thus "one of the main pillars" of this system (Xiao 2001, 391) and the basis for further negotiations. To get around the incongruity of "grafting" Hong Kong's systems into the socialist state, the possibility of establishing a Special Administrative Region "when necessary" was then added to the Chinese constitution.

When the Declaration was formally signed in December 1984, many saw it in different ways: a product of "dialectic Marxism and historical materialism" (Loh 2010, 124–143); "ingenious idea" (Carroll 2007,

181), and as "comprehensive protection" (Cradock 1994, 209) by Deng Xiaoping, Prime Minister Margaret Thatcher, and Percy Cradock, British Ambassador to China, respectively. In other words, it was the best that could be done under the circumstances, and it was presented to the public as a "take-it-or-leave-it" agreement, which greatly influenced how Hong Kong people regarded it. They had no choice but to "take it". In other words, the Joint Declaration was seen as an expedient way of achieving a strategic objective.

The Strategy of Negotiation and Its Realisation

Despite Britain feeling that it had largely achieved its objective (protection and maintenance of Hong Kong's systems) China's negotiation strategy was largely instrumental in shaping the final text of the Joint Declaration (Cottrell 1993; Bonavia 1985) which was the preliminary framework for the subsequent Basic Law of Hong Kong.

The main principle that China insisted before negotiations started was that Britain had to admit that Hong Kong belonged to China; Britain could not then logically argue that sovereignty and administration could be separated. Accepting this "principle", the Chinese could deduce other details by their own logic, putting the other side on the defensive. Concessions could then be extracted easily if the other side wants an agreement badly enough. This caused the British to believe that China was determined to take back Hong Kong at any cost, even as a "wasteland" (Cottrell 1993, 128). By instituting a firm deadline (September 1984), and saying that if this not kept, China would announce the terms of Hong Kong's constitution itself. This deadline was never questioned by the British.

One scholar saw these negotiations in terms of "game theory" (Ma 1997) and how the "game" was played out according to concurrent events which ultimately affected the resulting text. The negotiations can also be seen in terms of the discursive strategy of "strategic ambiguity" (Eisenberg 1984; Eisenberg and Goodall 1997). China's negotiation style was to emphasise general principles and the objective for using this style was so that details could be specifically realised according to changing situations.

The name of the document, its initial framing of the "One Country, Two Systems" principle (the phrase never actually appears in the document), the basic principles for governing Hong Kong and the tenets of continuity and preservation are all ambiguous. The actual Joint Declaration is 1166 words long, and with the annexes, makes up around 6000-odd words.[2] The former (and shorter) document is what the Chinese wanted and the latter is what the British "needed" (Loh 2010, 142). British diplomat and sinologist, David Wilson said stated "We [the British] wanted to write a book—which would have looked like the *Encyclopaedia Britannica*—while the Chinese wanted around 2–3 sides of A4 paper" (David Wilson cited in Blyth and Wotherspoon 1996, 79), this is somewhat ironic yet as Britain famously has no written constitution but mere a constitutional arrangement between Crown, Parliament and the Judiciary. These comments by Wilson mirror the typical differences in legislation between the two systems; the British following the common law system while the Chinese followed the civil law system. Under a civil law system, laws are "underspecified and written in the form of general principles" (Bhatia et al. 2008, 136; Cao 2004) leaving the interpretation to other bodies.

A Declaration, a Treaty, or a Series of Parallel Statements

China first resisted the idea of a treaty, wanting to record the understanding of the different sides as "parallel statements" (Ghai 1999, 53). Given the differences of views on the historical question of sovereignty, both sides wanted to state their own position, but that when the parties agreed, this would be stated in a common declaration (Ibid.). The title of the Sino-Joint Declaration creates uncertainty about the document's status. The term "joint declaration" (聯合聲明) seems to have no set definition in Chinese or English law or language (Henderson 1995; Foster 1998). Although the Chinese and English both agreed to use this term, their

[2] The Chinese Government website just has the Joint Declaration with no accompanying annexes. See their website: https://www.chinadaily.com.cn/china/HK15th/2007-06/20/content_15483595.htm

understandings of it diverged widely. The British regarded this as a binding international treaty and stated in the White Paper that accompanied it. The Chinese side in contrast, contrast consciously avoided the use of words like “treaty”, “convention” or “international agreement” which the British used that might suggest that they approved of the British position. Others thought it did not matter what the document was called as it was “equally binding”. Since China had seen the treaties ceding Hong Kong, Kowloon, and the New Territories as “unequal” and therefore “invalid”, there was no need for the Chinese to reach an agreement with Britain on the return of sovereignty in the first place.

The Chinese could view the Joint Declaration as “‘a domestic agreement’ that [the PRC] can unilaterally override” if need be (Henderson 1995; Foster 1998).[3] Moreover, once China exercised its sovereignty, it did not need the British to agree with its policies. The Chinese could then regard the Joint Declaration as a “transitional” document that would end on 1 July 1997 when the Basic Law, a domestic law, would come into force. In a joint declaration, both parties only declared that had to be done, without necessarily setting out clearly their rights and obligations.

The “buffer” of achieving a quasi “status quo” post-1997, which is what Britain wanted to instil confidence in Hong Kong and which the mainland also wanted to maintain stability and prosperity but without the humiliating “colonial content” (Xiao 2001, 237) resulted in the Declaration having four provisos on “no changes” (such as no changes to the existing social and economic systems); four on “maintenance” (such as the maintenance of its status as a free port and as a separate customs

[3] The Central Authorities now see the Sino-British Joint Declaration as a superseded document. This kind of thinking appears in textbooks after the introduction of the National Security Law. However, according to prominent Hong Kong barrister Gladys Li: “The Basic law does not supersede the Joint Declaration which is a treaty, Unfortunately the enforcement of it is not in the hands of the Hong Kong people but in the hand of the UK and they have been pretty supine until recently. The Joint Declaration is also used as an interpretative tool when construing the Basic Law in the courts so no way is it a ‘spent’ document.”—private email correspondence 17 January 2020. Regarding the UK issuing British Overseas National Passports after the NSL: “A correct comprehension of the Sino-British Joint Declaration (Joint Declaration) will allow one to understand that there is no single clause which provides for British rights or obligations to Hong Kong after the city’s reunification with the Motherland.” https://www.doj.gov.hk/en/community_engagement/sj_blog/20210130_blog1.html

territory); and two on "continuity" (for foreign exchange, gold, securities, and futures and the Hong Kong dollar will continue to circulate and remain freely convertible), actual Joint Declaration while in Annex I there are ten provisos on "maintenance", nine on "preservation" and seven that the SAR can make decisions on its own on a series of issues. Furthermore, "The HKSAR will be vested with executive, legislative and independent judicial power, including that of final adjudication. However, the laws currently in force in Hong Kong would remain *basically unchanged*" (italics added). "Basically unchanged" could be taken to mean some change.

Signalling the democratic road ahead, "elections" acted as a confidence booster in the future of Hong Kong in the drafting of the Basic Law. However, the ambiguity existing in specific provisions of the Joint Declaration left "creative room" for the Basic Law drafters while still allowing them to stay within its "broad contours", with which the new document had to "converge". The drafting of the Basic Law, being a domestic law of the People's Republic of China, would be largely in China's hands. In sum, the Joint Declaration was considered "site formation" work, preparation for the final construction of the "One Country, Two Systems":

> The draft agreement is like site formation work, has prepared the way for a well-constructed future. But it is only when work commences on the infrastructure of the Basic Law, that we shall begin to see the shape of what is to come, and when the superstructure of the Hong Kong Special Administrative Region is established, that we can judge if there are any structural faults. (Assessment Office 1984)

Metaphors from the Assessment Document (1984) about the draft described the agreement an "ill-fitting shoe" and a "partial agreement" while the Basic Law was likely to be a "blank cheque" and a "shotgun marriage", which emphasised its "take it or leave it" and compromising nature. This "draft agreement" was passed and later ratified without any changes to the text. Complicating matters, the period between the ratification of the Joint Declaration and the "handover" on 30 June 1997 was considered a "transitional" period; the British had to administer Hong Kong "with the object of maintaining and preserving its economic prosperity and social stability; and that the Government of the People's Republic of China will give its cooperation in this connection" (Article 4 of the Joint Declaration), and it had also to "ensure a smooth transition".[4] Three things were to occur in this interregnum: implementation of some initial democratisation; the drafting of The Basic Law; and preparations for the actual transition. This meant effectively that China had a say in Hong Kong affairs before the actual establishment of it as a Special Administrative Region.

The fundamental laws of states are usually "modelled" (Elkins et al. 2009), after countries that are similar to theirs (such as size, ethno-linguistic fragmentation, or security environment), reasoning that what is good for similar state would also be good for them. However, "in terms of its form, the political system is not entirely occidental nor is it completely oriental" (Rao and Zhenmin 2007), so its drafting could not mimic either of those systems. According to paramount leader Deng Xiaoping, it had to delineate the boundaries between national sovereignty and local autonomy; comply with the Joint Declaration; preserve and improve the existing system while removing the "colonial elements"; it also had to be following the principles of democracy and take consideration of different sectors of society. Despite the minimal political (democratic) changes suggested in the Hong Kong Government Green and White Papers of 1984,[5] the Chinese still considered them a bid to return the administration to the people of Hong Kong instead of to China by shifting policy-making control to the Legislative Council.

China described the British action as extremely clever because it had the effect of deepening "division and turmoil" (分裂和動亂) in society and diluting Chinese sovereignty by giving Hong Kong more autonomy

[4] Paragraph 4 of the Sino-British Joint Declaration: "The Government of the United Kingdom and the Government of the People's Republic of China declare that, during the transitional period between the date of the entry into force of this Joint Declaration and 30 June 1997, the Government of the United Kingdom will be responsible for the administration of Hong Kong with the object of maintaining and preserving its economic prosperity and social stability; and that the Government of the People's Republic of China will give its cooperation in this connection". https://www.cmab.gov.hk/en/issues/jd2.htm

[5] These papers concerned the development of limited representative government in Hong Kong prior to the handover. The colonial government said that "Maintenance of stability requires…should continue to be evolutionary rather than revolutionary", i.e., slow development.

(the so-called "democracy card" 民主牌). These tentative suggestions for possible advancements in representative government were also seen by influential business people who feared high taxes and possible "free lunches" to those who did not deserve them as a result (Loh 2010, 163).[6] In October 1985, Ji Pingfei (head of the Hong Kong and Macau Affairs Office) called upon the British to only alter the Hong Kong political system prior to 1997 in ways that "converged" with the Basic Law, which was just beginning to be drafted. If nothing was done, the British would have pushed ahead with the plan and Hong Kong "would be in chaos" (Ibid.). The British acquiesced in this so there would be little political reform before 1997. In return, Beijing would allow the legislature elected in 1995 to straddle the transition till 1999 if it conformed to the Basic Law. This arrangement was referred to as the "through train" (直通車). This could be described as "a useful cover for China's instinctive hostility towards democratic reform" (ibid.) as it kept the form of the governance framework pre-1997 but without British administration.

The conservative camp's view was that convergence of the political system before and after 1997 was essential for a seamless transition and thus stability and prosperity, while the more liberal camp thought faster democratisation would provide safeguards for Hong Kong and thus stability. A few months later, the events in Tiananmen Square on 4 June 1989 changed Hong Kong and altered how Beijing viewed the city. It also transformed Britain's attitude, and marked a turning point in Hong Kong's people's views on representative government; there were calls for faster democratisation, some seeing the incident as highlighting the "importance of One Country, Two Systems" and the need to firm up Hong Kong's "high degree of autonomy", otherwise it could be "Today's Beijing, Tomorrow's Hong Kong" (Loh 2010, 168).

In the British Parliament, there was a tone of "sympathy" for Hong Kong's plight, being a captive of "…its history and geography". On one hand, some urged faster democratisation for Hong Kong, they were also concerned that the people of Hong Kong had to "secure the least possible

---

[6] During the time of the Sino-British negotiations over Hong Kong's future, Beijing undertook "united front" (統一戰線) work to convince Hong Kong's elite that they had nothing to fear from the upcoming Chinese administration.

damage to their economic vitality as a result of what has happened in China, because China is their largest trading partner"; others thought it ironic that Britain was pushing for democracy in places where they had no responsibility and not pushing for it where they had responsibility: "If we are in favour of democracy in Eastern Europe and crave it for South Africa, why is it not also appropriate for Hong Kong?" (House of Commons 1990).

When the Basic Law was formally promulgated on 4 April 1990 by the National People's Congress (NPC), there were differences between the last public Draft of the Basic Law (February 1989) and its final form (April 1999). Beijing preferred a model that could prevent local liberals from dominating the legislature as under which only 25 percent of the legislature would be directly elected—this alleviated Beijing's fears that political parties in Hong Kong might spring up too quickly. The district-functional chamber should also prevent conflicts between liberals and conservatives from being able to grow into a split between the whole of the legislature and the chief executive.

Certain issues related to The Basic Law as an example of its genre that has a possible impact on how "elections" would be seen. The Basic Law has been called a "mini-constitution" as well as other names such as "political document", "constitutional edict", and a "quasi-constitution", among other designations. Although its status as a "constitution" could be disputed as Hong Kong is part of "one country" and should not have its own constitution, rather it is, in effect, at set of prescribing principles.

As Swales (1990, 54) writes, "A discourse community's nomenclature for a genre is an important source of insight" since it determines how we "read" the document in question. Many thus "read" the Basic Law as a constitution, so we will look at this document in this way as part of the genres of constitutions.[7] Constitutions "don't merely describe the national spirit community but bring it into being as a legal and political entity" (Pryor 2008, 9), they "perform" the state and define a nation and its goals. Because constitutions perform the state, and are regarded as a

[7] The *Oxford English Dictionary* defines a constitution as "A body of fundamental principles according to which a state is governed". Constitutions "don't merely describe the national spirit community but bring it into being as a legal and political entity"; they "perform" the state and define a nation and its goals (Pryor 2008, 9).

framework for that state, they are often treated as "sacred" documents (Ibid.).[8]

The General Principles of the Basic Law were described by one Mainland Basic Law drafter, as "like a tree and other chapters are the branches radiating outwards", that is, they explain the principles more broadly (Xiao 2001, 88). The following principles are considered by Mainland Basic Law drafter Xiao Weiyun as embodying the "second system" (Xiao 2001, 88–131) of Hong Kong and its "high degree of autonomy" and they largely follow the Joint Declaration's text:

- The Hong Kong Special Administrative Region is an inalienable part of the People's Republic of China (Article 1)
- The National People's Congress authorises the Hong Kong Special Administrative Region to exercise a high degree of autonomy and enjoy executive, legislative and independent judicial power, including that of final adjudication, in accordance with the provisions of this Law (Article 2)
- The executive authorities and legislature of the Hong Kong Special Administrative Region shall be composed of permanent residents of Hong Kong in accordance with the relevant provisions of this Law (Article 3)
- The Hong Kong Special Administrative Region shall safeguard the rights and freedoms of the residents of the Hong Kong Special Administrative Region and of other persons in the Region in accordance with law. (Article 4)
- The socialist system and policies shall not be practised in the Hong Kong Special Administrative Region, and the previous capitalist system and way of life shall remain unchanged for 50 years (Article 5)
- The laws previously in force in Hong Kong, that is, the common law, rules of equity, ordinances, subordinate legislation and customary law

[8] Exhibitions and websites about constitutions such as "Charters of Freedom" detailing the Declaration of Independence, the American Constitution and the Bill of Rights, www.archives.gov/exhibits/charters/ and the design of the "Magna Carta, Treasures in Full" website, www.bl.uk/treasures/magnacarta/index.html have a similar "iconic" atmosphere of reverence that is exhibited in discourse.

shall be maintained, except for any that contravene this Law, and subject to any amendment by the legislature of the Hong Kong Special Administrative Region. (Article 8)

A few of these Principles in particular impact on the future discourse of political change in Hong Kong. They are "high degree of autonomy" (Article 2); "50 years no change", "executive authorities and legislature…shall be composed of local residents" (Article 3), and the "maintenance of the previous capitalist system" (Article 5) and the "laws previously in force" (Article 8).

Article 2 (a synthesis of Items 2 and 3 of Paragraph 3 in the Joint Declaration), the "high degree of autonomy" is similar to that mentioned in the Joint Declaration. This article has implications for constitutional development as further democratisation implies increasing autonomy from the centre. Article 3, relates to the executive authorities and legislature being made up of local residents (relates to Item 4 of the Joint Declaration). The word "elections" is not mentioned at all in these General Principles. Although this is dealt later in the Basic Law under political structure, this still leaves scope for further definition of the term. Article 5 refers to the maintenance of the capitalist system and Hong Kong's "way of life" would remain unchanged for 50 years (Paragraph 3, Item 12 in the Joint Declaration). The "50 years no change" (五十年不變) of this Article is the period considered by Deng Xiaoping to be the time that China would "catch up" to Western developed countries economically.[9] These constrain Hong Kong's autonomy to within these specific parameters. Economic aspects are more textually detailed than the future political structure in the Basic Law. Economic matters have also figured largely in any post-1997 discourse of Hong Kong's political

[9] On occasion, the 50-year time period had been taken metaphorically as "a long time" or "maybe never"; for example, *wan sui* (萬歲) is what the crowds used to yell out for emperors. It is defined as "long life" but literally means "ten thousand years". In a speech at a Meeting with the Members of the Committee for Drafting the Basic Law of the Hong Kong SAR (Deng's 50 Years Statement on Taiwan), 16 April 1987: "…If the [opening up] policy is successful, yielding the desired results [increase in GDP] in the 50-year period after 1997, we shall have little reason to change it then. That is why I say that after the motherland is reunified under the 'one country, two systems' formula, our policy toward Hong Kong, Macao, and Taiwan will not change for 50 years and that it will remain unchanged even beyond that period" (Deng 1987).

reform and the possible effect of democracy on its financial systems and relationship to capitalism, and thus its stability and prosperity; this continues into the present.

From this historical overview, we can see certain themes that might emerge after the introduction of the National Security Law. The attempt of keeping Hong Kong's systems similar in many respects to the colonial period, but under Chinese sovereignty, and the emphasis on the danger of change that might risk Hong Kong's stability and prosperity. The drafting of documents in general principles and the emphasis on keeping the status quo indicates possible rhetorical conflict in the future.

The First Return

A century and a half of British rule had ended at midnight of 30 June 1997 and the first Chief Executive Tung Chee-hwa summed up the occasion with the words: "Now we are masters of our own house" (當家作主人)". In the early days, democrats (an inclusive term for several political parties) urged faster political reform (to achieve universal suffrage as promised); criticised the "small circle" who elected the chief executive and the profession-based functional constituencies. A broad range of questions about how Hong Kong was to be governed started to permeate political discourse.

While there were early controversies such as the Right of Abode saga and interpretation of the Basic law in 2004 (Huang and Huang 2016), it was after 2003 and the withdrawal of Basic Law Article 23 security legislation—a piece of legislation that democrats considered, but Beijing did not "undermines the rule of law," "ruins the "One Country, Two Systems", and "turns the public into enemies" (Ta Kung Pao 2003), that the mainland started to keep a closer eye on Hong Kong. Every year on July 1st there were large-scale protests about democratic development and other social issues.

Electoral reform was the major impetus for protests by democrats—and it was the OCLP (Occupy Central with Love and Peace) campaign in 2014 that would be carried out if the Hong Kong Government's proposed universal suffrage plan did not fall in line with what they considered international standards. Occupying Central, the main financial district in Hong Kong, would be the last civil disobedience act in the campaign, with the first three being public deliberation, public authorisation, and negotiation. Organisers of the OCLP felt that the government's plan fell below international standards, so this campaign took place, ending in December 2014. Although seen as a "failure", it led to significant official and public actions, in particular more youth involvement in politics and the rise in "localism (Kwong 2016).

There were changes in Hong Kong official discourse with the end of Occupy Central/Umbrella Movement. A subtle example of this, using "sleight of language" to manipulate a key concept of the "One Country, Two Systems" was the unannounced revision of the Basic Law Fact Sheet.[10] The abduction of booksellers critical of Beijing in 2015 (Chou and Siu 2016) and the snatching of a politically connected tycoon in 2017 (Haas 2017) saw boundaries between the systems being blurred.

Talk of "Hong Kong independence" was rare in Hong Kong prior to 2014 (Kwong 2016). The failure of significant political reform and the OCLP/Umbrella Movement meant a drop in trust towards the Beijing government (Ibid.). The failure of traditional democratic parties saw a shift to the discourse of the "local" rather than the "national". This was because "localists" (as they were called) had their focus on Hong Kong and called for either less intervention in the city by Beijing or even independence for Hong Kong (Kwong 2016). Slogans and talk advocating "Hong Kong independence" began appearing on university campuses in September 2017. There were four main topics could be gleaned from press releases issued by the Hong Kong Government at this time: (1) that freedom of speech is not absolute; (2) talk of independence is illegal; (3) education is necessary to educate students about the Basic Law and the "One Country, Two Systems"; and (4) projection of state power. These

[10] In December 2014 (just after the ending of OCLP), the phrase in English "Hong Kong people ruling Hong Kong" was replaced on the Factsheet with "Hong Kong people administering Hong Kong". The term in Chinese remained the same; the Chinese character could be interpreted as both "to govern" and "to rule". Although the term remained the same in Chinese, there was some change in its placement on the Factsheet. See Eagleton (2022, 208–209). The justification for the change in the English version was "consistency of word choice" as "administer" appeared elsewhere. The form of this Factsheet (a pdf) no longer exists. The current form of Basic Law facts can be found at https://www.basiclaw.gov.hk/en/basiclaw/facts.html

press releases also commented on the "legality" of mentioning or advocating independence either on a banner or shouted as a slogan was "illegal" (Eagleton 2022, 219–225). This could be seen as foreshadowing the future National Security Law and the focus on slogans that mentioned "independence".

Similarly, relative to the discussion of "freedom of expression" above, despite what Article 1 of the Basic Law says that Hong Kong is an "inalienable part of China", there was no "law" or legal statute in 2017 in which you could be prosecuted for raising the issue of Hong Kong independence. Despite labelling discussion of Hong Kong independence "illegal", none of the statements from state media, the city's leader, or universities' vice-chancellors logically articulated the legal basis for such a claim (Eagleton 2022, 223–224). The most often-cited basis was that Article 1 of the Basic Law, which declares that Hong Kong is an "inalienable part of China", meant that even simply discussion of independence broke the law.

During this time, the Hong Kong government intensified pressure on the city's democracy movement, prosecuting activists, blocking opposition politicians from running for election, and banning an independence-promoting political party in 2018 due to non-orthodox oath-taking The refusal to renew the visa of the *Financial Times*' Victor Mallet, president of the Foreign Correspondent's Club in 2018 after a representative of a pro-independence party spoke at a club luncheon was seen as a tactic borrowed directly from the mainland, which often uses issuing journalist visas as a means of control (Cheng 2018; Lahiri 2018). All these particular incidents relate to areas where Hong Kong and the mainland differ: in ideas of what could or could not be said, and who had the right to say it.

Also at this time, was the growing economic power (and confidence) of China on the world stage. Hong Kong, once the "rich cousin" generously helping its poor relations next door, was no longer seen as such. Both fiscally and physically, the "poor relation" is longer poor and thus there was less need for Hong Kong to be used as its "gateway" (Prasad 2019), although this metaphor is still being used to describe Hong Kong's function relative to mainland China. Fiscally, the Belt and Road Initiative (BRI—the Silk Road Economic Belt and twenty-first Century Maritime Silk Road) was a development strategy adopted by the Chinese government in 2013 involving infrastructure development and investments in nearly 70 countries in Asia, Europe, and Africa. In addition, the Pearl River Delta, now "the Greater Bay Area"—was the Chinese Central Government's scheme to link the cities of Hong Kong, Macau, and Zhuhai within a certain radius into an integrated economic and business hub. This has been likened to "a political manifesto masquerading as a business plan" (Heaver 2020).

Physical borders were also disappearing with the placement of a mainland customs station within the high-speed train terminus at West Kowloon, in which a portion of Hong Kong land was ceded back to become part of the mainland—and where technically a person can now be charged with crime from the mainland's jurisdiction (Li 2018). In addition, the construction of the Zhuhai-Macau-Hong Kong mega bridge was largely seen as a "white elephant" integration project since its current and projected use vis-à-vis the cost of its construction did not match up (Yip 2018). Hong Kong in the 1970s had traded up from manufacturing into financial services that the mainland still did not have. This meant that social and political contradictions could be put on hold until some mainland cities could bypass Hong Kong to a certain extent.

However, these inherent social/political contradictions became more apparent over time and alongside the delayed universal suffrage, and the seeming lack of warmth for their ancestral land, became increasingly obvious. The Extradition Bill of 2019 was seen by many as a "tipping" point towards further integration with the "One Country". It was seen as an affront to the rule of law, as the latter was always described as the "bedrock" and "foundation" of Hong Kong society (Cheng and Eagleton 2019), because once the people were on the other side of the border nothing could be guaranteed. In the earlier Occupy Central/Umbrella Movement, the Hong Kong Government said that protesters were threatening the rule of law, while the protesters said the opposite, that it was actually the government who was threatening the rule of law (Duhalde 2019; Hamlett 2019).

The Critical Analysis of the National Security Law and Its Aftermath

Much of this book involves discussion, justification, persuasion, and criticism about the National Security Law and its effects on life in Hong Kong. Critical discourse analysis is this book's main method in analysing texts. Critical Discourse Analysis (CDA) examines how these discursive sources are maintained and reproduced within specific social, political, and historical contexts (Fairclough and Wodak 1997). In a similar vein, Fairclough (1995) defines CDA as,

> Discourse analysis which aims to systematically explore often opaque relationships of causality and determination between (a) discursive practices, events and texts, and (b) wider social and cultural structures, relations and processes; to investigate how such practices, events and texts arise out of and are ideologically shaped by relations of power and struggles over power; and to explore how the opacity of these relationships between discourse and society is itself a factor securing power and hegemony. (pp. 132–133)

There is no one theoretical framework for CDA, its eclectic approach developing out of what Bell and Garrett (1998, 7) said is "best viewed as a shared perspective encompassing a range of approaches rather than just one school. This book uses the discourse-historical approach (D-HA) as it emphasises more strongly than the above approaches that "discourse is always historical, that is, it is connected synchronically and diachronically with other communicative events which are happening at the same time or which have happened before" (Wodak and Ludwig 1999, 21). As the name implies, the historical occupies a unique place in this approach. It denotes an attempt to integrate systematically all the available background of information in the analysis and interpretation of the many layers of text (Wodak 2010). The context of the discourse of Hong Kong under the National Security Law has a significant impact on the structure, function, and course of that discourse.

Characteristics of the D-HA Approach

The most important principles of this approach are briefly summarised below.

1. *The approach is interdisciplinary.* The description of the object of investigation of CDA is carried out from a widely differing perspective (involving concepts related to other fields, e.g., politics, law, etc.). This researcher had to do extensive research work into other disciplines, for example law, as the discussion involves legal genres and their implementation.
2. *It is problem-oriented*; like any other theoretical and methodological approach, is relevant as long as it can successfully study the relevant social issue under analysis (*no discourse is an island*). The researcher was interested in how the authorities justified the changes to Hong Kong's legal and electoral system in light of past discourse, vis-à-vis Hong Kong's "core values".
3. *Its theory and methodology are diverse and integrated* (in order to fully triangulate a topic); different parts of the book incorporate other theories and methods suitable for that particular topic, such as legal analysis of the articles of National Security Law. This is in order to gain a fuller understanding and explanation of the aftermath of the National Security Law.
4. *It incorporates an ethnographic component* (the researcher is often both a participant and observer)—this is a "study on the inside" to a certain degree as the author has closely actively followed Hong Kong events since taking up residence in October 1997, recording and writing about political issues as well as participating in them. The benefits of being a participant-observer in the discourse bring a unique perspective to this issue. With the use of multiple sources (triangulation), subjectivity can be minimised.
5. There is a constant flow between method, theory, and texts (*as each informs the other and each can be adjusted accordingly*). As emphasised by Meyer (2001), "data collection is not a phrase that must be finished before analysis starts but might be a permanently ongoing procedure" (Ibid., 18). As the researcher looks at some texts, other material comes

to light that impacts how later chapters will be shaped, thus the writing of the book involves moving backwards and forwards between chapters to ensure a holistic whole.

6. Multiple genres and fields of action are studied; the intertextual and interdiscursive relationships investigated (*since all texts have antecedents*); a "field of action" could be a "law-making procedure" and the political genre could be drafting the Hong Kong Basic Law or the National Security Law. Another field of action is "formation of political attitudes and will"; the genres could be opinion articles, editorials, and government press releases. Many of the documents referred to in this book relates to earlier texts—Article 23 of the Basic Law and government press releases about why the mainland has to step in and institute the National Security law. This "archaeology of texts" provides a deeper analysis to the documents analysed.
7. The historical context is always analysed and integrated into the interpretation of discourses and texts (*in order to more fully understand the context in which they appear*). Wodak (2010, 628) states that D-HA enables the systematic, explicit, and transparent analysis of the historical (that is, intertextual) dimension of discursive practices by exploring the ways in which particular genres of discourse are subject to change over time, and by integrating social theories to explain context. It follows from this that the historical orientation implies the reconstruction of how recontextualisation functions as an important process linking texts and discourses intertextually and interdiscursivity over time. This also involves changes in which "stories" are told.
8. The categories and tools for the analysis are defined according to all these steps; that is there is no one-size-fits-all approach to any study. Partly due to the researcher's long residence and study of Hong Kong social and political situation, she can tailor the study to Hong Kong's peculiar status in the category "One Country, Two Systems—limited to two, Hong Kong and Macau.
9. *There should be a practical application to the research findings*. It is this researcher's interest showing the public in how to critically analyse language used in talking about a controversial issue, what is the suggested meaning behind the words, and the meaning about what is "unsaid". (Adapted from Wodak 2001, 69–70)

There are three major concepts that are used in the D-HA approach and that is used here. These are critique, ideology, and power.

The D-HA follows a concept of social critique that integrates three related aspects: *text or discourse immanent critique*, the *socio-diagnostic critique*, and the *prospective critique.* At the micro level there is the "text of discourse immanent critique" which aims to discover and highlight the "inconsistencies, (self-) contradictions, paradoxes and dilemmas" inside a text or a discourse (Wodak 2001, 65). On the next, more macro level is the "socio-diagnostic critique" that aims to "demystify" the persuasive or manipulative aspect of the discourse practices employed in that discourse (Ibid.). To analyse this level of discourse the analyst needs to go "beyond the discourse" itself and use their background or contextual knowledge of the situation to insert the relevant social and institutional structures into the mix in order to show how the discourse is "framed" in an extended context.

The third level critique, "prognostic critique" which aims to put the results of the research to practical use in society by, for example, educating the public about the ideological use of language and in reducing language barriers (Wodak 1996). This critique arises out of critical discourse analysis's historical antecedent, using Horkheimer's definition that a critical theory is only adequate if it meets three criteria: that it is explanatory, practical, and normative all at the same time (Horkheimer 1993, 21). It follows from the above to infer that the understanding of critique implies that the D-HA should make the object under investigation and the analyst's own position transparent and should justify theoretically why certain interpretations and readings of discursive events seem more valid than others. The use of multiple methods or data sources (triangularisation) in qualitative research helps develop a comprehensive understanding of the phenomena.

"Ideology" actually refers to beliefs, assumptions, and expectations which people overlay on the world to give it "meaning" and which serve to direct our political or social activities (Eagleton 1991). Linguists see ideology as "...particular ways of representing and constructing society which reproduce unequal relations of power, relations of domination and exploitation" (Fairclough and Wodak 1997, 275). This is not so much about the explicit type of ideology, rather the more hidden ideology in everyday beliefs, which often appear disguised as conceptual metaphors and analogies. Van Dijk (2006) considers ideologies as "shared representations as "shared representations of social groups" (p. 115) which are "acquired, confirmed, changed, and perpetuated through discourse". He thus calls discourse analysis "ideology analysis" (van Dijk 1995). Thus, it is necessary to look at worldviews of individuals and groups through related mental representations, convictions, opinions, attitudes, and evaluations.

On July 1, 1997, Hong Kong became a Special Administrative Region of China (SAR) and the only example of the One Country, Two Systems principle. This principle was to build a new political order that embodies a new hegemony of beliefs and ideology (Loh 2010, 234).

A successful ruling ideology "…must engage significantly with genuine wants, needs and desires; but this is also its Achilles heel, forcing it to recognise the 'other' to itself and inscribing this otherness as a potentially disruptive force within its own forms" (Eagleton 1991, 45). Thus, for a governing ideology to be "monological" it must also address its opposite and thus be "dialogical" in order to be "unifying". There is thus a dialogue between ideologies which perhaps have different meanings for certain "essentially contested" concepts like "democracy" that may or may not be able to be reconciled (Gallie 1956; Gray 1977, 344).

The new ideology from 1997 onwards requires an acceptance that the HKSAR is subordinate to Beijing, and that a "high degree of autonomy" does not mean full autonomy and that those who share the values of the new political order of the "One Country" are ones that will best defend the beliefs and ideology of the new political order. As ideology also "rationalizes" social interests, "rationalizing" something is to imply that there is some potential conflict, an ideology, or potential course of action (Eagleton 1991, 51). For example, there are constant arguments that Hong Kong needs an "executive-led system", functional constituencies, and other interest groups to elect legislators and so on in order to remain an international financial hub and "Asia's world city".

Power is another crucial concept for critical analytical studies such as this one. It is regarded as constituting asymmetric relationships among social actors who assume different social positions or belong to different social groups. Power is not also exercised overtly or abusively by dominant group members, but maybe taken-for-granted in the actions of everyday life. Language can be the vehicle through which power is exerted. Texts are sites of social struggle and gatekeeping; they contain traces of ideological fights for dominance and hegemony. D-HA focuses on the ways in which linguistic forms are used in various expressions and manipulations of power. There is power in and behind discourse. For example, where language is ambiguous, vague, or couched in principles, designated "gatekeepers" have the authority to "interpret" the discourse, see for example the interpretation of the Basic Law in 2004 and now, the National Security Law.

Not all the participants in the communication process have "symmetry" (Blommaert 2005, 45) over contextualisation; those in power, who have the greater "right to speak" often have purchase on over powerful contextualising spaces such as linguistic definitions (for example, the "Basic Law guardians" [Legal academics from Beijing who were called this in 2004] have the right to contextualise potential ambiguities in the Basic Law). This relates to van Dijk's notion of the ideological basis of context (1995).

Some Tools of Analysis

Strategies are identified when analysing a specific discourse. D-HA is three-dimensional: after (1) having identified the specific contents or topics of a particular discourse, (2) discursive strategies (*ways of using language*) are investigated. Then (3) linguistic means are examined as types, and the specific, context-dependent linguistic realisations are examined. This suggests analysing the coherence of a text by first detecting the macro-topics and related subtopics. Second, it is important to understand the aim of the text producer in any genre (any genre can be "ideological"): Does the speaker intent to convince somebody and thus to realise a persuasive text? Depending on the aim, different strategies and linguistic, pragmatic, and rhetorical devices are used to realise the intended meaning. Wodak emphasises that in order to approach various discursive features and strategies, discourse-historical analyses systematically go through five questions (Ibid.). D-HA has a specific set of analytical techniques that can be drawn in their analysis. Specifically, this research draws on the typology of five discursive strategies outlined by Wodak (2001):

(1) *Nomination*: How are people/social groups referred to?
(2) *Predication*: The characteristics and qualities attributed to certain individuals/ groups.
(3) *Argumentation*: What explicit/implicit arguments are used to support these characteristics?
(4) *Perspectivisation*: The positioning of the speaker's point of view.
(5) *Intensification/mitigation*: "Modifying (intensifying or mitigating) the illocutionary force and thus the epistemic or deontic status of utterances" (Wodak 2001, 72–73).

In addition to these five core discursive strategies, this research also draws on the argumentation strategies developed by van Dijk (1993) which include: (1) Strategies of positive self-presentation and (2) Strategies of negative other-presentation (e.g., patriots vs non-patriots). The realisation of these discursive strategies occurs through the use of a number of rhetorical/linguistic devices. A key part of any discourse analysis, and the D-HA in particular, is the identification and contextualisation of these devices. These include the use of metaphors, tropes, topoi, stereotypes, hyperbole, fallacies, allusions, allocations, and rhetorical questions (Wodak and Meyer 2009).

Conclusion

We can see the possibility of why there are contested discourse and narratives between the state and society of Hong Kong as a Special Administrative Region of China and the central government authorities in Beijing, two radically different systems. The "One Country, Two Systems", and despite the objective to "maintain the metaphorical and constitutional distance" between China and Hong Kong and the desire of the former to "assert as formulated in the Basic Law is both a "wedge" separating the two systems is also a "bridge" connecting the two places sovereignty and achieve unity" (Wesley-Smith 1996, 106) comes into potential conflict, particularly with the wording dealing with Hong Kong's promise of universal suffrage, which implicitly infers further autonomy of the "Two Systems". This historical background and the knowledge way language works culturally, pragmatically, and politically enables the reader to get the most out of the book. Hong Kong has been a social movement society, and most of the confrontations and contestations lie in both street politics and struggles over interpretations of its core values and principles, such as the rule of law and now national security. These confrontations and contestations in discourse have become muted under the articles of the new National Security Law.

Layout of the Book

Chapter 2 looks at the notion of national security in the mainland Chinese context, followed by a textual analysis of the National Security Law (NSL) itself, and how the Law was promoted by the authorities before its promulgation as something that was "aligned with international practice" and the problems with this association. Chapter 3 deals a multimodal analysis of posters and videos used in publicity campaigns in which millions of dollars were spent in persuading the public that the NSL was necessary for Hong Kong's stability. Since in the early days of the NSL, the government's aim was to persuade the Hong Kong people that they would not be unduly affected by the implementation of the new law, and that life would largely remain the same, the core values being untouched.

Chapter 4 looks at the electoral changes of 2021 that meant that "patriots" would administer Hong Kong and the authorities' justification for how this change would not alter the basic tenets of Hong Kong's cherished tenets of the rule of law, freedom of expression and promise of universal suffrage as stated in Hong Kong's Basic Law. It will also look at the effect of these changes on the subsequent election in December of that year as well as related White Papers issued by the Chinese government about the development of Hong Kong's democracy. It also connects the issue of patriots to the earlier "patriotism debate" of 2004.

Chapter 5 looks at the importance of education under the National Security Law, its ideological implications for how Hong Kong is seen under the "One Country, Two Systems" framework, and how it links issues of identity and national security across the curriculum. The textbooks used in the classroom as well as how teachers must carefully navigate what they teach, the new code of conduct they must follow will also be shown, and how they must "police" possible infringements of the National Security Law as part of their mandate.

Chapter 6 places its emphasis on how the National Security Law impacts civil society, its systems and freedoms, with some seeing the changes as a "Cultural Revolution 2.0". All aspects of civil society such as the NSL's impact on the cultural scene—the arts, film, publishing, and freedom of speech, of association and protest will be discussed in a number of case studies.

Chapter 7 looks at dissidents and the discourse of exile, as the NSL saw an exodus of political activists because of the possibility or threat of arrest under this law. To contextualise this, there will be a brief discussion of the situation of the overseas Chinese democracy movement (the Tiananmen dissidents of 1989) and how their situation developed over time; speculation will be made about the future of these new Hong Kong exiles, as well as their similarities or otherwise to previous exiles.

Chapter 8, discusses how Hong Kong's "story" should be told and some thoughts about the future is envisioned (vis-à-vis the "50 years no change"). The current Chief Executive John Lee wants people to tell "good stories" about the city, while downplaying "bad stories", saying that these "bad stories" do not reflect the true reality. How the "Hong Kong Story" is told in museums, how past stories of Hong Kong are being repackaged and retold in the present, to better reflect the new present—the past thus becomes contested as well as the present and also the future. This serves as a conclusion to the book, summarising its findings and how "One Country, Two Systems", the formula promised by China to uphold Hong Kong's semi-autonomous status and its own systems distinctive from Chinese ones has been discursively positioned. In sum, the future of Hong Kong still remains an open "conceptual space".

References

Assessment Office. *Report of the Independent Monitoring Team, Hong Kong Assessment Office*. Hong Kong Government, Printer, 1984. Arrangements for Testing the Acceptability in Hong Kong of the Draft Agreement on the Future of the Territory; https://archive.org/details/arrangementsfort00comm/page/8/mode/2up

Bell, Allan, and Peter Garrett., eds. *Approaches to Media Discourse*. Oxford; Malden, Mass.: Blackwell, 1998.

Bhatia, Vijay K., Christopher C. Candlin, and Paola E. Allori., eds. *Language, Culture and the Law: The Formulation of Legal Concepts across Systems and Cultures*. Bern; New York: Peter Lang, 2008.

Blommaert, Jan. *Discourse: A Critical Introduction*. Cambridge, UK/ New York: Cambridge University Press, 2005.

Blyth, Sally, and Tim Wotherspoon. *Hong Kong Remembers*. Hong Kong: Oxford University Press, 1996.

Bonavia, David. *Hong Kong 1997: The Final Settlement*. Hong Kong: South China Morning Post, 1985.

Bruner, Jerome. *Acts of Meaning*. Cambridge, MA: Harvard University Press, 1990.

Callahan, William A. "National Insecurities: Humiliation, Salvation, and Chinese Nationalism," *Alternatives* 29 (2004): 199–118.

Cao, Deborah. *Chinese Law: A Language Perspective*. Burlington, V.T.: Ashgate, 2004.

Carroll, John. *A Concise history of Hong Kong*. Hong Kong: Hong Kong University Press, 2007.

Chan, H-h. "Hong Kong Exam Question on China and Japan Sparked Outrage – But Debates on Potential Good from Invasions and Bloodshed have Historical Precedent in Tests." *South China Morning Post*, May 21, 2020. https://www.scmp.com/news/hong-kong/education/article/3085351/hong-kong-exam-question-china-and-japan-hassparked

Cheng, Kris. "Pro-independence party Officially banned by Hong Kong Government in Historic Move Restricting Freedom of Assembly." *Hong Kong Free Press*, September 24, 2018. https://hongkongfp.com/2018/09/24/breaking-pro-independence-party-officially-banned-hong-kong-govt-historic-move-restricting-freedom-assembly/

Cheng, Winnie, and Jennifer Eagleton. "The Rule of Law and the Threat of Civil Disobedience in Hong Kong: Metaphorical Structures in Local Media." *Linguistics Journal* 13, no. 1 (September 2019): 173–196.

Chou, Oliver, and Phila Siu. "One Year On: Hong Kong Bookseller Saga Leaves Too Many Questions Unanswered." *South China Morning Post*, December 29, 2016. https://www.scmp.com/news/hong-kong/politics/article/2058000/one-year-hong-kong-bookseller-saga-leaves-too-many-questions

Cottrell, Robert. *The End of Hong Kong: The Secret Diplomacy of Imperial Retreat*. London: John Murray, 1993.

Cradock, Percy. *Experiences of China*. London: John Murray, 1994.

Deng, Xiaoping. "Our Basic Position on the Question of Hong Kong." Source: *Deng Xiaoping's Works*, September 24, 1982. https://www.marxists.org/reference/archive/deng-xiaoping/1982/184.htm

Deng, Xiaoping. *Deng Xiaoping on "One Country, Two Systems."* Hong Kong: Joint Publishing, 2004.

Deng Xiaoping. "Speech at a Meeting with the Members of The Committee for Drafting the Basic Law of the Hong Kong Special Administrative Region." April 16, 1987. http://www.china.org.cn/english/features/dengxiaoping/103351.htm

Duhalde, Marcelo. "The Rule of Law: Hong Kong vs China How Far Apart are the Two Systems in How they Apply the Rule of Law?" *South China Morning Post*, August 20, 2019. https://multimedia.scmp.com/infographics/news/world/article/3023351/rule-of-law/?src=social.

Eagleton, Jennifer. *Discursive Change in Hong Kong – Sociopolitical Dynamics, Metaphor, and One Country, Two Systems*. Maryland: Lexington Books, 2022.

Eagleton, Terry. *Ideology: An Introduction*. London; New York: Verso, 1991.

Eisenberg, Eric M. "Ambiguity as Strategy in Organizational Communication." *Communication Monographs* 51 (1984): 227–442.

Eisenberg, Eric M., and H. Lloyd Goodall. *Organizational Communication: Balancing Creativity and Constraint*, 4th edn. New York: St. Martin's, 1997.

Elkins, Zachary, Tom Ginsburg, and James Melton. *The Endurance of National Constitutions*. New York: Cambridge University Press, 2009.

Fairclough, Norman. *Media Discourse*. London/New York: E. Arnold, 1995.

Fairclough, Norman, and Ruth Wodak. "Critical Discourse Analysis." In *Discourse Studies: A Multidisciplinary Introduction*: *Vol. 2. Discourse as Social Interaction,* edited by Teun A. van Dijk. London, UK: Sage Publications, 1997.

Faulkner, William. *Requiem for a Nun*. Act I Scene III. Harmondsworth: Penguin in association with Chatto and Windus, 1960.

Foster, H. Frances. "Translating Freedom for Post-1997 Hong Kong." *Washington University Law Quarterly* 76, no. 1 (1998): 113–146.

Foucault, Michael. *The Archaeology of Knowledge*. Translated from the French by A.M. Sheridan Smith. Pantheon Books: New York, 1972.

Ghai, Yash. *Hong Kong's New Constitutional Order: The Resumption of Chinese Sovereignty and the Basic Law*. Hong Kong: Hong Kong University Press, 1999.

Gallie, Walter Bryce (1956). "Essentially Contested Concepts," *Proceedings of the Aristotelian Society* 56 (1956): 167–198.

Gray, John N., "On the Contestability of Social and Political Concepts," *Political Theory* 5, no. 3 (1977): 331–348.

Haas, Benjamin. "The Darkest time": Hong Kong Reels over Bizarre Disappearance of Chinese Billionaire." *The Guardian*, February 13, 2017. https://www.theguardian.com/world/2017/feb/13/the-darkest-time-hong-kong-reels-over-disappearance-of-xiao-jianhua-chinese-billionaire

Hamlett, Tim. "Hong Kong's Extradition Bill and the Rule of Law – More Complicated than You Think." *Hong Kong Free Press*, June 1, 2019. https://hongkongfp.com/2019/06/01/hong-kongs-extradition-bill-rule-law-complicated-think/

Heaver, Stuart. "Hong Kong and the Greater Bay Area: A Political Manifesto Masquerading as a Business Plan." *Hong Kong Free Press*, March 1, 2020. https://hongkongfp.com/2020/03/01/hong-kong-greater-bay-area-political-manifesto-masquerading-business-plan/

Henderson, John H., *The Reintegration of Hong Kong into the People's Republic of China. Vanderbilt Journal of Transnational Law* 28, no. 3 (1995): Article 8. https://scholarship.law.vanderbilt.edu/cgi/viewcontent.cgi?article=1888&context=vjtl1995

Horkheimer, Max. *Between Philosophy and Social Science: Selected Early Writings*. Translated by G. Frederick Hunter, Matthew S. Kramer, John Torpey, Thomas McCarthy. Cambridge: MIT Press, 1993.

House of Commons. *Hansard*. Hansard Debates UK Parliament, February 16, 1990. https://publications.parliament.uk/pa/cm198990/cmhansrd/1990-02-16/Debate-3.html

Huang, Zeping, and Echo Huang. "A brief history: Beijing's interpretations of Hong Kong's Basic Law, from 1999 to the Present Day." *Quartz*, November 7, 2016. https://qz.com/828713/a-brief-history-beijings-interpretations-of-hong-kongs-basic-law-from-1999-to-the-present-day

Kwong, Ying-Ho. "The Growth of "Localism" in Hong Kong: A New Path for the Democracy Movement?" September 2016 *China Perspectives* 3 (2016): 63–68.

Lahiri, Tripti. "China's Visa Revenge Tactics Against Journalists Have Come to Hong Kong." *Quartz*, October 5, 2018. https://qz.com/828713/a-brief-history-beijings-interpretations-of-hong-kongs-basic-law-from-1999-to-the-present-day

Li, Linda C., "High-speed Rail Sparks Co-Location Controversy in Hong Kong." *East Asia Forum*, April 7, 2018. https://eastasiaforum.org/2018/04/07/high-speed-rail-sparks-co-location-controversy-in-hong-kong/

Loh, Christine. *Underground Front: The Chinese Communist Party in Hong Kong*. Hong Kong: Hong Kong University Press, 2010.

Lovell, Julia. *The Opium War: Drugs, Dreams and the Making of China*. London: Picador, 2011.

Ma, Ngok. 'The Sino-British Dispute over Hong Kong: A Game Theory Interpretation." *Asian Survey* 37, no. 8 (1997): 738–751.

Meyer, Michael. "Between Theory, Method, and Politics: Positioning the Approaches to CDA)." In *Methods of Critical Discourse Analysis*, edited by Ruth Wodak and Michael Meyer (pp. 12–31). London: Sage, 2001.

Pepper, Suzanne. "National Security Law: A Second 'Handover' for Hong Kong?" *Hong Kong Free Press*, June 25, 2020. https://hongkongfp.com/2020/06/25/national-security-law-a-second-handover-for-hong-kong/

PORI. Survey on Hong Kong People's Views Regarding the Anti-Extradition Bill Movement. Hong Kong Public Opinion Research Institute, December 27, 2019. https://www.pori.hk/wp-content/uploads/2021/01/reuters_anti_elab_round1_ENG_v3_pori.pdf

Prasad, Eswar S., "Why China No Longer Needs Hong Kong." *New York Times*, July 3, 2019. https://www.nytimes.com/2019/07/03/opinion/hong-kong-protest.html

Pryor, Judith. *Constitutions: Writing Nations, Reading Difference*. Abingdon; England; New York: Birkbeck Law Press, 2008.

Rao, Geping., and Zhenmin, Wang. "'Hong Kong's One Country, Two Systems' Experience under the Basic Law: Two Perspectives from Chinese Legal Scholars." *Journal of Contemporary China* 16, no. 52 (2007): 341–358.

Swales, John. *Genre Analysis: English in Academic and Research Settings*. Cambridge; New York: Cambridge University Press, 1990.

Ta Kung Pao. "Openly Advocating 'Containment' Would Threaten Government Legislation - the 'democrats getting the Upper Hand causes More Rampant Disorder in Hong Kong" (公然鼓吹「圍堵」立會威脅政府—「民主派」得勢亂港更猖狂). *Ta Kung Pao*. 5 July 5, 2003. Accessed by WiseNews.

Ta Kung Pao. "Raymond Wu Adheres to Deng's Vision" (鄔維庸服膺鄧公遠見). *Ta Kao Pao*, July 27, 2004. Accessed by WiseNews.

US Gov. Hong Kong Human Rights and Democracy Act, January 13, 2019. https://www.govinfo.gov/content/pkg/COMPS-15534/pdf/COMPS-15534.pdf

Xiao, Weiyun. *One Country, Two Systems: An Account of the Drafting of the Hong Kong Basic Law*. Beijing: Peking University Press, 2001.

Van Dijk, Teun A. "Principles of Critical Discourse Analysis." *Discourse & Society* 4, no. 2 (1993): 249–285.

Van Dijk, Teun A. "Discourse Analysis as Ideology Analysis." Chapter 2, in *Language and Peace* (1st edition), edited by Christina Schäffner and Anita L. Wenden. Routledge, 1995.

Van Dijk, Teun A. (2006). "Ideology and Discourse Analysis." *Journal of Political Ideologies* 11, no. 2 (2006): 115–140.

Wesley-Smith, Peter. "Law in Hong Kong and China: The Meshing of Systems." *Annals of the American Academy of Political and Social Science* 547 (1996): 104–117.

Wodak, Ruth. Disorders of Discourse. London: Longman, 1996.

Wodak, Ruth. "The Discourse-historical Approach." In Ruth Wodak and Michael Meyer, eds. *Methods of Critical Discourse Analysis*, London: Sage, 2001: 63–94.

Wodak, Ruth. "The Glocalization of Politics in Television: Fiction or Reality?" *European Journal of Cultural Studies* 13, no. 1 (2010): 43–62.

Wodak, Ruth and Christof Ludwig., eds. *Challenges in a Changing World: Issues in Critical Discourse Analysis*, Vienna: Passagenverlag, 1999.

Wodak, Ruth and Michael Meyer, M., eds. *Methods of Critical Discourse Analysis*. 2nd revised edition. London: Sage, 2009.

Xu, George Q., "The Role of Rhetorical Topoi in Constructing the Social Fabric of Contemporary China. In Randy Kluver and John H. Powers, eds., *Civic Discourse, Civil Society, and Chinese Communities*, (pp. 41–52). Stamford, Conn.: Ablex, 1999.

Yip, Hilton. "Beijing is Foisting a White Elephant on Hong Kong." *Foreign Policy*, September 14, 2018. https://foreignpolicy.com/2018/09/14/beijing-is-foisting-a-white-elephant-on-hong-kong/

Zhai, Ivan. "Drugs Torched in Town that Provided Trigger for First Opium War." *South China Morning Post*, June 26, 2010. https://www.scmp.com/article/718170/drugs-torched-town-provided-trigger-first-opium-war.

Zhang, Xiaoming (張曉明). "The Stronger the Bottom Line of National Security, the Greater the Space for 'One country, two systems'" (國家安全底線愈牢，「一國兩制」空間愈大). Keynote speech (in Chinese) given by the deputy director of the Hong Kong and Macao Affairs Office of the State Council (Webinar on 30th Anniversary of the Promulgation of the Basic Law), June 8, 2020 (in Chinese). https://www.basiclaw.gov.hk/filemanager/content/tc/files/anniversary30/speeches_file2.pdf

2

National Security in the Chinese Context

In February 2019, the government of Hong Kong proposed legal amendments that would permit the extradition of criminal suspects from Hong Kong to mainland China. Many in Hong Kong viewed these amendments as undermining Hong Kong's autonomy and civil liberties, and many took to the streets to protest, forcing the government of Hong Kong to eventually withdraw the bill. However, the protests evolved into a broader expression of resistance against mainland Chinese interference in Hong Kong's autonomy and thus continued even after the bill's withdrawal. The Central Chinese Government began to cite the protests as justification for introducing sweeping national security legislation to Hong Kong. On June 30, 2020, the Chinese Central Government, without consulting Hong Kong, signed and passed the Law of the People's Republic of China on Safeguarding National Security in the Hong Kong Special Administrative Region (otherwise known as the National Security Law or NSL).

This chapter will first deal with China's promotion of the idea of "national security" in Hong Kong which came much earlier than the NSL's introduction in 2020. As early as 1989, China already considered

J. Eagleton, *Hong Kong's Second Return to China*,
https://doi.org/10.1007/978-3-031-84587-1_2

Hong Kong a "subversive base" that would possibly endanger national security. Then the chapter will deal with how the notion of national security continued to evolve in 2003, 2014, 2017, and 2019 in light of world and local affairs. The chapter will also include an overview of security in the Chinese context, in particular, Xi Jinping's concept of "holistic national security" prior to describing the initial reaction to the announcement that there would be a National Security Law (Wu 2010; Legarda 2021). This is followed by a systematic textual analysis of the contents of the NSL itself, related documents, and possible implications.

"National Humiliation" and Its Effects on National Security in China

In early twentieth century China, a new historical narrative arose around the idea of "100 years of national humiliation" (百年國耻). Highlighting their country's history as a victim of foreign aggression led Chinese leaders to rely on what Gries (2005, 3) calls "the moral authority of their past suffering" (i.e., a discourse of humiliation) and with a cartography to match. Chinese atlases had "national humiliation maps" (國恥地圖) to anchor in the public mind the danger of lost territories. Often these were "Inside-Out" maps, with borders showing the extent of lost territory, and they played up fears of the country being once again "carved up like a melon", a popular phrase that conjured the unequal treaties of the nineteenth century that saw a weak China ceding places like Hong Kong to foreign powers.[1]

These maps were still used in key political events of the recent past. They appeared in textbooks after the 1989 Tiananmen crackdown, during the handover of Hong Kong in 1997, and during the 60th anniversary of China's victory over Japan in World War II in 2005. Chinese foreign policy is thus not a security dilemma, but really an identity dilemma. The maps reflect a positive–negative dynamic that intertwines China's

[1] For a critical analysis of how "the century of national humiliation" relates to modern identity practices in China, see Callahan (2004).

domestic and international politics. "Territorial integrity", a common phrase used by Beijing, could be considered equivalent to "national identity".[2]

Hong Kong as an Early Subversive Base

Hong Kong's relationship with the mainland China has always been a precarious one. As a British colony, Hong Kong served multiple political functions, including as a base to be used by revolutionaries and dissidents of various types challenging the regime on the mainland. For example, Sun Yat-sen used Hong Kong as a base for preparing his revolution in China in 1911. According to the Hong Kong Tourism Board "What he [Sun] saw and heard in the territory gave birth to the epoch-making revolutionary ideas of this great Chinese statesman" (HKTB n.d.). The Communists and Nationalists fought fiercely in Hong Kong before 1949 when the Chinese Communist Party won the civil war. After the establishment of the People's Republic of China, the Nationalists used Hong Kong as a bridgehead to infiltrate and sabotage mainland targets and conduct extensive psychological warfare. The political role of Hong Kong as a place to flee to became more preeminent when Maoist policy campaigns on the mainland led to waves of refugees, political or economic, flocking to Hong Kong, and forming the political backbone of Hong Kong society.

Disgraced politicians and revolutionaries from outside China could also hide in the city and "disappear" (Torode 2008). Various political

[2] The best example of recent national humiliation maps is the mainland-produced book (in Chinese) *Maps of the Century of National Humiliation of Modern China* (1997), which has 86 pages of maps, pictures, charts, illustrations, and explanations (Callahan 2009, 157). From the Introduction to this book (Italics added): "The anniversary of the victory of the Anti-Japanese War has just passed, and Hong Kong is about to be returned to the motherland. At this commemorative time the People's Press publishes 'Maps of the Century of National Humiliation of Modern China'. It consists mainly of maps which are annotated with text, charts, and pictures. The book generalises the history of China *being bullied and invaded* by the Great Powers from 1840 to 1945. It takes this century where China lost sovereignty, to show through maps *the galling shame and deep humiliation* of the Chinese nation. The sovereign *territory that was trampled under iron heels and the bitter suffering of the masses come clearly into view*. These images are strong enough to arouse nationalist indignation and patriotic feelings."

figures spent time in Hong Kong with often little publicity either hiding out or passing through on the way to other political activities such as Anwar Ibrahim, Thaksin Shinawatra, and Ho Chi Minh. Earlier you might have been able to say that "Hong Kong is of the region but, politically and diplomatically at least, it is not really part of the region…Hong Kong may be a part of China, but it is still basically at arm's length …" and it was thought that "Hong Kong is a place where you can come to 'disappear' for a while," as one envoy said (ibid.), not so now.

The "foundation moments" of political parties in Hong Kong arose out of opposition to events in China. The first such group, founded in 1990, was the United Democrats of Hong Kong (UDHK). The UDHK developed as a result of a growing opposition within civil society against authoritarian rule during the 1980s, and the ongoing Sino-British negotiations culminating in party formation less than a year after the Tiananmen Square crackdown, an event with a huge impact on public support for democracy in Hong Kong. The United Democrats roundly condemned the Chinese Government who had deemed the protests "turmoil" rather than a patriotic "democracy movement" that the United Democrats saw themselves as, helping student dissidents to escape via "Operation Yellow Bird" (黃雀行動), an "underground railway" out of China that existed almost up to the time of the handover (O'Neill 2009).[3] The Hong Kong Democratic Party urged a faster pace of democratisation after 1989; for their actions in 1989, party members were barred from visiting the mainland; democratic leaders such as Martin Lee and Szeto Wah[4] were active in helping students exit China with foreign help which led Beijing's leaders to lack trust in Hong Kong's democrats. Furthermore, democrats later stated that the "source of the 1st July marches was June Fourth" (七一遊行源自六四).[5] (Luo 2004) and that "reversing the verdict on June Fourth is patriotic" (平反六四 才是愛國) (Lam 2004)

[3] The name "Yellow Bird" was after a Chinese proverb: "as the locust catches the cicada, the yellow bird is behind it waiting" (螳螂捕蝉，黄雀在后).

[4] Szeto Wah was head of the Hong Kong Alliance in Support of Patriotic Democratic Movements in China. The Alliance had five operational goals: release the dissidents; rehabilitate the 1989 pro-democracy movement; demand accountability of the June Fourth massacre; end one-party dictatorship, and build a democratic China.

[5] Large protests held each 1st July on Hong Kong Special Administrative Region Establishment Day.

rhetorically linking these two events as the Tiananmen protesters in 1989 had called their movement "patriotic". Thus, democratically leaning groups were seen by China as primarily wanting to end one-party rule.[6]

The return of Hong Kong to China did not alter Hong Kong's unique position as a "subversive base". It was after the massive public protest on 1st July, 2003 and the withdrawal of Article 23 security legislation—a piece of legislation that many considered "undermines the rule of law", "ruins the 'One Country, Two Systems'", and "turns the public into enemies", that the mainland started to keep a closer watch on Hong Kong (Ta Kung Pao 2003). Article 23 of the Basic Law was the demand from the Central Government for Hong Kong to enact national security legislation "on its own". The article as drafted was seen as vague, rushed, and problematic (HKFP 2018). As a result of the massive protest march and the withdrawal of Article 23 legislation, China had a "hands on" approach to Hong Kong and began to give priority to the concept of sovereignty, central control over Hong Kong affairs, and above all the effective protection of national security and the national interest.

The Occupy Central/Umbrella Movement of 2014, the upsweep of "localism" in 2016, and the rise of "independence talk" in 2017 were seen as negating the authority of the "One Country" which displeased the Central and Hong Kong Governments. Once a refuge for political dissidents as mentioned earlier, now various individuals with political backgrounds had difficulty entering Hong Kong (Lee 2017; Ng 2019).

President Xi Jinping's visit to Hong Kong in 2017 on the twentieth anniversary of the HKSAR, cautioned those who were "making everything political or deliberately creating differences" would "severely hinder Hong Kong's economic and social development" (Ramzy 2017). Xi

[6] The Hong Kong Democratic Party's manifesto (in 2012 when the author completed her PhD thesis) had the following points on their website: "Hong Kong is an indivisible part of China"; "Cares for China" and has the "right and obligation" to participate and comment on the affairs of China; Calls for amendment of the Basic Law to "achieve democracy as a safeguard to liberty during the transitional period"; says Beijing "crushed" the student movement in Tiananmen Square and "assaulted" the "will of the people"; urges the central government to "overrule" its position on Tiananmen and consider the student's actions a "patriotic movement"; and it would fight for amendment of Basic Law after 1997. Only the first three items of this list remain in their manifesto. See https://dphk.org/

warned that "any attempt to endanger China's sovereignty and security, challenges the power of the central government" or to "use Hong Kong to carry out infiltration and sabotage against the mainland is an act that crosses the red line and is absolutely impermissible" (ibid.). His comments on "infiltration and sabotage" in particular signalled that the government was likely try to resurrect Article 23 once again, regarding the issues of sedition and subversion. This was the first time Xi Jinping or any other Chinese leader had mentioned a "red line" concerning political actions in Hong Kong. China commentator Willy Lam stated that "It's a warning to the pro-independence or other so-called anti-China elements to not challenge the authority of the central government" (Ramzy 2017). The "ideal" Special Administrative Region was only next door to Hong Kong—that region was Macau.

The Exemplar Special Administrative Region

Praise has been constantly heaped on Macau, as the perfect SAR by President Xi Jinping (Xi 2019). On the twentieth anniversary of Macau SAR's founding in late December 2019, Xi, expressed faith in the "One Country, Two Systems" principle as practised there in four ways:

1. Macau has worked to safeguard the sovereignty and security of the country;
2. Macau always strives in the right direction; its citizens recognize that "one country" is the premise and precondition of the "two systems";
3. Macau people had always kept the country's overall interests in mind, and;
4. Macau residents had the "tradition of loving the mainland as well as a strong sense of national identity, belonging and pride" (based on Siu and Lam 2019; Siu and Cheung 2019).

While he made no mention of Hong Kong, these words could be seen to be a rebuke of Hong Kong in the light of previous remarks made earlier about the 2019 protests (Zhou 2019). It seemed obvious that Xi was deliberately contrasting his strong approval of Macau with his "silent disapproval" of Hong Kong's relationship with the motherland since its 1997 return to Chinese sovereignty. The following relates to the points made in Xi's speech:

- The call for "self-determination" and for "independence" by some in Hong Kong touched a sensitive nerve as this was seen as a threat to "sovereignty", always a sore point with the Chinese Communist Party (Point 1). Protesters seem to focus on the "second system":
- You cannot have a "second system" without the "one country", and the latter should take priority (Point 2);
- Hong Kong seemed to be more focused on their own affairs rather than Beijing's (Point 3); calling themselves "Hongkongers" rather than "Chinese"; and saying the oath of office wrongly, meant that potential legislators would not uphold the "One Country, Two Systems";
- Macau did not seem to have this kind of conflict (Point 4); furthermore, Macau was largely protest-free.

Hong Kong could be seen as a microcosm of what China claims is its larger national security threat that it faces. The long-standing fear that Hong Kong's high degree of autonomy, its growing advocacy of democracy, its political stagnation, and (and what Beijing calls it) its occasional "democratic violence" may have turned a city that was considered useful for China used to admire into an economic and political liability. China's economic development that made it not so reliant on Hong Kong in the past was also a factor seeing it proactively seek to design and implement this new law. This could also be seen to fit into Xi's concept of holistic national security.

The "Securitization of Everything": National Security Under Xi Jinping

The "securitization of everything", a phrase coined by Drinhausen and Legarda (2022), sums up Xi Jinping's concept of national security. This probably could be seen as the natural development of China's views on national security as it includes prior leaders' perspectives on the topic.

National security under Mao Zedong was mainly preoccupied with territorial and military security (Zhang 1992). The main aim was to keep the Chinese Communist Party in power and ensure political stability. Under Deng Xiaoping and Jiang Zemin, China's "open door policy" opened it up to the world at a time of global economic growth and industrial modernisation, thereby the concern become economic security. The 1989 Tiananmen protests triggered an emphasis on cultural or ideological and societal security, to prevent fundamental changes to the regime. Hu Jintao prioritised ecological and resource security, amidst widespread protests over pollution and lack of labour protection (Cabestan 2009). The Jiang Zemin and Hu Jintao eras also saw regular warnings about the danger that ideological dissent, social protests, online media, and official corruption posed to the party's grip on power. Xi Jinping's concept of holistic national security incorporated these areas into a more organised conceptual framework: national security included everything.

Holistic National Security

Xi's concept of holistic national security (總體國家安全觀) was introduced in 2014 and comprises twenty policy areas deemed essential to China's development and the party state, being closely linked to achieving the "rejuvenation of the Chinese nation" by 2049, the concept has been revised in the Party Constitution in various party documents and laws (Drinhausen and Legarda 2022). *Zongti* "總體" in the name could be translated as *total, holistic,* or *comprehensive*, while *guan* "觀" could be translated as *concept, outlook,* or *approach* reflecting that this security paradigm is *maximalist* in conception, while "觀" in the name indicates ambiguity and flexibility about what could be included in the concept. The following from the Hong Kong Government's National Security Day website neatly sums up neatly this holistic view of what is national security. Clicking on the icons in the website (given in the footnote) for the twenty major fields gives more information on what security means in each of these fields.

> National security covers twenty major fields, including political security, military security, homeland security, economic security, financial security, cultural security, societal security, science and technology security, cyber security, food security, ecological security, resource security, nuclear security, overseas interests' security, outer space security, deep sea security, polar security, biosecurity, artificial intelligence security and data security.[7]

Of all the types of security: political security (safeguarding the party state) was seen as the "bedrock" (*genben* 根本) of all securities, followed by economic safety being the basis of the system; to be dealt with danger before it materialises, while fields such as cybersecurity and maritime security, for example, are described as urgent tasks. Promoting China's overseas interests were also seen as being crucial in national security. National security for stability is framed as the highest political priority and preconditions for continued economic development. This paradigm could be seen a dialectic of "confidence and paranoia" (Drinhausen and Helena Legard 2022, 4).

This holistic concept melds together the relational pairs of hard and soft power, internal and external threats, transgressing the differences between the worlds of economics, culture, and diplomacy. Security must be "total". Therefore, anything that threatens any one of these "securities" could be legislated against. Western powers posed threats to certain countries by instigating revolution from within (i.e., "colour revolutions"). The collapse of the Soviet Union demonstrated what happened to a party who ignored this threat; the Chinese Communist Party thus has to remind people that the state is under constant threat from forces both inside and more particularly, outside the Party. Party authorities consistently describe their country as the object of hostile strategies designed to subvert China's domestic stability and the ruling party's unquestioned rule (i.e., they were "containing China"). In response to fears of greater global and domestic instability, Xi, sought a unified theory that combined internal and external security threats and that would guide overall policy strategies. This was not only a way to remain in power, but to shore up risk to its legitimacy if economic growth slowed. Collective security,

[7] Taken from https://www.nsed.gov.hk/national_security/index.php?l=en&a=national_security_main_focus

meaning a controlled but stable society, thus a "strong China" was a way hopefully to inspire national confidence in the people and respect internationally. This was in exchange for the downplaying of ideology after 1989. The overall goal is to give "top priority to national interests"; Hong Kong, as an "inalienable part of the People's Republic of China", comes under this security umbrella. In many respects "Xi has turned national security from policy goal to mode of governance" (Drinhausen and Legarda 2022, 5).

Announcing Hong Kong's National Security Law

The decision to have a new National Security Law (NSL), full title: Law of the People's Republic of China on Safeguarding National Security in the Hong Kong Special Administrative Region (中華人民共和國香港特別行政區維護國家安全法) was announced without warning on 22 May 2020 and endorsed by the National People's Congress Standing Committee (NPCSC) on 28 May. All drafting and legislative formalities in time for its promulgation by 1st July 2020, the 23rd anniversary of Hong Kong's return to Chinese rule. No time had been allowed for public consultation; nor was there a circulation of a first draft (as had occurred for the Sino-British Joint Declaration and the Basic Law). The full text would not be available until after the law was actually promulgated. The NSL is annexed to Annex III of the Basic Law as part of the national laws that apply in the HKSAR and took effect at 11 pm on 30 June 2020. The next section will look at the initial reaction after the announcement that the Chinese Central Authorities would devise this law for Hong Kong. This will help to see if these predictions would come to pass or not in later chapters of this book.

Reactions to the Law's Announcement

Reactions to the announcement of the NSL, the contents of which were unknown, were immediate: For example, such a law "eroded rule of law principles" and "it is a weaponised law that threatens…" (Creery 2020); it would "sound the death knell for One Country, Two Systems framework"

(Chang 2020); "Beijing reveals its Orwellian plan to shackle Hong Kong, but can they kill an idea?" (Vines 2020); and "top Hong Kong barristers say 'unprecedented' security law draft has 'worrying and problematic features' (Ho 2020). On the other hand, according to former Chief Executive Tung Chi-hwa, "Legislation for safeguarding national security is not a savage monster, it is good medicine to save Hong Kong from the gridlock", to use a strange combination of metaphors (Ho 2020); "The relevant national security law will not undermine the principle of 'one country, two systems' or erode the systems on which Hong Kong's success as an international city depends, including the legal system" (Ta Kung Pao 2020). The views were polar opposites: The NSL was considered both a serious threat to and a means of salvation of the "One Country, Two Systems".

These photographs were both taken by the author on May 23, 2020, the day after the announcement that a National Security Law would be introduced. Figure 2.1 is a Hong Kong Federation of Trade Unions (a pro-Beijing group) stall asking people to sign their support for the upcoming law. The graffiti in Fig. 2.2 represents one of many that soon appeared all over Hong Kong.

The following are more specific views of law scholars, human rights organisations, Hong Kong activists, political parties, and Beijing-affiliated entities as well as the international community on what the possible effect of the NSL would be on Hong Kong and its systems. At the end of these excerpts, their current position/status is listed (as of 2024), which already implies certain connotations about life under the NSL:

Legal expert Johannes Chan, speaking to Citizen News: "If Article 23 can be legislated in such a way, can we possibly avoid other laws? It means that all laws in China can be applicable in Hong Kong." … "If we accept everything Beijing mandates, the judiciary can barely play its role." (Wong 2020a). Chan is the former Dean (2002–2014) of the Faculty of Law, University of Hong Kong. He retired from the University in July 2021 and was appointed an adjunct professor after his retirement.[8]

[8] Beijing supporters tried to thwart the appointment of legal scholar Johannes Chan as a university pro-vice-chancellor. He was criticised by the pro-Beijing media, which stressed his unsuitability for the job given his public support for Occupy Central in 2014. According to Chan, "They are trying to send a message that if someone is sympathetic to Occupy Central … there will be repercussions" (Reuters 2015).

Fig. 2.1 Pro-NSL Group

Law scholar Eric Cheung: "The Central Government is enacting a tailor-made law designed for the situation in Hong Kong under the guise of enforcing a nationwide law through the use of Appendix III of the Basic Law, which indicates that the Central Government is legislating laws on Hong Kong's behalf. This act would utterly violate the Basic Law, and annul the One Country Two Systems model" (Wong 2020a). Eric Cheung is on the academic staff, Faculty of Law, the University of Hong Kong.

Fig. 2.2 One country, one system

Activist Joshua Wong: "I know everyone is panicking and worrying. I also wonder what will become of Hong Kong after the National Security Law has passed. How many will be prosecuted? How many [political] groups will be replaced? To what extent will the oppression be? Will we be transferred to China? Arrest or imprisonment? (Wong 2020a). Joshua Wong is currently serving various prison sentences.

Activist Nathan Law: "We are blessed with an ideal battlefield nonetheless…One of the major reasons the Chinese Communist Party has opted for doing it now is to restrain the international community from standing with Hong Kong, but we must strive for the world's support" (Wong 2020a). Nathan Law, a former legislator, is now in self-exile in the United Kingdom with a Hong Kong Government bounty on his head.

Pro-democracy lawmaker Dennis Kwok: "When the world is not watching they are killing Hong Kong, killing one country, two systems, and using social distancing rules to keep people from coming out to protest… This is the most devastating thing to happen to Hong Kong since the Handover" (Wong 2020a). Dennis Kwok is in self-imposed exile with a Hong Kong bounty on his head. A former Hong Kong lawmaker representing the legal functional constituency in the Legislative Council. He is currently a partner in a law firm in New York City as well as serving as a visiting professor at a range of academic institutions in the United States.

Joshua Rosenzweig, Amnesty International: "China routinely abuses its own national security framework as a pretext to target human rights activists and stamp out all forms of dissent. This dangerous proposed law sends the clearest message yet that it is eager to do the same in Hong Kong, and as soon as possible." (Amnesty International, May 22, 2020). The organisation no longer operates in Hong Kong. Overseas, the reaction was similar:

European Union: "The EU considers that democratic debate, consultation of key stakeholders, and respect for protected rights and freedoms in Hong Kong would represent the best way of proceeding with the adoption of national security legislation, as foreseen in Article 23 of the Basic Law, while also upholding Hong Kong's autonomy and the 'One Country Two Systems' principle" (EU, May 22, 2020).

The establishment/government camp saw the NSL as a solution to longstanding problems:

New People's Party: "Over the past year, there has been all kinds of violence, terrorism and separatism with a hint of subverting the country and the SAR government, but Hong Kong lacks the legislation to tackle it… Therefore, the New People's Party supports the country to take the initiative to enhance national security and perfect "One Country, Two Systems" (Wong 2020a). The New People's Party is considered a pro-Beijing political party in Hong Kong. Chaired by Regina Ip, she is currently the convenor of the Executive Council (ExCo) and a member of the Legislative Council of Hong Kong. Ip was the secretary of security in 2002 when the draft of Article 23 was released. [9]

---

[9] Ip became a controversial figure for her role advocating the passage of the national security legislation (Article 23 of the Basic Law) in 2003 and after this legislation was withdrawn, she became the

State-run China Daily editorial: "The overreaction of those rioters and their foreign backers, who see such legislation as a thorn in their side, only testifies to the pertinence of the decision and the urgent need for such legislation, which will accelerate the construction and improvement of China's legal system regarding national security, and enhance the efficiency of the country's response to national security concerns. Thus, it is an integral component of the country's overall efforts to modernize its governing capacity and system" (*China Daily*, May 21, 2020).

The State-run Global Times: The national security legislation for HKSAR is fundamentally necessary for the "one country, two systems" principle. Hong Kong opposition forces and Western media have said the draft decision would destroy it. On the contrary, the draft law is a move aimed at preventing external forces from meddling in HK affairs. It would also deter the power HK extremists. The decision would reestablish a stable environment where the "one country, two systems" principle could work smoothly" (*Global Times*, May 22, 2020).

We can see from many of the opinions above that this law would likely have profound changes in the "One Country, Two Systems', that Hong Kong would have less autonomy, that China would not perform according with international norms of behaviour, and that human rights and rule of law would be compromised. On the other hand, Beijing-affiliated sources and pro-Beijing parties and newspapers saw the NSL as something necessary and that would enhance law and order as well as perfecting the "One Country, Two Systems". Remember these views were given *before* the contents of the NSL were known. This section serves as a kind of foreshadowing of future discourse on the NSL and whether predictions were accurate or not about aftermath of the NSL.

In the next section there will be a systematic analysis of the content NSL itself vis-à-vis the Basic Law and international covenants that are mentioned in the NSL. Although greatly informed by the recent edited

---

first principal official to resign from the administration of Chief Executive Tung Chee-hwa. She was famous for saying that "Hitler was elected by universal suffrage" Don't believe that democracy will be a panacea and that "Adolf Hitler was returned by universal suffrage and he killed seven million Jews" (「希特勒就是一人一票選出來，他殺了700 萬猶太人。」). "At Forum City University Students Oppose Legislation" (論壇上即場表態城大學生反立法), *Ming Pao Daily*, October 29, 2002.

book on the NSL published by the University of Hong Kong's Faculty of Law (Fu and Hor 2022), the analysis is carried out as a fairly educated reader would understand it, rather than the detailed analysis by a legal scholar and also in general linguistic terms as a product belonging to the legal genre. There will also be some comments on how some of these articles have already worked in reality.

A Content Analysis of the National Security Law

Textual (content) analysis is a technique that serves to describe, in an objective and systematic way, the content of communication. A textual and critical analysis of the NSL will show what ambiguity and vagueness lie in many of its provisions (Wong and Kellogg 2021). In a nutshell, this new law criminalises any act of: *secession*—that is, breaking away from the country; *subversion*—that is, undermining the power or authority of the central government, *terrorist activities*—that is, using violence or intimidation against people, and fourthly, *collusion with a foreign country or with external elements to endanger national security* –involvement with outside entities that are not in the nation's interests. The following lays out the structure of the document.

Chapter I	General Principles
Chapter II	The Duties and the Government Bodies of the Hong Kong Special Administrative Region for Safeguarding National Security
Chapter III	Offences and Penalties: Secession, Subversion, Terrorist Activities; Collusion with a Foreign Country or with External Elements to Endanger National Security; Other Provisions on Penalty; Scope of Application
Chapter IV	Jurisdiction, Applicable Law and Procedure
Chapter V	Office for Safeguarding National Security of the Central People's Government in the Hong Kong Special Administrative Region
Chapter VI	Supplementary Provisions

Chapter I: General Principles (Articles 1–6)

The NSL is enacted to implement the principle of "One Country, Two Systems" (OCTS) and to protect the lawful rights and interests of residents of the HKSAR (Article 1), which is similar to the role of the Basic Law. This implies that the OCTS has not been implemented fully. Article 2 makes specific mention of abiding by the provisions of the Basic law, while Article 3 states that the Central People's Government (CPG) has an "overarching responsibility" on national security affairs, while Hong Kong has to "perform the duty accordingly", which fits in with the holistic security concept discussed earlier. Since the CPG has this "overarching responsibility" for national security which is "holistic", it could in fact have impacts on the provisions of the Basic Law itself. There is a general principle to protect human rights (Article 4). This is particularly important article, bringing in an international context concerning "freedoms" vis-à-vis constrictions on freedoms that will be later apparent:

> Human rights shall be respected and protected in safeguarding national security of the Hong Kong Special Administrative Region. The rights and freedoms, including the freedoms of speech, of the press, of publication, of association of assembly, of procession and of demonstration…shall be protected in accordance with the law.

The "law" referred to here is the Basic Law and the International Covenant on Civil and Political Rights (ICCPR) and the International Covenant on Economic, Social, and Political Rights (ICESPR). However, there are no detailed measures in this article on how to protect this exercise of the freedom of expression and of the press in more specific terms, or to reconcile the potential conflict between the exercise of these freedoms in this or any subsequent article. This legislation is often broad and vague, and perhaps purposely so, i.e., left for the courts to work out later. This will later become apparent (for one has to see the NSL as a whole as other articles impact on individual articles).

Article 5 of the Hong Kong National Security Law clearly stipulates that law enforcement agencies must adhere to "the principle of the rule of law when taking law enforcement actions against offences endangering national security". Furthermore, "a person is presumed innocent until convicted by a judicial body." In addition, no one shall be liable to be tried or punished again for an offence for which he or she has already been finally convicted or acquitted in judicial proceedings. However, the government has sought to overturn by appeal a verdict that the government does not like.[10]

Article 6 deals with the "common responsibility" of the people and organisations of Hong Kong to safeguard and not endanger the security of the nation. In particular people standing for public office "shall confirm in writing or take an oath" to swear allegiance to the HKSAR.

Chapter II: Duties and Government Bodies

Part 1 Duties (Articles 7–18)

Article 7 concerns the enacting of security legislation Article 23 "as stipulated in the Basic Law" as "early as possible". This article will: "prohibit any act of treason, secession, sedition, subversion against the Central People's Government, or theft of state secrets, to prohibit foreign political organisations or bodies from conducting political activities in the HKSAR", and will also prohibit political organisations/bodies from establishing ties with foreign counterparts. These offences are not covered by the NSL.[11] Article 8 urges law and judicial authorities to "fully enforce" the NSL to prevent, suppress and punish acts endangering national security, by using this law and "laws in force for the region"; the combination

[10] The DOJ to get more power to challenge NSL acquittals: Hong Kong's prosecutors will be given more opportunities to appeal against any acquittals in national security trials, under new legislation planned by the government. "The Department of Justice (DOJ) explained that at present, prosecutors do not have the right to turn to the Court of Appeal if a three-judge Court of First Instance panel acquits a defendant in a national security trial, 'even though its reasons for verdict may disclose an error of law'". This contrasts with acquittals by magistrates or District Court judges, which can be subject to appeal under existing law. Another change planned to the Criminal Procedure Ordinance will give prosecutors the ability to appeal if the judge in a High Court criminal trial with a jury rules the defendant has no case to answer" (see https://news.rthk.hk/rthk/en/component/k2/1701820-20230523.htm).

[11] From the Security Bureau: https://www.sb.gov.hk/eng/bl23/faq.html (see Question 1). Article 23 was introduced in early 2024. Prior to Article 23, the old colonial law on sedition was used to prosecute individuals deemed in violation of the National Security Law.

of "laws in force" ultimately have some contradictions with Article 4 as well as subsequent articles on extended police powers and special national security committees.

Under Article 9, the government should take "necessary measures" to "strengthen" public communication, guidance, supervision, and regulation over matters concerning national security, including those relating to schools, social organisations, the media, and the Internet. These necessary measures are not defined. Article 10 is similar to Article 9 in that it is also "raise the awareness of Hong Kong residents of national security and of obligation to abide by the law" and reiterates that the law has to be obeyed as a solemn duty.

Part 2 Government Bodies: (Articles 12 to 19)

The NSL creates new security structures, the Committee for Safeguarding National Security (CSNS). The CSNS is created under Article 12 of the NSL, and operates as a hybrid body, which includes senior Hong Kong government officials and a National Security Advisor appointed by the Central People's Government). However, Article 12 also makes clear that the Committee only answers to Beijing: "It shall be under the supervision of and accountable to the Central People's Government"; therefore, it is not accountable to the people of Hong Kong.

The scope of the Committee is rather broad and vague. Under Article 14 of the Law, the Committee has both an analytical and coordinating role, and is also responsible for "advancing the development of the legal system and enforcement mechanisms… for safeguarding national security." The work of the Committee is thus largely beyond the reach of the Hong Kong legal system: its decisions are not subject to judicial review, and information relating to its work is not subject to public scrutiny: "No institution, organisation or individual relating to the work of the committee shall be subject to disclosure. Decisions made by the Committee shall not be amenable to judicial review" (Article 14).[12] The NSL could

[12] Judicial review is a procedure by which the Court of First Instance of the High Court exercises its supervisory jurisdiction over the activities of administrative bodies and inferior courts. "The administrative bodies concerned are usually government departments and those public bodies

thus undermine judicial independence in at least three ways. First, by not being able to be judicially reviewed, it is in effect placing the NSL above other laws, making it beyond public or legal inspection. Second, "being not subject to disclosure" in the name of national security (i.e., no transparency); and third, as there is a mainland-appointed security advisor who will sit on the meetings of the Committee (Article 15)—and as the representative of state power would likely wield significant power on the committee.

The police force will also "establish a department for safeguarding national security" (Article 16) within the Hong Kong Police Force. The police's duties and functions in this special department (Article 17) are different from the usual duties of the police force. It has extra tasks of intelligence gathering concerning national security, planning, and coordination of operations for safeguarding national security and conducting counter-interference investigations and national security reviews (Article 17). The latter function could presumably involve counter-espionage operations directed at foreign governments and entities. These duties are similar to what intelligence services do (DCAF 2017, 2).

Chapter III: Offences and Penalties

The NSL has four core criminal provisions: secession, subversion, terrorism, and collusion with foreign entities, as well as incitement to engage in these actions, or other forms of support for them.

Part I: Secession (Articles 20 & 21)

"Secession" according to the *Cambridge Dictionary* is "the act of becoming independent and no longer part of a country, area, organization, etc."

which were set up according to certain ordinances. The first important note is that judicial review does not aim at reviewing the merits of an administrative decision. Instead, the court will review the relevant decision-making process. In other words, the court will not examine whether the decision under challenge is right or wrong, but it will check whether there was any error made during the decision-making process." Community Legal Information Centre, Law and Technology Centre, the University of Hong Kong (see https://clic.org.hk/en/topics/civilCase/judicial_review).

A definition of secession is not given, but as "acts": "A person who organises, plans, commits or participates in any of the following acts, whether or not by force or threat of force, with a view to committing secession or undermining national unification shall be guilty of an offence":

(1) *separating* the Hong Kong Special Administrative Region or any other part of the People's Republic of China from the People's Republic of China;
(2) *altering by unlawful means* the legal status of the Hong Kong Special Administrative Region or of any other part of the People's Republic of China; or
(3) *surrendering* the Hong Kong Special Administrative Region or any other part of the People's Republic of China to a foreign country.

Use of force or the threat of force is not a required element of the crime, just saying it seems to be enough. Article 21 of the NSL affects not just an individual who "organises, plans, commits" but also someone who "participates in" or "incites, assists in, abets" or otherwise provides help for the acts of secession (Article 21). The three points above seems to indicate that a collective or group, rather than an individual, would be more likely able to do these acts. Furthermore (italics added):

> A person who is a principal offender or a person who commits an offence of a *grave nature* shall be sentenced to life imprisonment or fixed-term imprisonment of not less than ten years; a person who *actively participates* in the offence shall be sentenced to fixed-term imprisonment of not less than three years but not more than ten years…
>
> If the circumstances of the offence committed by a person are of a *serious nature*, the person shall be sentenced to fixed-term imprisonment of not less than five years but not more than ten years; if the circumstances of the offence committed by a person are of a *minor nature*…

The phrases "a grave nature, "a serious nature", and a "minor nature" are not defined. Under a civil law system, which China follows, laws are "underspecified and written in the form of general principles" (Bhatia et al. 2008, 136; see also Cao 2004) leaving the interpretation to other bodies, also meaning the changing of principles "according to the actual situation".[13] The broad wording could mean that anyone who uttered statements in support of Hong Kong's autonomy, "a bystander who at the spur of the moment joined a pro-independence protest, or a person giving water to protesters could perhaps be charged with an offence.

States can prohibit acts of secession, provided that such provisions are usually narrowly tailored to primarily cover violent acts that are meant to overthrow the state, or to end its sovereignty or control over a particular piece of territory, or clear an unequivocal incitement to such acts of violence. In many countries, the "peaceful advocacy of political independence is generally protected by international law: (Wong and Kellogg 2021, 20). With its vague and overbroad language, terms like "surrendering" and "altering by unlawful means" used in the Article are both broad and not legally defined. Beijing is particularly sensitive to pro-independence talk, something that emerged even before the 2019 protests in 2017. In 2018, for example, the Hong Kong SAR government banned the pro-independence Hong Kong National Party (HKNP). The topic of "independence", is so sensitive, that even acts of possessing pro-independence literature and shouting pro-independence slogans have been considered serious enough for charges to be laid on a number of individuals since the law as introduced.

Subversion (Articles 22 & 23)

Article 22 of the NSL covers subversion, which includes "overthrowing or undermining" the People's Republic; "seriously interfering in, disrupting, or undermining the performance of duties and functions" of the People's Republic of China or the Hong Kong government; or "attacking or damaging the premises and facilities" of the Hong Kong government (italics added).

[13] The word "elections" were left undefined in the Sino-British Declaration, for later "definition-giving" by legal gatekeepers. "According to the actual situation" are in Article 45 of the Basic Law about when universal suffrage for the election of the chief executive could be introduced into Hong Kong.

The law defines four vague acts of subversion (summarizing the actual text):

(1) "*overthrowing or undermining*" the basic system of mainland China
(2) "*overthrowing*" the body of central power of mainland China or Hong Kong
(3) "*Seriously interfering in, disrupting, or undermining* the performance of duties and functions" by the Chinese or Hong Kong governments; and
(4) "attacking or damaging the premises and facilities" used by the HK government to perform its duties and functions such that it is incapable of performing them.

Expressive activity related to these acts is also included since the law covers such acts whether committed "by force or threat of force or other unlawful means". The law captures anyone who "organises, plans, commits or participates in" or who "incites, assists in, abets or provides pecuniary or other financial assistance or property" (Article 23) for the commission of the subversive acts. These provisions are vague and any activity could be viewed as possibly "disrupting or undermining" the actions of the Chinese or Hong Kong governments under Article 22(3), from disagreeing with a government policy to contesting elections on a pro-democracy slate (which came to pass in the Legislative Council elections of 2021 with the instigators of "unofficial primaries" are now being prosecuted). The law fails to define what specific actions would count as "disrupting or undermining", for example. Thus, these provisions mean that the Central and Hong Kong authorities could arrest almost anyone they view as a threat to national security.

As with secession, force or the threat of force is not an element of the crime of subversion. In regards to the International Covenant on Civil and Political Rights (ICCPR) and International Covenant on Economic, Social and Cultural Rights (ICESCR) the list of acts in Article 22 is rather vague; it is not just "overthrowing" the government but also "undermining the performance of duties and "functions" of the local and central governments.

The same problem with broad and imprecise language in Article 20 on secession can also be found in Article 22: peaceful political protests that block access to government buildings, for example, it is fairly common sense that you could easily make arrests in certain instances, according to regular law. Acts of vandalism against government buildings or other state property might also be deemed subversion under the NSL.

As a result, Article 22 would not be proportional (the punishment fitting the crime in other words).[14] Experts in Hong Kong expressed concern that this provision was meant to target peaceful protesters who took part in protests that later turned violent, which was the case in Hong Kong in 2019.[15]

Article 23 of the NSL covers incitement and aiding and abetting individuals engaged in subversive acts, including the provision of financial support. As with secession, force or the threat of force is not an element of this article; subversion is "generally seen by legal experts as a "political" criminal act, used to punish a government's political enemies, and generally not used to tackle genuine threats to the existing political order" (Wong and Kellogg 2021, 22).

Part 3: Terrorist Activities (Articles 24–28)

Article 24 covers terrorist activities, and targets the use or threat of violent acts as part of an effort to "coerce" the central government or the Hong Kong government to do certain actions. Listed actions include "serious violence against a person or persons" and "explosion, arson, or dissemination of poisonous or radioactive substances". Article 25 covers individuals who organise terrorist organisations while Article 26 covers

[14] "The proportionality test is a four-stage test. It requires the restriction in question to be justified in terms of four matters: first, the restriction must serve a legitimate aim. Second, there has to be a rational connection between the legitimate aim and the restriction. Third, the restriction must be no more than is necessary to achieve the legitimate aim. Fourth, the benefits of achieving the legitimate aim must not be disproportionate to the encroachment and inroads made into the fundamental right concerned, and in particular, the restriction must not impose an unacceptably harsh burden on the individual involved" (Cheung 2019).

[15] Protest marches have been approved after the lifting of Covid-19 restrictions in 2023; however, groups have withdrawn their request for a "letter of no objection" after being persuaded by police of liability if "radical elements" hijack their protest (see Chap. 6).

those who aid and abet such activities. Finally, Article 27 covers advocacy of and incitement to terrorism.

"Terrorism" as such is not defined in the article; rather a simple list of terrorist acts is set out. Terrorist activities here were acts causing or intended to cause "grave harm" to society with a view to "coercing the Central People's Government and the Government of the HKSAR or an international organisation or intimidating the public in order to pursue political agenda". These include serious violence; explosions or arson; dissemination of poisonous or radioactive substances; sabotage of transport or transport facilities; serious interruption or sabotage of electronic systems or public services such as water, electricity, power, gas, transport, telecommunications or the internet; and "other dangerous activities which seriously jeopardise public health, safety or security." This could include activities such as throwing petrol bombs at the police; committing arson as well as damaging the mass transit rail system, setting fire to traffic tunnels, smashing traffic lights, etc. that all occurred during the 2019 protests. The law could also be extended to include the blocking of major public roadways, which also took place in 2019 as well as "doxing" (i.e., publishing private personal information on the Internet) of police officers and government officials. Thus, the definition is left wide open.

Violence, target, motivation, and organisation seem to be key to any definition of terrorism. First, terrorism requires violence as its objective element (Zhou 2015). The United Nations' definition concerns intentional violence that causes (a) death or serious bodily injury to any person; (b) serious damage to public or private property; or (c) damage to property resulting or likely to result in major economic loss. The European Union definition provides a long list of the most serious offences against persons or property. International definition of terrorism in OECD countries are classified under the following headings: (1) Status of definition of terrorism (2) Intention of terrorist act (3) Identification of those behind the act (4) Means used (these mostly involve "acts of violence or "threats of violence" (5) Targets/effects (OECD n.d.). The US definition[16] requires the premeditated use of violence:

[16] The FBI website (https://www.fbi.gov/investigate) is blocked in Hong Kong. The author's friend in Australia accessed the site on her behalf for this definition.

> International terrorism: Violent, criminal acts committed by individuals and/or groups who are inspired by, or associated with, designated foreign terrorist organizations or nations (state-sponsored). Domestic terrorism: Violent, criminal acts committed by individuals and/or groups to further ideological goals stemming from domestic influences, such as those of a political, religious, social, racial, or environmental nature. (FBI see endnote 16)

Part 4: Collusion with a Foreign Country or with External Elements to Endanger National Security (Articles 29 & 30)

The term "collusion" does not appear in the actual texts of Articles 29 and 30 and is only present in the title to this crime. Article 29 is comprised of two offences. The first criminalises the provision of state secrets or intelligence concerning national security to foreign countries or other foreign actors. The second criminalises cooperation with foreign actors (broadly defined to include "conspiring with" or the indirect instructions or funding from such actors) to commit five specific acts (Italics added):

(1) *waging war against China* or using force or threatening to use force to "seriously undermine the sovereignty, unification and territorial integrity" of China (Article 29 (1));
(2) "*seriously disrupting* the formulation and implementation of laws" by the governments of China or Hong Kong (Article 29(2));
(3) "*rigging or undermining* an election" in Hong Kong (Article 29(3));
(4) *imposing sanctions*, blockades or engaging in "other hostile activities" by "unlawful means" against Hong Kong or mainland China (Article 29(4));
(5) *Provoking by unlawful means* hatred among Hong Kong residents towards the Central People's Government, which is likely to cause serious consequences.

Point (1) for example, could refer to efforts to collaborate with a foreign organisation to "seriously disrupt… the formulation and implementation of laws or policies by the Government of the Hong Kong Special Administrative Region". Such a provision could be used to cover lobbying efforts to change Hong Kong laws carried out jointly by Hong Kong and international groups, or Western foundations/organisations to fund such efforts by Hong Kong activist organisations.

Point (2) could perhaps involve disruptive acts performed in the Legislative Council during discussion of legislation and police matters, delaying passage of bills. Point (3) directly relates to 11 and 12 July 2020—although the unofficial primaries were held just after the NSL's introduction, the planning of the primaries was done some time earlier, which the government had known about and firmly criticised. The primaries, which were largely about maximising democratic candidates' chances of being elected, was not specifically against the Basic Law but explicitly authorises the Legislative Council to reject the budget and—if done twice—force the city's leader to resign (in Article 52).[17] Jonathan Sumption, who resigned as a non-permanent overseas judge from the Court of Final Appeal in June 2024, commented on recent convictions regarding these primaries: "The [ruling's] result is that Legco cannot exercise an express constitutional right for a purpose unwelcome to the government….(Tse 2024).

Point (4) relate to action of Hong Kong protesters calling for overseas sanctions during the 2019 protests (and even earlier) and relate to current political activists in exile. Point (5) introduces a new concept of "provoking by unlawful means hatred". Perhaps this assumes that the "hatred" will mean a violent act against the government. How can you tell the someone has provoked hatred rather than criticism? Article 20 of the ICCPR also mandates against inciting war and hatred, that may assist in defining "hatred" in the political context. The United Nations have a robust test (The Rabat Threshold Test) for Article 20, paragraph 2 of the ICCPR: "Any advocacy of national, racial or religious hatred that constitutes incitement to discrimination, hostility or violence shall be prohibited by law", since this article "requires a high threshold because limitation of freedom of expression must remain an exception".

[17] Article 52: The Chief Executive of the Hong Kong Special Administrative Region must resign under any of the following circumstances: When he or she loses the ability to discharge his or her duties as a result of serious illness or other reasons; When, after the Legislative Council is dissolved because he or she twice refuses to sign a bill passed by it, the new Legislative Council again passes by a two-thirds majority of all the members the original bill in dispute, but he or she still refuses to sign it; and When, after the Legislative Council is dissolved because it refuses to pass a budget or any other important bill, the new Legislative Council still refuses to pass the original bill in dispute.

The basic definition they give for "hatred" and "hostility" is an "intense and irrational emotions of opprobrium, enmity, and detestation towards the target group". There is six parts to the Test that needs to be fulfilled in order for a statement to amount to a criminal offence: context, speaker, intent, content, and form, extent of the speech act, and likelihood, including imminence (OHCHR n.d.). It is noted that in the NSL article there is a qualification that the provocation must be "by unlawful means" (which is not defined), and hence the incitement itself must also be against the law. Penalties range from life imprisonment for a "grave nature" down to three years (see other articles which have penalties of a similar vague nature), while Article 30 concerns a person "who conspired with or directly or indirectly receives instructions, control, funding or other kinds of support from a foreign country or an institution, organisation, or individual outside the mainland, Hong Kong, and Macao" will incur a "severe penalty".

Articles 29 and 30 are not meeting the standard as required by Article 15(1) of the ICCPR,[18] and similar concerns could be raised about proportionality. These provisions might affect the right of free association as protected by Article 22 of the ICCPR and by Article 27 of the Basic Law.[19] This could have implications with Hong Kong's oft-cited role as a conduit and "gateway" between the international community and groups and individuals in Hong Kong with mainland China.

Most jurisdictions have laws that outlaw collusion with foreign powers in ways that are detrimental to national security. Such laws generally cover matters such as intelligence gathering, or efforts to impede or degrade a state's national defence. However, Article 29 uses broad language that could be used to criminalise peaceful and common—civil

[18] Article 15(1): "No one shall be held guilty of any criminal offence on account of any act or omission which did not constitute a criminal offence, under national or international law, at the time when it was committed."

[19] Article 27 of the Basic Law: "No one shall be held guilty of any criminal offence on account of any act or omission which did not constitute a criminal offence, under national or international law, at the time when it was committed. Nor shall a heavier penalty be imposed than the one that was applicable at the time when the criminal offence was committed. If, subsequent to the commission of the offence, provision is made by law for the imposition of the lighter penalty, the offender shall benefit thereby."

society activity, such as contacts between human rights groups in Hong Kong and international non-governmental organisations in the United States, Europe, and elsewhere (the fact that a number of human rights organisations have left Hong Kong embodies these fears). For example, it does not explain what it means to "participate" in secession or subversion, and it is also not clear what it means to "indirectly receive" support from external "elements" to "undermine" Chinese sovereignty in the case of foreign collusion.

At the core of all four criminal provisions is the problem of vague and overbroad language, which could be used to punish peaceful acts of expression, association, and assembly. A core element of both international human rights laws and of the rule of law more generally, is the principle of legal certainty,[20] which holds that criminal laws should be narrowly defined, so that citizens are aware which specific behaviours constitute a criminal offense. Overly broad laws (principles) can be arbitrarily applied to opposing political views.

Part 5: Other Provisions on Penalty (Articles 31–35)

Article 31 relate to fines for entities such as companies or organisation which commits an offence under the NSL and Article 32 relates to "financial aid, gains and rewards, and funds and tools used or intended to be used in the commission of an offence"; thus, those charged may have their funds suspended, rightly or wrongly, while till their trial takes place. Article 33 "A lighter penalty may be imposed, or the penalty may be reduced or, in the case of a minor offence exempted, if an offender, criminal suspect, or defendant" does the following: "voluntarily discontinues" performing the offence; "voluntarily surrenders" themselves and "gives a truthful account of the offence"; or "reports on the offence by another person" (if true), or provides "material information" which helps in solving other criminal cases. To date, there appears that lighter sentences have not been given for these factors.

[20] ICCPR, Article 15(1). https://www.lexisnexis.co.uk/legal/glossary/legal-certainty

Part 6: Scope of Application (Article 36–39)

In a nutshell, the NSL has wide application—even outside Hong Kong, that is the Law has extraterritoriality. In Article 36, a potential criminal act will be considered as having "committed in the region" if "an act constituting the offence or the consequence of the offence occurs in the Region" (even if the perpetrator is outside the region). A "vessel or aircraft", if registered in the region will also come under the NSL is an act occurs on the vessel or aircraft. Hong Kong permanent residents and incorporated/unincorporated bodies registered in Hong Kong can be charged with an offence even outside the region (Article 37). Article 38 states that the Law even applies to persons who are not permanent residents of the region in circumstances where the offence is allegedly committed outside the region. This would seem difficult to enforce and perhaps are designed more for its deterrent effect and will stop these persons travelling to Hong Kong. With the withdrawal of extradition agreements made by other countries with Hong Kong, will see it difficult for people to be prosecuted. Article 39 just states that "This Law shall apply to acts committed after its entry into force for the purpose of conviction and imposition of punishment."

Chapter IV: Jurisdiction, Applicable Law, and Procedure (Articles 40–47)

Moving on from the Offences and Penalties in the previous section, Article 40, states that Hong Kong "shall have jurisdiction over cases concerning offences under this Law, except under the circumstances specified in Article 55 of this Law" (that is, where serious or complex cases can go to mainland courts—more on this article later).

The written consent of the Secretary for Justice is required before proceeding with a prosecution under the NSL. Trials would be on indictment in the High Court, which would be open unless involving state secrets or public order. In such circumstances, the trials would be closed or partially closed to the public and media. Nevertheless, the judgment would be delivered in open court (Article 41). In a reversal of the presumption of bail (based on the presumption of innocence until proven guilty), in cases involving the NSL, "no bail would be granted unless the Judge has sufficient grounds for believing that the defendant would not continue to breach acts endangering national security" (Article 42). There have been few cases of bail given since 2020, implying that perhaps a presumption of guilt is implicit, since the fear that other crimes may be permitted. In this article "concerning matters such as the detention and time limit for trial" the legal and judicial authorities of Hong Kong "shall ensure that cases concerning offence endangering national security are handled *in a fair and timely manner* so as to effectively prevent, suppress and impose punishment for such offences (emphasis added).[21] This would appear to be the case from Article 17 of the NSL in which the Hong Kong police are empowered to perform their duties as necessary for enforcement of the NSL.

The Hong Kong Police Force has to set up a designated department in-charge of offenses endangering national security offences (Article 43). The national security department of the police are exempted from key due process requirements, including the need to seek judicial authorisation to engage in certain forms of electronic surveillance and other searches of criminal suspects. The CSNS "shall be responsible for supervising the implementation of these measures."[22]

Articles 44 to 47 relate to the appointment of judges: The Chief Executive of Hong Kong can "designate" a number of officials to hear NSL cases from Magistrates and Recorders up to Judges of the Court of Final Appeal. In this regard, the Chief Executive may consult with the Chief Justice, as well as with the Committee for Safeguarding National

[21] This is in reference to people in jail for the primaries. They were arrested on 6 January 2021 and the cases have still not been concluded as of June 2024.

[22] Another major change is that a suspect under the NSL would be required to answer questions and produce materials, in the same manner as currently required under the Securities and Futures Ordinance, Cap 571, Laws of Hong Kong ("SFO") at section 187. However, the difference under the SFO is that the person can actually claim privilege against self-incrimination so that his answers are not used against him in a criminal trial. There may be a future test case in which a suspect tries to invoke the right to silence under Article 14 of the International Covenant on Civil and Political Rights ("ICCPR").

Security. The Chief Executive Carrie Lam stated that, from the panel of qualified judges, she would not be choosing individual judges for particular cases, but instead would rely upon the existing procedures by leaving the matter to the Chief Justice.

These judges are appointed for one year only, and judges can be removed if they are deemed to be a threat to national security, the criteria for which is unspecified (Article 44). The short appointment term and the lack of removal criteria seem to be contrary to the idea of judicial independence; and the definition of what is a "serious" or "grave" offence could have a tendency to be subjective. One Hong Kong lawyer observed that in practice, conviction-oriented judges were rewarded with promotions to higher courts, whereas those who followed traditional common law standards would see their careers stagnate (Lau 2020). For example, at least two judges were reassigned to handle non-criminal matters after they had acquitted protesters and were subject to criticism by pro-government figures (Wong 2020b). The Hong Kong government has generally appealed cases of acquittal and as of April 2023, there has been a 100 percent conviction rate in NSL cases, Hong Kong's security minister seeing this as "defending the rule of law and upholding justice" (Ho 2023).

Chapter V: Office for Safeguarding National Security (Articles 48–61)

Article 48 of the NSL allows for the creation an Office for Safeguarding National Security of the Central People's Government of the Hong Kong Special Administrative Region (to give its full name; hereafter OSNS). Unlike the Committee, which has a Hong Kong-Mainland structure, the Office is a solely a Mainland body, staffed by officials sent by the central government. The OSNS's mandate in Article 49 is wide-ranging: it includes a policy advisory role, an oversight role, and an intelligence collection and analysis role: "Analysing and assessing development in relation to safeguarding national security" in Hong Kong and "providing opinions and making proposals on major strategies and making proposals on majors strategies and important policies". The OSNS is also empowered to directly "handle cases concerning… national security in accordance with the law." This suggests that the OSNS could take part directly in such activities as questioning witnesses, gathering information on suspects through electronic surveillance and other means, and so on.

Article 50 states that the OSNS must "perform its mandate in strict compliance with the law," and that the staff of the Office will "abide by the laws of the HKSAR." However, if the CSNS and OSNS were only to advise on the Hong Kong SAR government's day-to-day work, that advisory role would still infringe on the Hong Kong government's authority. The two new groups could take on a direct role in implementing the NSL, and the National Security Advisor could exercise direct authority over cases being investigated and tried under the law.

Articles 51–53 largely detail organisational matters of the OSNS, its funding by the Central People's government, that the Hong Kong Government needs to "strengthen working relations and cooperation with the Liaison Office of the Central People's Government" and "establish a mechanism of coordination" with the CSNS. This suggests a holistic type of control over most workings of the Hong Kong Government and a lesser role for the Basic Law. The Office also plays a special role in the "management of and services of organs of foreign countries and international organizations" in Hong Kong, as well as non-government organisations and new agencies of foreign countries," obviously seeing them as potential threats to national security, whose activities need to be watched more closely than prior to the introduction of the NSL (Article 54).

Article 55 of the NSL also allows the Office to simply take over a case, without obligation to work with Hong Kong institutions, if it believes that such cases are sufficiently "complex" to warrant doing so ("complexity" is undefined), especially if it is "due to the involvement of a foreign country or eternal elements, thus making it difficult for the Region to exercise jurisdiction over the case"; in addition, if a "serious situation" where Hong Kong is "unable to effectively enforce this law" (if Hong Kong had Article 23 in place in 2019, the CPG would not have had to act), or if it believes that a "major and imminent threat to national security has occurred", this article can be invoked. Again, the situations or threats are not defined.

Article 56 also allows for the designation of Mainland courts to handle such cases using Mainland criminal procedure and other laws if the

OSNS "initiates investigation into the case", and further that the "Supreme People's procuratorate shall designate a prosecuting body to prosecute it". Ironically, this somewhat resembles the original extradition bill ordinance that led to the massive protests in 2019. This undermines the judicial independence promised by Article 85 of the Basic Law,[23] and the jurisdiction of the courts "over all the cases in the Region" established by Article 19(2) of the Basic Law.[24] Even more importantly, perhaps, Article 55 casts doubt on the right of individuals accused of a crime in Hong Kong to a fair trial, guaranteed by Article 87 of the Basic Law,[25] if one compares criminal trials in China where there is little transparency.[26] Articles 57–59 mostly relate to procedural matters relative to Article 55, also about the right for a lawyer to represent him or her.[27]

However, Article 60 makes clear that staff of the office "shall not be subject to the jurisdiction of the Hong Kong Special Administrative Region." As with the Committee, the Office would also seem to be above the laws of Hong Kong, making any promise that it will abide by Hong Kong law unenforceable or difficult to enforce.

The CSNS and the OSNS can be seen to have shared mandates and overlapping division of labour, illustrating what is a key element of the NSL: That it has multiple layers of control. The Law's provisions give

[23] Article 85 of the Basic Law: "The courts of the Hong Kong Special Administrative Region shall exercise judicial power—not a lawyer of this choice independently, free from any interference. Members of the judiciary shall be immune from legal action in the performance of their judicial functions."

[24] Article 19 (2) of the Basic Law: "The courts of the Hong Kong Special Administrative Region shall have jurisdiction over all cases in the Region, except that the restrictions on their jurisdiction imposed by the legal system and principles previously in force in Hong Kong shall be maintained."

[25] Article 87 of the Basic law" "In criminal or civil proceedings in the Hong Kong Special Administrative Region, the principles previously applied in Hong Kong and the rights previously enjoyed by parties to proceedings shall be maintained."

[26] The conviction rate is similar to the Mainland's; Hong Kong security chief hails 100% conviction rate in national security cases; "Hong Kong's security minister hailed the national security law and the prosecution's chief said that 'defending the rule of law and upholding justice is in the DNA of our prosecutors' (Ho 2023).

[27] The *Apple Daily's* proprietor Jimmy Lai was unable to retain overseas counsel for his NSL trial. Hong Kong's leader "will refrain from explaining his decision to bar any overseas lawyers from national security trials under a new vetting system, as doing so could pose a risk to the state". Secretary for Justice Paul Lam Ting-kwok said that "'fundamentally' overseas lawyers should not take part in national security cases, but added no outright ban would be adopted" (Yau and Chan 2023).

Beijing a number of different ways to react to any perceived national security threat: it can work through the OSNS, or through the CSNS, with the National Security Advisor overseeing the latter's work. It can work with the Hong Kong prosecutor to try national security cases in Hong Kong courts, or it can move to have key cases tried in Mainland courts.

If both the CSNS and the OSNS are involved in day-to-day policing and policy functions, then they would seem to be directly overriding the functions of Hong Kong SAR government in some fashion as with cases taken over by the OSNS under Article 55) or in part. This would seem to go against some provisions of the Basic Law, including Article 12, which states that the SAR will "enjoy a high degree of autonomy", and Article 16, which grants executive authority to the SAR government, and ensures that it will administer Hong Kong "on its own", and also Article 22.[28] We know that "a high degree" is something that can be negotiable.

Chapter VI: Supplementary Provisions (Articles 62–65)

Article 62 states that the NSL "shall prevail" over provisions of local laws of Hong Kong in cases of direct conflict. This would likely mean that local laws like the Bill of Rights Ordinance) would be subordinate to it, and that they could not be used to offset the impact of, the NSL's vague and broad criminal provisions, despite the human rights norms what was stated in Article 4 of the NSL. As a law passed by the National People's Congress, the Basic Law itself is not covered by the Article; one could therefor argue that it possesses a somewhat higher status than the Basic Law, which was passed by the Standing Committee of the National People's Congress (SCNPC). Therefore, local judiciary would be limited in how it could interpret the NSL.

Article 63 emphasises the confidentiality of the information concerning an offence that endangers national security that "law enforcement and judicial authorities and their staff" hold (including defense counsels

[28] Article 22 of the Basic Law: "No department of the Central People's Government and no province, autonomous region, or municipality directly under the Central Government may interfere in the affairs which the Hong Kong Special Administrative Region administers on its own in accordance with this Law."

or legal representatives) as well as any "relevant institutions, organisations and individuals who assist in handling the case", therefore much will remain hidden to the public.

Article 64 provides for how these mainland-style penalties (the three penalty ranges—see Article 20) The terms used to express penalties are similar to the PRC legal system and will be "converted" into punishment that fits the Hong Kong's legal system (Chen 2022, 29). Article 65 limits the role of the judiciary in interpreting the NSL. Under this Article, as the Standing Committee of the National People's Congress has the power of interpretation of the Law. It may not do so in some case, but it could be used to give a conservative reading of the NSL's core provisions, limiting what the courts could do judicially to minimise the effects of the law. As a final statement to the Law, Article 66 simply states that "This Law comes into force on the date of its promulgation."

Conclusion: Legalising Security

From Beijing's perspective, the events of history as a subversive base, with the events of 2019 as a tipping point: Beijing seemed to view the HKSAR government as being incapable of dealing with the protests on its own. Beijing also saw the protests as a direct challenge to its own authority (with the calls for independence by some for a "revolution of our times"). While the introduction of the NSL without consultation from Hong Kong seemed to touch on Hong Kong's "high degree of autonomy" (It had to "shall enact laws on its own to prohibit any act of treason, secession, sedition, subversion against the Central People's Government…" (Article 23, Basic Law); the 13-year delay in Article 23's implementation was seen as unacceptable.

The multiple layers of control in the National Security Law (special committee, national security advisor) indicate Beijing's desire for a high degree (almost "holistic") authority over Hong Kong matters, and its lack of trust in the Hong Kong SAR government. According to the Mainland, if this law were not implemented, the political situation in Hong Kong would likely continue to deteriorate.

The Basic Law tried to "freeze" Hong Kong's political and legal systems what they were in the 1980s despite the change in sovereignty (refer back to Chap. 1). The NSL attempts to readjust legal norms and institutions in Hong Kong to render "convergence, compatibility and complementarity" (Lam 2023) between Hong Kong and national Chinese laws. The dual nature of the NSL means Chinese legal elements are inserted into Hong Kong's legal system, expands the presence of the Central Authorities in the SAR, and deepens the intersection as well as conflict between mainland law and Hong Kong's common law, thus imposing challenges to the rule of law. Although the Hong Kong system has often grappled with and absorbed Chinese legal conventions, the decisions of Hong Kong courts are often enforced in mainland China by mainland courts.

The constant mention of "endanger(ing) national security" by the Hong Kong Government (not only in the NSL where it occurs 31 times), could mean many things, given the vagueness and ambiguity of the language used in the Law's various articles as previously described. The four offences (Parts I-IV in Chapter III) are broadly defined, thus have the potential to act as "catch-all offences" according to the situation at the time.[29] Although vagueness often occurs unintentionally in everyday language, it can also be used as a deliberate rhetorical strategy to avoid dealing with an issue or responding directly to a question (this was done with inserting the word "elections" into the Sino-British Declaration and certain phrases in Article 45 of the Basic Law dealing with the introduction of universal suffrage). Vagueness can be used to allow someone to redefine a concept useful for a particular occasion (Macagno and Walton 2014). Interpretation is thus the key in how the National Security could be enforced, particularly when vague. "Guidance" is thus needed in determining the meaning of some of the vague/ambiguous words mentioned in the articles of the NSL. Courts and legislators are likely to seek government officials' interpretations of vague statutory terms, in this case, it would be the mainland-appointed National Security Advisor.

[29] A "catch all" is something intended to include everything. A catch-all offence or a "pocket crime", the charge has been used by Chinese authorities against human rights activists and dissidents for a wide range of behaviours. 'Picking quarrels and provoking trouble': how China's catch-all crime muzzles dissent (Guo 2021).

The National Security law (in line with the concept of holistic national security) also imposes controls over education, journalism, and social media, and to areas outside Hong Kong; the investigating authorities (the special police department) have extra powers and the Chinese Central Government now has a national security arm in Hong Kong, one that is not subject to oversight. Human rights' protections are given in Article 4 of the law, but there is risk that they could be overridden given the nature of other articles in the law. The is so vague it prevents anyone from knowing how and when they might transgress it (cross the so-called "red lines").[30] The effects of this law have been immediate in Hong Kong society, and these aspects will be dealt with in Chap. 5, the effects on civil society in practice. The next chapter will see how the government "sells" the NSL to the Hong Kong people prior and immediately after the implementation of the Law.

References

Amnesty International. "China: Dangerous National Security Law Plan is Fundamental Attack on Human Rights in Hong Kong." Amnesty International, May 22, 2020. https://www.amnesty.org/en/latest/news/2020/05/china-dangerous-national-security-law-plan-is-fundamental-attack-on-human-rights-in-hong-kong/

Bhatia, Vijay, Christopher N. Candlin, and P. Evangelisti Allori, eds. *Language, Culture and the Law: The Formulation of Legal Concepts across Systems and Cultures*. Bern/New York: Peter Lang, 2008.

Callahan, William, A. "National Insecurities: Humiliation, Salvation, and Chinese Nationalism." *Alternatives* 29 (2004): 199–218.

Callahan, William, A. "The Cartography of National Humiliation and the Emergence of China's Geobody." *Public Culture* 21, no. 1 (2009): 141–173.

Cao, Deborah. *Chinese Law: A Language Perspective*. Burlington, V.T.: Ashgate, 2004.

[30] The "three red lines" are as follows: not endangering China's national security; not engaging in political infiltration in Hong Kong; and not slandering or damaging Hong Kong's development prospects (Chan 2023).

Cabestan, Jean-Pierre. China's Foreign- and Security-policy Decision-making Processes under Hu Jintao. *Journal of Current Chinese Affairs* 38, no. 3 (2009): 63–97.

Chan, Kahon. "Hong Kong National Security Law: Beijing's '3 Red Lines' have 'Zero Effect' on My Work, US Envoy to City Gregory May Says." *South China Morning Post*, March 22, 2023. https://www.scmp.com/news/hong-kong/politics/article/3214410/hong-kong-national-security-law-beijings-3-red-lines-have-zero-effect-my-work-us-envoy-city-gregory

Chang, Albert. "Beijing's National Security Law Sounds the Death Knell for 'One Country, Two Systems' and Democracy in Hong Kong." *South China Morning Post*, May 29, 2020. https://www.scmp.com/comment/opinion/article/3086482/beijings-national-security-law-sounds-death-knell-one-country-two

Chen, Albert H. Y. "The National Security Law of the HKSAR: A Contextual and Legal Study." In Hualing Fu and Michael Hor, eds., *The National Security Law of Hong Kong Restoration and Transformation*. Hong Kong: Hong Kong University Press (2022), 20–48. http://dx.doi.org/10.2139/ssrn.3958261

Cheung, Andrews. "Conflict of Fundamental Rights and the Double Proportionality Test." A Lecture in the Common Law Lecture Series 2019 delivered at the University of Hong Kong on September 17, 2019. https://www.hkcfa.hk/filemanager/speech/en/upload/2236/Common%20Law%20Lecture%20(Final%20Version).pdf

China Daily. "Proposed Security Legislation to Better Safeguard Hong Kong's Development: China Daily editorial." Chinadaily.com.cn, May 21, 2020. https://global.chinadaily.com.cn/a/202005/21/WS5ec687fea310a8b241157686.html

Creery, Jennifer. "'Double Standards and Hypocrisy': Hong Kong Gov't Rebukes Foreign Criticism over National Security Law Plan." *Hong Kong Free Press*, May 25, 2020. https://hongkongfp.com/2020/05/25/double-standards-and-hypocrisy-hong-kong-govt-rebukes-foreign-criticism-over-national-security-law-plan/

DCAF. "Intelligence Services: Roles and Responsibilities in Good Security Sector Governance." Geneva Centre for the Democratic Control of Armed Forces, "Intelligence Oversight", SSR Backgrounder Series. Geneva: DCAF, 2017. https://www.dcaf.ch/intelligence-services-roles-and-responsibilities-good-security-sector-governance

Drinhausen, Katja, and Helena Legarda. "'Comprehensive National Security' Unleashed: How Xi's Approach Shapes China's Policies at Home and Abroad."

MERICS, Mercator Institute for China Studies. September 15, 2022. https://www.merics.org/en/report/comprehensive-national-security-unleashed-how-xis-approach-shapes-chinas-policies-home-and

EU. "Declaration by the High Representative, on Behalf of the European Union, on the announcement by China's National People's Congress Spokesperson Regarding Hong Kong." Council of the EU, May 22, 2020. https://www.consilium.europa.eu/en/press/press-releases/2020/05/22/declaration-by-the-high-representative-on-behalf-of-the-european-union-on-the-announcement-by-china-s-national-people-s-congress-spokesperson-regarding-hong-kong

Fu, Hualing, and Michael Hor. *The National Security Law of Hong Kong Restoration and Transformation.* Hong Kong: Hong Kong University Press, 2022.

Global Times. "National Security Legislation Offers Overdue Remedy for HK." *Global Times,* May 22, 2020. https://www.globaltimes.cn/content/1189137.shtml

Gries, Peter Hays. *China's New Nationalism Pride, Politics, and Diplomacy.* University of California Press, 2005.

Guo, Rui. "Explainer 'Picking Quarrels and Provoking Trouble': How China's Catch-all Crime Muzzles Dissent." *South China Morning Post,* August 25, 2021. https://www.scmp.com/news/china/politics/article/3146188/picking-quarrels-and-provoking-trouble-how-chinas-catch-all

Ho, Kelly. "Another Hong Kong Magistrate Reassigned after Criticism of Protest Rulings." *Hong Kong Free Press,* October 14, 2020. https://hongkongfp.com/2020/10/14/another-hong-kong-magistrate-reassigned-after-criticism-of-protest-rulings/

Ho, Kelly. "Hong Kong Security Chief Hails 100% Conviction Rate in National Security Cases." *Hong Kong Free Press.* April 14, 2023. https://hongkongfp.com/2023/04/14/hong-kong-security-chief-hails-100-conviction-rate-in-national-security-cases/

HKFP. "Article 23 (Part I): The Rise and Fall of Hong Kong's 2003 National Security Bill." *Hong Kong Free Press,* February 17, 2018. https://hongkongfp.com/2018/02/17/reviving-article-23-part-i-rise-fall-hong-kongs-2003-national-security-bill/

HKTB. "Stroll Through History on the Sun Yat Sen Historical Trail." Hong Kong Tourist board, n.d. https://www.discoverhongkong.com/eng/explore/culture/dr-sun-yat-sen-historical-trail.html

Lam, Paul. (RTHK-NSL Chronicles II) Convergence, Compatibility and Complementarity Should be How We Correctly Describe the Relationship between the National Security Law and the Common Law system." *The Standard.* August 19, 2023—*The standard* https://www.thestandard.com.hk/breaking-news/section/4/207091/(RTHK-NSL-Chronicles-II)-Paul-Lam:-convergence,-compatibility-and-complementarity-should-be-how-we-correctly-describe-the-relationship-between-the-National-Security-Law-and-the-common-law-system

Lam, Pun-lee (林本利). "Vindicating June 4th is Patriotic" (平反六四才是愛國). *Apple Daily*, June 4, 2004. Accessed WiseNews Database.

Lau, Chris. "Hong Kong Protests and National Security Law: Are the Courts Becoming Politicised and Are Judgments Biased?" *South China Morning Post*, September 14, 2020. https://www.scmp.com/news/hong-kong/law-and-crime/article/3101505/hong-kong-protests-national-security-law-and-judiciary

Lee, Danny. "British Human Rights Activist Refused Entry to Hong Kong." *South China Morning Post.* October 11, 2017. https://www.scmp.com/news/hong-kong/politics/article/2114938/british-human-rights-activist-refused-entry-hong-kong

Legarda, Helena. "China's New International Paradigm: Security First." Chapter 3 of the MERICS Paper on China, *The CCP's Next Century: Expanding Economic Control, Digital Governance and National Security*. June 15, 2021. https://merics.org/en/chinas-new-international-paradigm-security-first

Luo Fu (羅孚). "The Source of July 1st is June Fourth" (七一遊行源自六四). *Apple Daily*, July 23, 2004. Accessed by WiseNews Database.

Macagno, Fabrizio, and Douglas Walton. *Emotive Language in Argumentation*. Cambridge University Press, 2014.

Ng, Kang-chung. "Tiananmen Square Dissident Feng Congde Refused Entry to Hong Kong Ahead of June 4 Commemorations." *South China Morning Post,* June 2, 2019. https://www.scmp.com/news/hong-kong/politics/article/3012785/tiananmen-square-dissident-feng-congde-held-hong-kong

OECD. Definition of Terrorism by Country in OECD Countries. OECD Platform on Risk Insurance, undated. https://www.oecd.org/daf/fin/insurance/TerrorismDefinition-Table.pdf

O'Neill, Mark. "Another Kind of Orient Express." *Asia Sentinel,* June 10, 2009. www.asiasentinel.com/index.php?option=com_content&task=view&id=1926&Itemid=407)

OHCHR. "OHCHR and freedom of Expression vs Incitement to Hatred: The Rabat Plan of Action." *Office of the High Commissioner for Human Rights*, n.d. https://www.ohchr.org/en/freedom-of-expression

Reuters. "HKU Under Pressure on Johannes Chan Role." Cnbc.com, September 29, 2015. https://www.cnbc.com/2015/09/29/hku-criticised-by-pro-beijing-supporters-over-johannes-chan-role.html

RTHK. "DOJ to Get More Power to Challenge NSL Acquittals." Radio Television Hong Kong, May 23, 2024. https://news.rthk.hk/rthk/en/component/k2/1701820-20230523.htm

Ramzy, Austin. "Xi Delivers Tough Speech on Hong Kong, as Protests Mark Handover Anniversary". *New York Times*, July 1, 2017. https://www.nytimes.com/2017/07/01/world/asia/hong-kong-china-xi-jinping.html

Siu, Phila, and Jeffie Lam. "Macau Handover Anniversary: Xi Jinping Begins Visit by Heaping Praise on City for Sticking to 'One Country, Two Systems' Policy." *South China Morning Post*, December 18, 2019. https://www.scmp.com/news/hong-kong/politics/article/3042620/macau-handover-anniversary-activists-and-more-journalists

Siu, Phila, and Tony Cheung. "Chinese President Xi Jinping Holds Up "One Country, Two Systems" as Only Way Forward for Hong Kong and Macau." *South China Morning Post*, December 20, 2019. https://www.scmp.com/news/hong-kong/politics/article/3042920/chinese-president-xi-jinping-heaps-praise-macau-citing

Ta Kung Pao. "Openly Advocating 'Containment' Would Threaten Government Legislation—The 'Democrats Getting the Upper Hand causes More Rampant Disorder in Hong Kong" (公然鼓吹「圍堵」立會威脅政府—「民主派」得勢亂港更猖狂). *Ta Kung Pao*, July 5, 2003. Accessed by WiseNewsDatabase.

Ta Kung Pao. "SAR Government: If America Changes its Hong Kong Policy It Will Damage its Own Interests" (特區政府:美若改對港政策損自身利益). *Ta Kung Pao,* May 28, 2020. Accessed by WiseNews Database.

Torode, Greg. "Hong Kong: A Free Port in Every Storm." *South China Morning Post*, January 27, 2008. https://www.scmp.com/article/624451/hong-kong-free-port-every-storm

Tse, Hans. "Beijing's Offices in Hong Kong Hit Out at British Judge who Quit Top Court, as Another UK Justice Pledges to Stay." *Hong Kong Free Press,* June 14, 2024. https://hongkongfp.com/2024/06/14/beijings-offices-in-hong-kong-hit-out-at-british-judge-who-quit-top-court-as-another-uk-justice-pledges-to-stay

Vines, Stephen. "Beijing Reveals its Orwellian Plan to Shackle Hong Kong, But Can They Kill an Idea?" Hong Kong Free Press, May 22, 2020. https://hongkongfp.com/2020/05/22/beijings-reveals-its-orwellian-plan-to-shackle-hong-kong-but-can-they-kill-an-idea/

Wong, Lydia, and Thomas E. Kellogg. "Hong Kong's National Security Law: A Human Rights and Rule of Law Analysis." Center for Asian Law, Georgetown Law, February 2021. https://www.law.georgetown.edu/law-asia/wp-content/uploads/sites/31/2021/02/GT-HK-Report-Accessible.pdf

Wong, Rachel. "'This is the End of Hong Kong': Reactions Pour in as Beijing Proposes Security Law." May 22, 2020a. https://hongkongfp.com/2020/05/22/this-is-the-end-of-hong-kong-reactions-pour-in-as-beijing-proposes-security-law/

Wong, Rachel. "Hong Kong Magistrate Transferred, as Pro-Beijing Lawmakers Hit Out Over Protest Rulings—Local Media." *Hong Kong Free Press*, September 8, 2020b. https://hongkongfp.com/2020/09/08/hong-kong-magistrate-transferred-as-pro-beijing-lawmakers-hit-out-over-protest-rulings-local-media/

Wu, Baiyi. "The Chinese Security Concept and its Historical Evolution." *Journal of Contemporary China* 10, no. 27 (2010): 275–283.

Xi, Jinping. "Speech on the 20th Anniversary of Macao's Return to China and the Inauguration of the Fifth-Term Government of the Macao Special Administrative Region." *Qiushi* (CPC Central Committee Monthly). December 20, 2019. http://en.qstheory.cn/

Yau, Cannix, and Kahon Chan. "Hong Kong National Security Law: City Leader Won't Offer Explanation if Foreign Lawyers Barred from Trials, Justice Minister Says." *South China Morning Post*. April 8, 2023. https://www.scmp.com/news/hong-kong/politics/article/3216419/hong-kong-national-security-law-city-leader-wont-offer-explanation-if-foreign-lawyers-barred-trials

Zhang, Shuguang. "'Preparedness Eliminates Mishaps': The CCP's Security Concerns in 1949—1950 and the Origins of Sino-American Confrontation." The Journal of American-East Asian Relations 1, no. 1 (1992): 42–72. http://www.jstor.org/stable/23613366

Zhou, Laura. "Xi Jinping Again Backs Hong Kong Police Use of Force in Stopping Unrest." *South China Morning Post,* November 14, *2019.* https://www.scmp.com/news/china/politics/article/3037811/xi-jinping-again-backs-hong-kong-police-use-force-stopping

Zhou, Zunyou. "How China Defines Terrorism," *The Diplomat,* February 13, 2015. https://thediplomat.com/2015/02/how-china-defines-terrorism/

[illegible]

3

Selling the National Security Law

The Hong Kong Government spent millions of dollars on boosting public understanding of the need for a National Security Law even before anyone actually knew the content of the Law, although the Hong Kong Government may have had a guess of its likely contents. This chapter deals with how the government tried to persuade the public that the NSL was necessary, and that it would not negate existing freedoms in Hong Kong, but in fact enhance them. This will be done first through textual analysis of the chief executive's "Letter to Hong Kong Citizens" and its place in the wider sociocultural context, followed by a multimodal analysis of one billboard/poster (before the NSL was introduced), and a number of videos (for a six-month period after the introduction of the NSL). When these videos were initially shown much was unknown about how the NSL would actually work in practice and its effect on civil society. To instil confidence and allay fears, the Hong Kong Government used these videos to paint a positive picture of what the NSL could and would or would not do. These analyses form a basis to compare the actual impact of the NSL on civil society which is detailed in Chap. 6.

J. Eagleton, *Hong Kong's Second Return to China*,
https://doi.org/10.1007/978-3-031-84587-1_3

Promoting the National Security Law Before Its Introduction

The government spent over six million Hong Kong dollars on promoting the NSL before it came into effect (Ho 2020), indicating the importance of the "product" to be "sold". Public calls for support of the Law appeared everywhere despite the Hong Kong government not knowing its actual content. The then Chief Executive Carrie Lam's Letter to Hong Kong Citizens on 29 May 2020 (Lam 2020) was to convince the public the need for such a law, again without knowing its contents herself. This letter, which was published in all major newspapers and on government websites, serves as the first "selling" of the law based on trust in the unseen.

The Chief Executive's Letter to Hong Kong Citizens

The "Letter to Citizens" came a few days after China approved plans for the National Security Law. It was addressed to "Fellow Citizens", and overall, the letter's contents seem to refer to those who were not responsible for the violence that occurred during 2019; the topic sentences of each paragraph are used to address issues raised in the letter.

Topic Sentence 2: *Hong Kong, the home we all treasure, is defined by the "Lion Rock spirit" by which we join hands to pursue our dreams while putting aside our differences.*

The "Lion Rock spirit" Lam speaks of here is the spirit of "resilience, proactive attitude, passion for innovation, optimism, persistence and caring for others", in other words a spirit of "can do".[1] This is informed by the idea of "harmony" in society, an oft-quoted theme in traditional Chinese discourse. Lam also reiterated that Hong Kong was "enjoying a high degree of autonomy and *unique advantages* under 'One Country, Two Systems'" (italics added). This "high degree of autonomy"—and "unique advantage"—would be threatened if no security law is in existence.

---

[1] Many older Hongkongers arrived in the tiny territory on China's southern coast as refugees with nothing, fleeing from turmoil in mainland China between the 1930s and 1960s when Hong Kong was still a British colony. It was their resilience and hard work, that transformed their city into a global financial centre in a short time. "Below the Lion Rock" (獅子山下) was a popular TV show about the lives of Hong Kong citizens demonstrated this "spirit of resilience".

Topic Sentence 3: *Over the past year, the Hong Kong community has been traumatized.*

With an estimated 1–2 million Hong Kong people reportedly participating in some forms of civil protest over several months, it was true that stress, anxiety, and depression would go up because of the daily disruptions caused both to the general public and to the active protesters (Hou et al. 2021). However, Lam indicates or at least presumes, that this trauma was caused by "violence by rioters" alone that pose a "terrorist threat", not the generalised public anger over the anti-extradition law, or that trauma may also have occurred by actions of the police force, that many considered "heavy handed" and "excessive" (Mahtani et al. 2019).[2]

Those protesting against the extradition bill took issue with them being framed as "rioters" throughout the protests (Ting 2019). The word "rioters" has a negative semantic prosody of being "out of control" compared to "protesters".[3] The chief executive also mentions "opposition forces and organisations" interfering in Hong Kong's affairs as well as those "advocating independence, self-determination, and foreign sanctions against the city" as well as "blatantly challenging the authority of the Central Authorities, making Hong Kong "a *gaping hole* in national security" (italics added) and putting Hong Kong's "prosperity and stability at risk". Even earlier during the Occupy Central/Umbrella Movement, the authorities thought that protests were orchestrated (and funded) from foreign sources and were not a local movement (info.gov.hk 2014).

Topic Sentence 4: *Regrettably, the current legal system and enforcement mechanisms for Hong Kong to safeguard national security are inadequate or even "defenceless".*

---

[2] A police spokesman emphasised that the force is adhering to "strict" guidelines in policing the protests, "benchmarked against international standards." A review of more than 100 pages of police guidelines and training manuals obtained by *The Washington Post* details these protocols surrounding use of force. "The guidelines, however, were often ignored by police, who have misused chemical agents and used excessive force against protesters not resisting, according to experts in policing who examined dozens of incidents in consultation with Post journalists and in comparison, with the police protocols" (Mahtani et al. 2019).

[3] "Generally speaking, a protest in the sense relevant here is "a usually organized public demonstration of disapproval" (of some law, policy, idea, or state of affairs), while a riot is "a disturbance of the peace created by an assemblage of usually three or more people acting with a common purpose and in a violent and tumultuous manner to the terror of the public" (both according to *Merriam-Webster's Dictionary of Law*). Some protests in 2019, did end in violence, usually by a few.

Now the letter moves on to discuss "improving the legal system". The Basic Law was held to be "scientific" and a "guiding light" for Hong Kong at the time of its implementation by Beijing, the implication being that it was almost a sacred text. However, the Basic Law was now seen as inadequate and defenceless, but not because it had intrinsic problems, but because "Hong Kong has yet to enact laws to curb acts that threaten national security in accordance with Article 23 of the Basic Law", the current political and social situation making it "difficult for Hong Kong authorities to complete on its own legislation to safeguard national security in the foreseeable future". Therefore, it was now the task of the Central Government to initiate a similar law.

By saying that the Central Authorities' action "demonstrates the commitment" they have to "fully and accurately implement 'One Country, Two Systems' as well as their care for Hong Kong people", this infers that the "One Country, "Two Systems" was not correctly secured in place prior to the introduction of the National Security Law; This fits in with the idea of a "second return" (i.e., the "real return") of Hong Kong as a part of China, which is the main theme of this book. Being against such a law is negating the constant care and concern that China has for Hong Kong. The fifth paragraph of the letter gets to the actual criminal acts that the NSL will legislate against.

Topic Sentence 5: *The objective of the legislation is to prevent, curb and sanction secession, the subversion of state power, the organisation and carrying out of terrorist activities that seriously endanger national security, and interference by foreign and external forces in the affairs of the HKSAR.* Lam states that an "extremely small minority of illegal and criminal acts and activities" will be affected. However, from June 9, 20219 until March 31, 2024, 10,279 people were arrested in connection with the protests and unrest (Hutton 2024).[4] Lam seeks to assure us that constitutional freedoms (freedom of speech, of the press, of assembly, of demonstration,

[4] "Five years since the first arrests linked to Hong Kong's 2019 protests were made, only 28 per cent of the more than 10,000 people arrested have been prosecuted, leaving question marks over what will happen to the remaining 72 per cent." And "From June 9, 2019, until March 31, 10,279 people were arrested in connection with the protests and unrest. Fewer than 3,000 of them have had their cases go through the courts five years after the introduction of the NSL, with police saying only that they will "handle the remaining cases *in accordance with the law*" (Italics added) (Hutton 2024).

of procession) will be maintained after the introduction of the NSL, and that prosecutions will be conducted, "in *accordance with the law*". This is assumed to be the NSL, but could also imply laws under the Basic Law and general policing. This is actually is different from *the rule of law* (Maden 2020).

The Chinese term for rule of law is 法律. Both "in accordance with the law" and "rule by law" are, in Chinese, 依法, though 法治 is sometimes used for the latter (see also Cao 2004). So, both languages have two different terms. The Hong Kong government still frequently mentions Hong Kong's "rule of law"; however, some see that the number of times this has been used has fallen. Terms like "independent judiciary" and "follow the law" has become more prominent. "Important as judicial impartiality is, it is but one component of rule of law: the impartiality of the prosecution service and the process by which legislation comes into being—to name but two—are as important" (Maden 2020).

Topic Sentence 6: *Fellow citizens, every country has its own laws to safeguard national security for the long-term security of their country and the stability of people's lives.*

The government positions the new legislation as being simply in line with that of national security legislation in other jurisdictions, making the case for a smooth comparison. However, the national securities laws of other jurisdictions in liberal democracies have mitigating factors in their implications (more on this later). This legislation will "enable Hong Kong society to find a way out of the impasse" as it will be able to "restore stability as soon as possible" so that the economy can develop.

Lastly, the letter ends with "I appeal for your full understanding and staunch support for the Decision passed by the National People's Congress." The public now has to wait for the actual wording of the Law to emerge. Invoking a degree of fear if such a law is not in place, it has also to be taken on trust, since no one, including Chief Executive Carrie Lam herself knew the contents of the National Security Law at the time of writing the letter.

Apart from the letter just analysed, one particular billboard/poster (with slight variations) could be found on many static surfaces (sides of building, inside government facilities, etc.) as well as moveable surfaces (buses and trams) around Hong Kong.

The National Security Billboard/Poster

There was really only one major billboard/poster that was seen everywhere in Hong Kong. The words "National Security Law" in English and Chinese printed followed by a slogan. Slogans are forms of concise discourse that convey ideas, values, and are often guides to action. As guides to action effectively, they need to be short. Usually, to make these slogans memorable, their authors might use rhetorical devices such as metaphors, alliteration, or simple, vivid language (Denton 1980; Song and Gee 2019). Essentially, they work as a special subset of advertising texts. Apart from this, semantic features of slogans often associate with the emotional appeal of the created phrases.

Slogans in China are still are an important means to encourage people to see themselves as part of the state at the giving them "ideological goals" to strive for that serves the state's interest and normalises that these ideological goals are (Song and Gee 2019). Chinese slogans in China use concise statements to simplify complex ideas and teach people certain socio-political values and to encourage them to follow those values. For example, the phrases "Smash the Gang of Four" (打倒四人帮)—1976; "Seek Truth from Facts" (实事求是)—1978; and "Have More Children, Raise More Pigs" (少生孩子多养猪)—1979 are all commissive speech acts, extorting the people to do something. Since this billboard/poster involves two modes, both text and image, there will be first some brief comments on multimodal analysis.

Multimodal Analysis

"Multimodal analysis refers to the process of interpreting and making sense of qualitative data in projects that mix verbal and nonverbal forms of information" (Dicks 2019, Abstract). This all communication: gesture, facial expressions as well as images, video and sound. Investigating *how* meanings are made is more important in this case than just simply *what* is being said. The study of one mode in isolation (when many modes are present) overlooks the complexity of how textual, aural, linguistic, spatial, and visual resources integrate with each other (Kress 2010, 1). Analysis of these as a holistic unit draws out the full meaning of the text.

Each mode has a specific potential meaning: the image is quicker to "read" than text. Colour is used to highlight specific aspects of the overall message, for example emotion and tone (including hue, brightness, saturation, or modulation). Together, these modes/semiotic resources have a synergistic effect.

> In analyzing multimodality, analysts pay attention to many of the same kind of things they do when they analyze spoken language, especially sequentiality, how elements are ordered in relation to one another; and simultaneity, how elements that occur at the same time affect one another. (Jones 2009, 37)

Visual information is remembered for longer and *often affects people negatively* in more covert ways, as visual manipulations tend to be easily overlooked and as the common saying puts it "seeing is believing"; messages can then become "multimodal misinformation" when the visual information is reflected in the text alongside it. Video information (fake or misformed) seems to be more credible than text or audio: especially for issues where a person is less informed or interested (ICDS News 2021).

The following is the standard billboard/poster mentioned above that was found everywhere in Hong Kong in the lead up to the introduction of the National Security Law (either in vertical or horizontal format) and then just after its introduction (Fig. 3.1).

In this horizontal billboard/poster, transparent orange arises out of the east, possibly mimicking a sunrise moving up from the lower right-hand corner in the direction of the words "National Security Law" in large bold black letters, underneath in much smaller font is "Preserve One Country, Two Systems" while underneath that is "restore stability" (first in Chinese, then in English).

Cohesion of text and image can be achieved by "colour coordination" (with all parts or elements relate, blend, or match to a particular colour scheme). This means certain areas of the text have roughly the same degree of brightness, and/or saturation. Where there is not much written text, the function of colour is important as in this poster, since ideas can be expressed in colour (Kress 2010, 348; see also Kress and Van Leeuwen 2002). Colours are visual "speech acts" and signal identity by association

Fig. 3.1 National Security Law billboard/poster, photograph taken by the author in early June 2020

and their physical properties—hue, saturation, differentiation, modulation, purity. The orange (a colour representing optimism and enthusiasm as well as transformation in Confucianism, also could symbolise "gold"—stability and prosperity, and wealth—think of lunar new year celebrations) becomes more transparent and merges into a light blue (represents tranquillity and peace); the "sky" that is above the pixelated (transparent) skyscrapers across the horizontal edge of the poster.

The National Security Law is the "actor" in this instance, indicating the "dawning" of a new age in stability and so on. As it is a commissive speech act, it implies that the "One Country, Two Systems" has been threatened and that this law promises to save it; the result being the restoration of "stability". Since the law was still to be enacted, the present tense is not yet used as in "protects" and "restores". "National Security Law" is given in large, bold letters—perhaps implying strength. We are just told what it promises; that we need to "trust" that it would promise to do. The poster, being in multiple locations, means that the repetition of the commissive speech act increases the probability of it being registered in the memory of the viewer, and perhaps in the believability (or not) of the promise. That is the "ideological goal"—to paint the period of protest as undermining of Hong Kong's "stability", that is based on the smooth implementation of the "One Country, Two Systems".

On enactment of the NSL, the next task was to inform the public of the specific contents of the Law, what the changes to systems were, and allay any fears about it that may exist in society.

Promoting the National Security Law After Its Introduction

The government also produced public informational videos about the new National Security Law for dissemination just after the introduction of the NSL. Free-to-air broadcasters were obligated to transmit these as they have to do for all government messages. These were around one-minute-long films with Cantonese narration with English subtitles, each dated nearly every day from 29 June till 18 December 2020, an almost six-month period to "provide relevant information on safeguarding National Security in Hong Kong to members of the public". These can be found on the Safeguarding National Security in Hong Kong website.[5] These videos consist of a male narrator as well an authority figure from the Hong Kong government, judiciary, legislature, or academia, thus providing "credible sources" for what the law means and would likely do. If we think of the rhetorical triangle, this use of authority figures could be considered to be both *logos* and *ethos*, as the sources supposedly help support the logic or reasoning of the text, and also help portray the text as having the authority to speak. The film backdrop to these texts often consists of crowds of people, skyscrapers, flags, streets aflame, signs, and slogans held by protesters. Words of the narrator(s) are coordinated with the narrator(s) "glosses" from the images—making them understandable because they are accompanied (i.e., emphasised) by words. The episodes are numbered consecutively but are divided into the following three sections:

[5] https://www.isd.gov.hk/nationalsecurity/eng/videos.html

Secure Homeland	35 episodes, 29 June to 2 August 2020
National Security Law—Heralding A New Era	30 episodes 10 August—8 November 2020 (October is omitted)
National Security Law—Bedrock of Community	35 episodes 2nd November—18 December 2020

The three headings perhaps could be seen as establishing, firming, and solidifying national security as a mainstay or new core value of Hong Kong (Leung 2023).

At this time, there were many uncertainties about its contents, and much speculation about whether the new law would fundamentally change Hong Kong (remember the initial reaction to the NSL's announcement in Chap. 2). Generally speaking, these videos had an educational function for the ordinary Hong Kong resident. They were to tell them that (a) Hong Kong is now peaceful, stable, and returning to normal; (b) Hong Kong's rights, freedoms, and rule of law are not compromised by the NSL; (c) the NSL will be effective in ensuring and maintaining stability; and (d) the central authorities have Hong Kong's best interests at heart. Similar topics were raised in each of the three categories, although some topics were more prominent in each. "Secure Homeland" seems to emphasise legitimacy, law, and policing matters that the system is much the same; "Heralding A New Era" focused on the meaning and use of slogans during the protests; while "Bedrock of Community" seems to emphasise that all states have national security laws, and in fact that Hong Kong's law is quite mild in comparison.

Analysing the Videos

Episodes to be analysed came from the three categories above. The date was recorded for each video analysed, a list of the series of images used in the video is given, and the complete English subtitles were transcribed. A Cantonese-speaker checked that the English subtitles reflected the Chinese narration, which they did. Pertinent words and phrases in the transcriptions were italicised for emphasis. The name and affiliation of authorities who speak in the videos are underlined. Originally, the plan was to have a representative screenshot of each video analysed. Permission was sought by the Information Services Department who passed on the request to the Security Bureau, who, after a month, refused permission to do so, despite the videos being on a publicly available website. This highlights the sensitivity of this topic outside the intended audience of these videos (which was the Hong Kong public).[6] Videos were selected that were replies to particular criticisms of the National Security Law or reflected the discourse of officials.

The first four videos (one from "Secure Homeland", one from "Heralding A New Era" and two from "Bedrock of Community) below deal with the stability has been restored and normalcy returns theme, then followed by videos about an illegal slogan, law and policing, education and publishing. Since the videos are quite short, the entire narration is included so that the reader can see the discourse in its proper context and surrounding co-text. Italicised words in square brackets with the subtitles indicate scenes from the video that match up with the narration.

The Restoration of Stability

Secure Homeland: Episode 8, 6 July 2020

Scenes: National People's Congress Standing Committee; close-up of NPCSC members; protesters holding barriers, and then walking up a street; building displaying the Hong Kong and Chinese flags; crowds on street; a drone shot of skyscrapers; PRC insignia on wall; cover of Basic Law booklet; meeting of State Council Information Office; Zhang Xiaoming Deputy Director, Hong Kong Macau Affairs Office); Hong Kong and China flags fly on flagpoles; skyscrapers; old Legislative Council building; Zhang Xiaoming; drone skyscraper shot.

English Subtitles: (male narrator): After the NPCSC [*various shots of the NPCSC*] passed the National Security Law, Zhang Xiaoming said it is now possible to prevent, curb, and punish criminal acts [*protesters being violent*] that endanger national security [improve the constitutional

[6] The author had mentioned these screen shots were to be used for an academic book about the NSL.

framework of the "One Country, Two Systems" and safeguard national sovereignty and development interests [*row of Hong Kong and China flags*]. He said the issue of ensuring Hong Kong's long-term security, prosperity, and stability is of profound and far-reaching significance. This law (the National Security Law), after the Basic Law [*Cover of copy of the Basic Law*], is the second piece of important legislation [*State Council room*], that the Central Government has *specially enacted* for Hong Kong. It fully and faithfully implements the policy of One Country, Two Systems further puts into the law the principle and bottom line of One Country, Two Systems, strengthen the HKSAR's ability to safeguard national security and has a far-reaching impact of ensuring the successful implementation of "One Country, Two Systems" [*drone shot of skyscrapers*]. The National Security Law *is a milestone* for the practice of "One Country, Two Systems".

Analysis: Zhang Xiaoming, Deputy Director, Hong Kong Macau Affairs Office is the authority figure who speaks in this video. There are only a few scenes of protesters causing mayhem (unlike many subsequent videos), the main emphasis here is of which is the legality and the legitimacy, necessity and solemn nature of enacting the NSL that fits in with Hong Kong's guidance framework. The use of superlative language such as "profound and far-reaching" and "milestone" paint the law as a significant solution. The images of official bodies in the video serve to legitimise the introduction of the new law, which is depicted as "specially enacted" out of Mainland concern for the city. Similar things were also said about the Basic Law when it was introduced. Zhang Xiaoming is the mainland official in Chap. 1 who had quoted the Singapore official that the NSL was a "shield".

Heralding A New Era: Episode 10, 19 August 2020

Scenes: (male narrator): Burning placards; fires near MTR station; <u>Yun Chan, Chairman, New Territories Association of Societies</u>; a trashed shop; protesters about to smash a window; fires and protesters; Bauhinia Square near the harbour, police lined up in front of large signboard saying "National Security Law"; cars going through tollway to tunnel with a NSL poster above the tollway; Yun Chan; Hong Kong and China flags fly in front of the Legislative Council; wide-angle shot of the Hong Kong Government complex; crowds in the street; fires burning; protesters holding flags of other countries; crowds and trams crossing the street.

English Subtitles: (male narrator): Starting in June last year, *anti-extradition protests triggered large-scale street violence.* Acts of arson and vandalism [*fires and protesters*] were seen in many parts of Hong Kong. (Yung Chan now speaks): Over the past year, with its members over 280,000, the New Territories Association of Societies and its affiliate clubs have experienced *black violence* and widespread smash-and-burn in Hong Kong [*a shop being trashed; protesters about to smash a window*]. Since Hong Kong implemented the National Security Law, so far none of our offices or volunteers have been threatened, surrounded, or vandalised like before. (Male narrator now speaks): He believes the National Security Law helps maintain social stability. (Yun Chan speaks till end of video) The National Security Law is *like a giant protective shield* [*crowd of people*] safeguarding Hong Kong from the attack of extreme criminal activities and preventing *evil foreign forces* from making the *Hong Kong people collateral damage* [*protesters with foreign flags*]. This new law can restore stability to the city we call home. We believe the National Security Law can keep our nation safe, our city stable, and help our people feel assured.

Analysis: The authority speaking in the video is from The New Territories Association of Societies (新界社團聯會), a pro-Beijing umbrella political group which consists of many New Territory organisations. This is one of the few videos to actually mention "anti-extradition law protests" by name, rather than just "violence" or "violent acts" in isolation. The term "black violence" will later become a common way of the government describing the protests because many protesters wore all black: "first of all, it is not the 2019 protests. It is the 'black violence'"—said by Chief Executive Lee in 2023—(Grundy 2023). Here, too the NSL, rather than being a metaphorical sword, becomes a metaphorical "shield". The "evil foreign forces" [*image of crowds holding foreign flags*], which are never named, indicate this. Hongkongers depicted as "collateral damage" puts the blame on these foreign forces, perhaps implying Hong Kong people are easily seduced by outside views. Earlier in transitional Hong Kong, the maturity of the local people would be called into question by establishment figures to indicate that they were not ready for universal suffrage (Eagleton 2012).

Bedrock of Community: Episode 14, 19 November 2020

Scenes: (male narrator): Secretary of Justice, Secretary of Security, and the Chief Executive, each hold a copy of the NSL; people walking across a footbridge; crowds of people on the street; officials with masks and protective gear entering housing; registering for vaccines; workers wearing protective gear spraying disinfectant on street; community kitchen and food pantry in the US; people in US waiting for handouts; black-clad protesters, fire in a trolley cart; US rows of police and protesters throwing things at them; US clashes on the street; a number of empty US streets are shown; Maria Tam Deputy Director of the Basic Law Committee; Hong Kong protestors, holding umbrellas and barricades; Hong Kong protesters running away, fires burning; crowds walking on footbridge.

English Subtitles: (male narrator): After the enactment of the National Security Law, social stability has been restored in Hong Kong and people can enjoy their normal daily lives [*people walking cross a footbridge*]. Deputy Director of the Hong Kong Basic Law Committee Maria Tam thinks it also helps the HKSAR government and Hong Kong citizens *cope with the coronavirus epidemic.* [*Picture of suited-up health workers*] (Maria Tam now speaks till the end of the video): Let's look at the current situation in the US. On one side of the picture, we find a hot fire with rioting and civil strife on the streets. [*Americans lining up for food, riots, etc.*] The other side is in deep water with the rampant spread of Covid-19. [*Deserted streets in the US—Covid-19 lockdowns*] It'd be very hard for us to pull through. But the National Security Law has managed to make the hot fire subside…suppress it, and give us the chance to start over. The National Security Law has restored social order allowing us to enjoy stable daily lives and give us the opportunity to plan our development with the Greater Bay Area. It has an enormous stabilising power.

Analysis: The authority figure in the video is Maria Tam, a Basic Law Committee member. Hong Kong's situation is contrasted with images from the US which seems in a state of chaos. During the Covid-19 pandemic, the National Security Law helps to douse the "hot fire" with its calming and stabilising influence. Since the protesters' tactic during 2019 was known as "being water", the NSL ironically acts like "water" in this instance. The pandemic helped ease the protest situation even before the NSL. This also implies that the "help" of "evil foreign influence" mentioned in other videos may be not so beneficial after all. "Suppressing" the fire, does not imply the full "putting [it] out" of the fire.

Bedrock of Community: Episode 31, 14 December 2020

Scenes: setting fire to cardboard boxes; more fires burning; crowd of protesters; John Lee, Secretary for Security; protesters, barricaded and fire…; protesters trashing a room; Secretary of Justice, Secretary of Security, Chief Executive each hold a copy of the NSL; cars entering a tollway with a NSL Law signboard above; Hong Kong independence flags; protesters waving US, UK, and Israeli flags; another view of crowd waving these flags; John Lee; Hong Kong independence flag; crowd of protesters under umbrellas; two black-clad protesters defacing police sign outside Tsim Sha Tsui police station; black-clad protesters amidst a cloud of tear gas, and running on street; John Lee.

English Subtitles: (John Lee, Secretary for Security speaks): Since the implementation of the National Security Law, incidents of violence have gone down, advocacy of Hong Kong independence has become considerably less evident, social order has been restored and people are no longer running scared [*John Lee speaks*]. What struck me the most was that a loophole in national security could bring about such devastating damage to a place [*fire with protesters*]. That's when a law-abiding culture reaches the brink of collapse. [*Protesters smashing things*] When our situation was at its worst the [implementation of the] National Security Law rectified the situation, (male narrator now speaks): Secretary John Lee also mentioned the deterrent effect of this law led to the voluntary disbandment of some local groups [*group of independence flags*] and the backing off of external forces. [*Protesters holding foreign flags*] It's also the key facts behind the restoration of peace to society. (John Lee speaks again till the end of the video): Yet, we have some worries, despite that law that wrong thinking has not yet been eliminated—the notion of Hong Kong independence still remains, as well as the notion of violence. We must not let our guard down again if we want to return to what it was like before June last year, before the violence broke out, [*various shots of protesters moving in groups, graffiti on police station*] so we can go back to work as usual and people can live normal life again.

Analysis: John Lee, Secretary for Security is the authority in this video, a former policeman, later to become the Chief Executive of Hong Kong. The Hong Kong people are "no longer running scared" seems to be a hyperbole as public opinion on the protests were largely supportive, especially after the landslide democratic win in the District Council elections of November 2019. "Law-abiding culture reaches the brink of collapse" also seems hyperbolic. The people who are protesting are likely radicals, the few who are jeopardising the "law abiding" Foreign flags shown in the video are linked to collusion with "foreign forces" without directly mentioning them; "deterrent effect of this law led to the voluntary disbandment of some local groups and the backing off of external forces", implying that these local groups may have had "guilty consciences" for possible evil acts that they had done. "We cannot let our guard down" implies that the "independence movement" has not been eradicated; the remaining threat will be somewhat neutralised in the early implementation of the NSL. This could also imply that more laws will be necessary, which could be an indirect reference to future enactment of Article 23 of the Basic Law.

The Illegality of 2019 Protest Slogans

A particular slogan was criticised during the protests, seen as advocating independence, self-determination, and separatism, concepts always been sensitive in China (foreign powers carving up the nation, the sense of humiliation of not administering its own territory) was not the first time after 1997 that slogans were seen as advocating independence.[7] First, one

[7] Making noise and shouting slogans is "the only thing that the Democratic Party knows" (直斥民主黨只懂喊口號) according to the pro-Beijing/pro-establishment camp in the early 2000s. One such slogan, "Return power to the people" (還政於民) was used by democrats on democracy marches. Such a slogan was seen by the pro-establishment and Beijing as advocating "independence for Hong Kong". To them, with the "One Country, Two Systems" and the departure of Great Britain power had truly returned to the people" (Qiao 2005).

video from "Secure Homeland" will be analysed followed by a number episodes in "Heralding A New Era" since Episodes 24–30 all dealt with what the government saw as the intended meaning of "liberate Hong Kong, revolution of our times", the repetition of this an indicator of a particular point that the authorities wanted to get across.

Secure Homeland: Episode 16, 14 July 2020

Scenes: China and Hong Kong flags fly on flagpoles; close up of Hong Kong flag; crowd peacefully marching; police, wearing protective vests, filming suspects; suspects are handcuffed entering a police van; close up of Hong Kong independence flag; reporters taking pictures of a lone protester holding a Hong Kong independence banner and on the ground before him are a row of British colonial flags; Teresa Cheng Yeuk Wah, Secretary for Justice; protesters near Peninsula Hotel; close up of these protesters; crowd of protesters with US flags; black-clad protesters holding banners; protesters carrying Hong Kong independence flags; close up of Hong Kong independence flag; Teresa Cheng.

English Subtitles (male narrator): On this year's establishment day, crowds took to the streets, and police arrested around 370 people, 10 of which were charged with breaches under the National Security Law [*people getting arrested*]. Is it illegal to shout out slogans "Hong Kong independence" or "self-determination"? [*independence flags shown*] The Secretary for Justice Teresa Cheung points out that one must consider the overall objective facts. [*picture of the entrance to the high court*] (Teresa Cheung now speaks till the end of the video): Regarding the issue of shouting slogans, it cannot be solely based on the slogans, if someone is guilty. For instance, when someone shouts a slogan, does it objectively constitute subversion of the government from an objective perspective? [*Cheung speaks, and then some protesters moving*] We must look at the act itself and the criminal intent. How could shouting out that slogan be objectively understood and perceived as shouting out "Hong Kong independence"? In a situation like this, we must also consider the evidence, whether it can prove the criminal intent of the act.

Analysis: Teresa Cheng, Secretary for Justice of Hong Kong is the authority figure here. Cheng, who is also a lawyer, poses a number of questions, the answers that she gives is rather unclear. She mentions "objective facts", but does not suggest what these could be (no hypothetical situations are given), just that shouting slogans alone would not be sufficient for prosecution. The criminal intent of the act would have to be ascertained, perhaps implying that a real state (an act) of "Hong Kong independence" is the intent.

Heralding A New Era: Episode 24, 2 September 2020

Scenes: Star Ferry crossing harbour; Hong Kong flag flying; protesters with slogan "liberate Hong Kong, Revolution of Our Times" on a banner; protesters holding the British colonial flag; be water; independence; building in Forbidden City, Beijing superimposed with "gwang fuk"; Prof. Lau Chi-pang, Department of History, Lingnan University; "gwang fuk" appears as he is speaking; a crowd of overseas protesters; crow close-up; crowd clapping; Prof. Lau Chi-pang; old walled buildings in Beijing; another old building (with Chinese text superimposed on it that gradually grows larger); picture of Qing dynasty men; Prof. Lau.

English Subtitles: (male narrator): After the implementation of the NSL, the Hong Kong government has stated the slogan "gwong fuk Heung Gong" (liberate Hong Kong), "Si doi gap ming" [*protesters with slogan "liberate Hong Kong, revolution of our times*"] on a banner (revolution of our times) equals a separatist call for Hong Kong independence and subversion. In modern Chinese history, the term "gwong fuk" was commonly used in the late Qing [*Qing dynasty building in Forbidden City, Beijing superimposed with "gwang fuk"*]. (Prof. Lau Chi-pang speaks till the end of the video): What is meant behind this word? The literal meaning of "gwong fuk" is to restore something to its original state. For example, taking back a place, a city, a country, a sovereignty. [*Catalan independence activist—a crown and a closeup of an individual*] In China, "gwong fuk" is a rather contemporary concept. [*Buildings within the Forbidden City*]. It was commonly used in the late Qing dynasty by the Restoration Society which, as well as the Revive China Society and the

Society for the Revival of China [*old building (with Chinese text superimposed on it that gradually grows larger*], were all anti-Qing organisations [*historical photograph of a group of men in Chinese costume*]. They later merged and became the Chinese Revolutionary Alliance. The Restoration Society wanted to liberate the country [*close up of some people from the group*]. Its struggles of course were against the Manchus.

Analysis: The official in the video is Prof. Lau Chi-pang, Dept. of History, Lingnan University. The narration almost seems a simple historical account of the term "gwong fuk". As mentioned, the Gwong Fuk Hui in Cantonese (光復會), was a revolutionary group opposing the Qing dynasty, who used the phrase "Restore Han Rule" (光復漢族), as one of their mottoes. This was the name of an organisation established by the Republic of China after the communist revolution on the mainland with the purpose of restoring the light (the literal meaning of 光—light, 復—restore) on Mainland China (Lee 1970). The latter organisation was dissolved in June 1990. This particular slogan would annoy Beijing as 1949 was considered China's "Liberation". It needed no further restoration. Finally, it is also of interest to note that the term 光復 (liberate) in the slogan could also be translated into English as "liberate" "restore", "reclaim", or "revive", thus showing that the term has a wide range of meaning. Here, the word is just taken literally. Thus, the slogans are taken to be "a separatist call for Hong Kong independence and subversion" by mapping the words used in a previous historical context.

Heralding A New Era: Episode 25, 3 September 2020

Scenes: protesters surrounding tram; close-up of protesters banner of "independence/liberate Hong Kong banner; Catalan protester with "Lliberte" banners (liberty, freedom in Catalan); picture with three revolutions—the French Revolution, 1911 Revolution, Russian Revolution in Chinese text vertically arranged; Prof Lau Chi-pang, Dept. of History, Lingnan University. Catalan protesters close-up; same crowd clapping; different flags, black estrada flag and a shot of a blue Estrada flag. Prof. Lau Chi-pang; mausoleum in Guangzhou; old back and white photo of the 72 martyrs; picture of settings of 1911 revolution and the Russian Revolution name moves; Prof. Lau.

English Subtitles: (male narrator): During last year's anti-extradition bill movement, demonstrators often chanted the slogan "liberate Hong Kong, revolution of our times". The government had already stated it equals a separatist call for Hong Kong independence and subversion. [*Protesters with independence banners*] The term "revolution" was used in modern world history [*group of Catalan independence protesters*]. For example, the French Revolution, the 1911 Revolution, and the October Revolution [*picture of three places where three revolutions took place and the names of these in Chinese, vertically arranged*] (Prof. Lau Chi-Pang Dept. of History, Lingnan University speaks till the end of the video): The original intention of a revolution is to bring about certain large-scale changes that can range from peaceful to violent. [*Catalan protesters close-up; same crowd clapping; different flags, black estrada flag*] Through the history of mankind, there has been some very large-scale or perhaps very impactful changes [*Tomb of the 72 Martyrs*] and at changing the political system [*historical photographs with weapons*]. The majority of the *violent revolutions*, such as the 1911 Revolution in China, October Revolution in Russia and many other revolutions around the world they were all the same. Force and violence were used to achieve their goals.

Analysis: Prof. Lau Chi-pang, Dept. of History, Lingnan University repeats his role as the authority figure. Again, the slogan "liberate Hong Kong, revolution of our times" is seen as a separatist act advocating independence, and again stresses the classic meaning of "revolution" as a violent act; the following sentence "The original intention of a revolution is to being about certain large-scale changes that can range from peaceful to violent" could cover the Hong Kong protesters' acts which wanted to change aspects of the system, many of which were largely peaceful. The "potential" of violence is emphasised.

It is doubtful that the average Hongkonger would know what the foreign flags were or their significance as advocating liberation. It was the Senyera Estelada flag (four red stripes on a yellow field and a blue triangle with a star on the left side), symbol of the claim of independence of the autonomous community of Catalonia with the Spanish state. The implication here was that they were all the same, using force and violence despite mentioning that some were "peaceful". The 1911 Revolution led to the start of changes in the Chinese political system which ultimately were deemed necessary. The revolution in 1911, ended China's last imperial dynasty, the Qing dynasty, and led to the establishment of the Republic of China, after a decade of agitation, revolts, and uprisings. It ended over 2,000 years of imperial rule in China and saw the saw the beginning of China's republican era.[8]

Heralding A New Era: Episode 26, 4 September 2020

Scenes: Crowd with Liberate Hong Kong, Revolution of our Time flags, British flags; dense crowd holding US flags; close-up of Hong Kong independence banner; protest crowd with umbrellas (peaceful); black-clad protester and fire; close-up of a protest banner; Lau Siu Kai Vice-President Association of Hong Kong and Macau Studies; protester with "liberate" and Hong Kong independence flags; different pictures of protesters; line up of protesters with Hong Kong independence, "be water", and liberate Hong Kong banners; protesters with British colonial and US flags; close up of Hong Kong independence flags; liberate Hong Kong banner; protesters holding US and Israeli flags; Lau Siu-kai.

English Subtitles: (male narrator): During last year's social movement, demonstrators often brandished banners with the slogan "Liberate Hong Kong, Revolution of Our Times" on them [*banners with this slogan on them]*. On the implementation of the National Security Law, some people still took part in protest marches. Major clashes broke out [*fire*] and banners with "Liberate Hong Kong, Revolution of Our Times" were found. (Lau Siu-Kai speaks to the end of the video): Purely *from the literal meaning* of the slogan, "liberate Hong Kong" and "revolution of our times", it really *carries the idea* of succession and the intention of overthrowing the HKSAR government and the political system of the HKSAR as its goal and content [*protesters hold "Hong Kong independence" and liberate Hong Kong and Revolution of our times banners*]. But at the individual level, it depends upon on where someone over a long period of time, has repeatedly made these remarks or participated in activities of

[8] The 72 martyrs were buried together near where they died, and a large tomb and memorial remind visitors of the sacrifices they made to bring China into the modern world. There was a small "Statue of Liberty" atop the tomb. Complicated (not shown in the video).

this nature, or joined some organisation that advocates Hong Kong independence or various kinds of separatist organisations, or held any ties with external elements [*protesters waving the flags of foreign countries*], leading others to believe that when he or she chanted the slogan, he or she was not simply ignorant of the meaning of this slogan.

Analysis: Lau Siu-Kai Vice-President Association of Hong Kong and Macau Studies is the authority figure in the video. Like the previous episode, the focus is on the literal definition of the word "revolution". Revolutions are not necessarily violent, they can be societal, political, economic, or cultural (that is, of a metaphorical nature). It can also be used *metaphorically* to "describe a kind of revolutionary consciousness or aptitude"; in contemporary Hong Kong, like elsewhere, the term "革命" (revolution) could be in a non-political context is *digital revolution* (數碼革命) or information revolution as in the headline "How a digital revolution is redefining the way property owners design, operate and manage real estate in Hong Kong" (Anderson 2022) and "A silent revolution is underway in Hong Kong's fintech industry, helping city catch up to Greater Bay Area neighbours" (Bray et al. 2021). Therefore, the meaning of "revolution" really depends on the "company it keeps", that is, its collocates (Firth 1957, 11). In the slogan, "革命" (revolution) is postmodified by "時代" (era/times). "時代 革命" (literally, revolution of an era/times) does not clearly the say what is the aim of the change; obviously in this case major social and political change. The phrase is therefore can have any number of interpretations, although it of course does not exclude physical violence.

Heralding A New Era: Episode 27, 5 September 2020

Scenes: Crowd of turban-wearing men; a series of wide shots of same crowd holding signs in Arabic); one protester in a crowd is holding a gun with a flower in it; map of Georgia with Georgian flag superimposed on top of it, "rose revolution" in Chinese vertically; Ukraine Orange Revolution in 2004—same configuration; Arab Spring 2000—row of African countries; Hong Kong protesters wearing black, helmets, and gas masks with a fire in their midst; Hong Kong protesters throwing a firebomb; a liberate Hong Kong banner held by two protesters; a close up of a liberate Hong Kong flag; close up of protesters; Ronny Tong, senior barrister; photo of handover ceremony on 30 June 1997; the Hong Kong and China flags; protesters breaking into the Legislative Council building; a worker taking down an old British crown emblem; liberate/independence banners, Hong Kong colonial flag on floor; Ronny Tong; flags on balcony; a protest with fire; a firebomb being thrown; protest crowd with foreign flags; a group with US flags.

English Subtitles: (male narrator): In the past decade or two, Central Asia and Eastern Europe have witnessed many social movements, anti-government demonstrations often used colours or flowers as their symbols [*protester holding a gun with a flower in it*]. For example, the Rose Revolution in Georgia; Orange Revolution in Ukraine in 2004, and the Arab Spring in 2010 [*graphics of these places*]. During a series of violent social incidents in Hong Kong last year [*protesters and fire*], demonstrators often raised banners with the slogan "liberate Hong Kong" on them [*pictures of these banners*]. Will they be considered anti-government symbols? Ronny Tong speaks till the end of the video: "liberate Hong Kong" means restoring the previous system. Now Hong Kong's reunification with the motherland, [*the handover ceremony*] the previous system refers to the colonial government. [*Colonial government insignia being lowered from governor's residence*] Thus, it has the meaning of subverting the government or inciting subversion of state power. [*Independence flags and banner, Hong Kong colonial flag on floor*] So, even without a specific time frame, the slogan "liberate Hong Kong" itself is problematic. Together with last year's anti-extradition bill movement and subsequent social events, the slogan can be easily construed as a call for overthrowing the current system and restoring the colonial system.

Analysis: Ronny Tong, who is a senior barrister, is the authority in the video. He frequently mentions "colour" revolutions through the protests, while images of violent protest in Hong Kong are shown alongside them and are thus compared with them. Since "restoring" means returning to the colonial government's administration, this reminds us of British PM Margaret Thatcher's suggestion that China could hold sovereignty of Hong Kong while Britain would administer it. This was totally unacceptable to the Chinese authorities. Tong sees the protest slogan as "a call for overthrowing the current system" as being "easily construed" as such. The protesters haven't given "a specific timeframe" for the actual revolution, presumably the potential is there for it to occur in the near future. The intention is likely to introduce fear of instability and thus acceptance of the NSL.

Heralding A New Era: Episode 28, 6 September 2020

Scenes: A foreign scene with the word "Separatism" in large Chinese characters and English letters (the narrator says the word in English); The word overlays scenes of a protest; Catalan separatists protesting—red and blue Estrada flags are held on poles; protester holding a black Estrada flag; a red flag is also present; tram in Hong Kong surrounded by protesters; Hong Kong independence and liberate flag held between two protesters; the Hong Kong independence, be water, liberate Hong Kong and British colonial flag; two protesters hold liberate banner; Lau Siu-Kai; drone shot of Hong Kong skyscrapers; Golden Bauhinia Square on 1st July, National Security law signboard behind; Hong Kong crowds walking; old Legislative Council building; container terminal; skyscrapers; Lau Siu-kai Kai Vice President of the Chinese Association of Hong Kong and Macau Studies; a Hong Kong independence flag waved on high; a group of protesters holding the Hong Kong independence flag; Lau Siu-kai.

English Subtitles: (male narrator): The term separatism (said in English) usually means advocacy of separation of a certain domain [*looks like Arab Spring protests*] from an existing sovereign state to set up an independent state [*Catalan protests with their Estrada flag*]. Lau Siu-kai believes the slogan "Liberate Hong Kong Revolution of Our Times" has the connotation of separatism. (Lau Siu-Kai speaks till the end of the video): It implies that Hong Kong is facing external threats mainly coming from the Chinese mainland, and Hong Kong's degree of autonomy, its value systems, its institutions, and its systems have been damaged [*pictures of old Legislative Council building, container terminal, skyscrapers*]. Hence, the advocates think it's necessary to separate Hong Kong from the external forces, the Chinese mainland, and only by freeing the city from the interference and influence of these external forces can it defend its local interests, its institutions, its value systems, and safeguard Hong Kong's autonomy.

Analysis: Lau Siu-Kai is again the authority figure in video. The fact that the word "separatism" is voiced in English is significant and is obviously used for emphasis. Lau says that the protesters see the mainland China as a threat to Hong Kong's system which is against what the government and Beijing officials say about the "One Country, Two Systems", that it has been "benevolently" bestowed on Hong Kong. The protesters seem to be focusing on the "second system" of Hong Kong's governance framework, when it really needs to "one country" in order to exist. The "external threat" seen by the protesters is not an outside force, but the homeland which is an incorrect view.

Heralding A New Era: Episode 29, 7 September 2020

Scenes: Chinese official walks towards camera; four students hold cut-out Chinese characters that say "self-determination"; close up of Hong Kong independence flags; independence flags/protesters from a distance; a group of students/protesters wearing different coloured T-shirts hold the cut-out characters for "self-determination"; people going into a polling station; people queuing up to vote; people coming out of polling station; Ronny Tong, senior barrister; close up of Hong Kong independence flag; another shot of the Hong Kong independence flags; protester holding up "I stand for Hong Kong independence; close up of the cut-out Chinese characters for "self-determination" (the Chinese character for self "自" appears a little higher than the other characters); Hong Kong independence flag being waved; crowd with independence flag visible; various banner for independence, etc.; Ronny Tong;

English Subtitles: (male narrator): In 2018, Li Fei, chairman of the Hong Kong Basic Law Committee [*Li Fei is interviewed while walking*] pointed out "self-determination" is in breach of the Basic Law. It's a euphemism for advocacy of Hong Kong independence, [*independence flags being waved*] using different words, but both are essentially the same. Some who are against Hong Kong independence but advocate "self-determination" signed up for the Legislative Council election earlier. They were disqualified by returning officers on grounds of openly promoting self-determination of Hong Kong independence. [*people entering voting venue*] (Ronny Tong speaks till the end of the video): Hong Kong is now part of China. Therefore, there does not exist a choice of "self-determination" to set up a separate nation or an independent state. So, if you put this slogan of self-determination in practice or push for political reform, such acts will carry the connotation of overthrowing the existing system of the country and building a new political system [*more independence flags*]. If you build a new political system, it's obvious you may contravene the law against secession. Therefore, you may contravene the law in relation offences of secession and subversion of state power at the same time.

Analysis: The video begins with Li Fei, chairman of the Hong Kong Basic Law Committee walking, being quoted by the male narrator that "self-determination breaches the Basic Law), thus adding the illegality to this concept. Barrister Ronny Tong is the second authority figure in this video. "Self-determination" like the "high degree of autonomy" promised in the Basic Law might mean more autonomy, not necessarily "full autonomy", but this is not the way that government authorities or Beijing see it. It is simply an "euphemism" for independence. Hong Kong has no "self" apart from being the "second system" of the "one country". Putting "self-determination in practice" or even merely making a "push for political reform", you are committing of the offences of secession and subversion of state power.

Heralding A New Era: Episode 30, 8 September 2020

Scenes: protest crowd chanting; protest crowd near Peninsular Hotel covering the whole street; protesters on street tearing up paper; drone shot of crowd; Hong Kong independence and liberate Hong Kong flags being carried between two protesters; balcony with liberate and Hong Kong independence banners hanging; State Council Information Office (SCINO) meeting/panel; close up of spokesman of SCINO; crowd of protesters holding liberate, UK, UK, and other countries' flags; protest crowd sitting down; more of other countries' flags; more protest crowd scenes; crowd waving numerous liberate Hong Kong flags; a line of protesters holding Hong Kong independence, "be water", liberate and British colonial flags; Ronny Tong senior barrister; protesters throwing bricks; fires; protesters holding liberate Hong Kong, revolution of our times banners (in Chinese); Ronny Tong.

English Subtitles: (male narrator): During last year's anti-extradition movement, demonstrators often displayed and chanted [*chanting could be heard*] "Liberate Hong Kong, Revolution of Our Times". A spokesman for the State Council of Hong Kong and Macau Affairs Office [*scenes from the state council shown*], pointed out that last year the demonstrators' political motive was obvious to everyone. Their target: "One Country" [*pictures of protesters*] under the "One Country, Two Systems" principle. In fact, after the implementation of the National Security Law, which law could be breached by promoting this slogan? (Ronny Tong, senior barrister, now speaks till the end of the video) [*as he is speaking bricks, there are scenes of fires and protesters*]: This is likely an offence of subversion of state law, as a subversion of state power means overthrowing the current political system and the current government so as to set up a new system. "Liberate Hong Kong" has that connotation. So, obviously it's an offence of subversion of state power.

Analysis: A spokesman from the State Council was to have said that "the demonstrators' political motive was obvious to everyone", while Tong said that the "connotation" of "liberate Hong Kong" was the setting up of a new political system, thus "obviously" this is an offence of subversion of state power. This is also similar to what Tong had said in an earlier video. Since is "obvious" to these authority figures, the general public should take it as a given, that is, the intention behind chanting such slogans is criminal.

In summary, we can also think of the slogan "liberate Hong Kong, revolution of our times" as a commissive speech act. It declares an intention or desire to "liberate Hong Kong" by participating and/or supporting a "revolution of our times". But who is the speaker, and who is the receiver of the slogan? Are the events where this is chanted the same? "Liberate Hong Kong, revolution of our times" was not first used in the 2019 protests. It was first suggested by Hong Kong localist activist

Edward Leung as a slogan for an election. At the press conference where Leung originally announced his bid for the 2016 New Territories East by-election, his campaign slogan was "Walk the talk, innovation for our generation" (知行合一，世代革新); it was later changed to "liberate Hong Kong…"

The slogan "liberate Hong Kong, revolution of our times" is vague and general. Political discourse often uses hyperbole (exaggeration) and "linguistic indeterminacy" (instability of meaning). Contextual clues are also important; the slogan may well be the "expression of hopefulness and encouragement to other participants, as well a determination to the government and to international media" (Leung 2024: 657). As shown in earlier videos, the vague and general framing of the slogan enables a number of interpretations. "Intentionality simply cannot be ascertained by the literal meaning of the slogan" (ibid. 2024, 658).

Law and Policing

Secure Homeland: Episode 3, 1 July 2020

Scenes: View of skyscrapers; black-clad protesters holding iron poles; black-clad protesters running around; Leung Chun-ying vice chairman of the Committee of the CPPCC; view across harbour to Hong Kong island; protesters/reporters, smoke rising at protest scene; black-clad protesters running; MTR station entrance blocked; scenes of the 13th meeting of the NPC; Leung Chun-ying; Chinese and Hong Kong flags on flagpole; close up of the Chinese flag; Hong Kong Island as seen from Tsim Shi Tsui; close up of the Convention Centre; crowd crossing street; close up of crowd crossing street; Leung Chun-ying.

English Subtitles: (male narrator): Last June the anti-extradition bill movement triggered large scale street violence and vandalism that had yet to be settled [*scenes of violent protest*] (Leung Chun-ying speaks): Hong Kong was always a very safe city with excellent law and order, yet over the past year, *we have seen the emergence of terrorism, which has the potential to keep expanding and growing.* (Male narrator): On May 22, the third session of the 13th National People's Congress (NPC) commenced and announced the enacting of a national security law in Hong Kong. (Leung Chun-ying speaks till the end of the video): One of the objectives of national security legislation, to prevent and *curb the emergence of terrorism* [*more violent acts are shown*]. In Hong Kong the rule of law prevails. Hence, we are resorting to legislative means to stop this, with a view to safeguard lives and property and to resist and *oppose the "burn with us mentality"*.

Analysis: The National Security Law has been enacted to "curb the emergence of terrorism"; which has the "potential" to keep expanding and growing" if nothing was done—a discourse of fear of instability and thus the loss of cherished prosperity is raised. Again, the context of this "terrorism" has not been given for this "very safe city with excellent law and order" where the "rule of law" prevails (equating "rule of law" with "breaking the law"). This accords with what Chief Executive Carrie Lam said earlier in her letter to citizens. The phrase "burn with us" comes from the book/film *The Hunger Games*: "If we burn, you burn with us" fighting words that rallied support behind the symbol of the rebellion: *The Mockingjay*. The phrase *lam chau* (攬炒), which was used to express this in Cantonese, literally means "embrace fry", which has a similar meaning. It also came to mean "mutually assured destruction". It is also used more broadly to refer to the idea of sanctions against Hong Kong and was invoked in the unofficial primaries in July 2020, which was to increase democratic presence in the Legislative Council and to ensure that the chief executive would need to step down from their post (as required by the Basic Law).

Secure Homeland: Episode 6, 4 July 2020

Scenes: scenes from 13th meeting of the NPCSC; crowd of protesters with British and US flags; large protest crowd with flags of many countries; Demosisto website; Hong Kong National Front website; Studentlocalism website; Chief Executive Carrie Lam; picture of Tiananmen Square with Forbidden City entrance in the distance; "Long Live the Great Unity of the World's Peoples" (世界人民大团结万岁) on the front part of this;

Carrie Lam; Hong Kong and Chinese flags on flagpoles; the Hong Kong High Court; close up of sign saying "High Court"'; Carrie Lam.

English Subtitles: (male narrator): After the National People's Congress passed the National Security Law, many parties that advocated localism, self-determinism and Hong Kong independence announced their dissolution before the law was officially implemented [*Demosisto website; Hong Kong National Front website; Studentlocalism website*]. According to the Chief Executive Carrie Lam under the principle of the current rule of law, *bygones will be bygones*, the law starts implementing on the day it comes into effect. (Carrie Lam now speaks till the end of the video): Even though it is a natural law, drafted based on the legal system of the mainland, it does not mean laws enacted on the mainland will completely violate the legal principles we value. People are concerned about whether these criminal offences will be retroactive. Both Deputy Directors (Zhang Zemin and Deng Zhonghua) have indicated, in general that the law will not be retroactive and *bygones will be bygones*.

Analysis: Chief Executive Carrie Lam, as leader of Hong Kong and representative of the Central People's Government gives authority to what "Let bygones be bygones" is an idiom (既往不咎) repeated twice in the video; it means to forgive someone for something done or for a disagreement and to forget about it. First it is used after the dissolution of some organisations/political parties and used also to refer to the NSL as not being retroactive. The latter serves to calm fears of past actions coming back to haunt people, giving a "clean slate" to people who might have been "radical" in the past but who are no longer so. Attempting to emphasise that Hong Kong's laws will be retained, the sentence "It does not mean laws enacted on the mainland will completely violate the legal principles we value", implies that laws on the mainland *will partially violate* the valued legal principles, since "not…completely violate", leaves room for such violation. Prior to this statement "natural law" is mentioned. This is a reference to the idea that civil law "should be based on morality, ethics, and what is inherently correct. This is in contrast to what is called 'positive law' or 'human law' which is defined by statute and common law and may or may not reflect the natural law".[9] This could refer to

[9] See Investopedia—https://www.investopedia.com/terms

"unspoken" mainland Chinese norms that society is expected to know, which is likely to differ to Hong Kong's norms. It is unclear if the ordinary Hongkonger would realise this.

Secure Homeland; Episode 12, 10 July 2020

Scenes: drone shot of skyscrapers; black-clad protesters holding sheets of corrugated iron; black-clad protesters crouching down holding up umbrellas; reporters taking pictures of protesters breaking glass to get into a building; people walking across street; close-up of crowd walking; close up of flag pole with Hong Kong flag flying; ferry crossing harbour; view of Hong Kong Island shore from Tsim Sha Tsui Star Ferry; Rita Fan former member of the Standing Committee; drone shot of tall buildings; dense crowd of protesters holding British and US flags and Hong Kong independence flags; close up of US flags; close up of Hong Kong independence flags; scene of umbrellas open amidst tear gas; protesters throwing firebombs on street; Rita Fan; protesters throwing firebombs at barricades across streets; trashed businesses; Rita Fan.

English Subtitles: (male narrator): The National Security Law aims to prevent and curb four types of acts and activities that severely endanger national security [*black-clad protesters holding sheets of corrugated iron*]. It targets an extreme minority of people said the basic rights and freedoms of the Hong Kong people are still protected with the Basic Law. Also, though the laws of Hong Kong, the International Covenant on Civil and Political Rights and the International Covenant on Economic, Social and Cultural Rights are implemented. Their relevant provisions will not be restricted. (Rita Fan speaks till the end of the video): Hence our daily lives will not be restricted. Hence our daily lives will not be affected. But if I raised a British or American flag [*protest scene of British and US flags*] and shout "I want independence for Hong Kong" and then proceed to commit arson and assaults, I believe such acts will be restricted. This (law) actually protects ordinary citizens who are not violence-related [*scenes of violence*] as well as the rights to free expression. When you impede on the people's freedom, it is not called freedom…you are breaking the law. The law is the law. As long as your means are peaceful, the freedom you have always enjoyed under the Basic Law will not be affected.

Analysis: This video seems to imply that violence is necessary to be charged with a crime under the National Security Law. This seems to be somewhat contradictory to what has been said before in an earlier video. Most security laws in other jurisdictions need violent intent in order to be prosecuted as an offence, and "as long as your means are peaceful", you have the right to voice the slogan, although this is not directly stated.

Secure Homeland; Episode 15, 13 July 2020

Scenes: mainland body full of people; same people in white shirts; close-up of these people's hands—turning pages; picture of Tiananmen Gate with picture of Mao on top; Close-up of PRC insignia; crowd of Hong Kong people walking; picture of Hong Kong's Legislative Council building; view looking down from the Peak on skyscrapers and harbour; China/Hong Kong flags flying on flagpoles; people filling Victoria Park for June Fourth commemoration; the park at night full of people with lit candles. Priscilla Leung member of the Basic Law Committee; close up of a blue and white flag; protesters seen from above; protesters on street tearing up paper; scenes of protesters handling barricades; Priscilla Leung.

English Subtitles: (male narrator): Do the provisions of the NSL and the International Covenant on Civil and Political Rights contradict each other? According to the statement of the Ministry of Foreign Affairs, The NSL clearly stipulates that in safeguarding national security, human rights should be respected and protected and the residents of the region shall be protected *in accordance* with the Basic Law and International Covenant on Civil and Political Rights and the International Covenant on Economic, Social and Cultural Rights including freedom of assembly, procession and demonstration. [*People filling Victoria Park for June Fourth commemoration; the park at night full of people with lit candles*] (Priscilla Leung now speaks till the end of the video) [*Close-up of a blue and white flag*]: Actually, not just this law. The common law also deals with the principles. Why did you go there? Why did you show up? When others were shouting "Hong Kong independence" Why didn't you leave? Why did you stay? Why did you act as if you were backing them up? And just when you got into trouble, you'd then deny everything. Actually, on many occasions, honestly, very often, we apply a *very reasonable third-party* standard: *How others will interpret your actions on that day.*

Analysis: There are scenes of people filling up Victoria Park for the June Fourth vigil with candles while Priscilla Leung is discussing freedom of procession and demonstration. In the light that subsequently commemorating June the Fourth has not been allowed since is telling. A new flag [*Blue and white flag on the words*] while Leung says "Why did you go there? is interesting. In an editorial in *Stand News*, an online newspaper, we are told that the colour blue stands for freedom while white represents democracy and independence. *Daily Record*, an online news source that reports primarily on the anti-government movement, wrote in a Facebook post that is no longer available that "the upper blue symbolises the Hong Kong's past as a British's colony as well as symbolises freedom. The white colour reinstates the urge of a peaceful life that many Hongkongers look for." The general public may not know what the blue flag means unless actively following the protests. The questions posed by Leung relate to the common law, and the "third-party standard": How others would interpret your actions on that day; this would be the police and the judiciary, and probably a NSL trial without a jury of their peers.

All Countries Have National Security Laws

Carrie Lam said after the enactment of the law that "Compared to the national security laws of other countries, it is a very mild law. Its scope is not as great as that in other countries, even China" (BBC 2022) and was mentioned in Lam's "Letter to Hong Kong Citizens". The government and supporters of Hong Kong's National Security Law accuse the West of hypocrisy and double standards in their own national security laws, as every country has a right, and indeed a duty, to protect national security and sovereignty. As a government spokesperson put it "To suggest that our sovereign, China, does not have the right to legislate to protect national security in the Hong Kong Special Administrative Region (HKSAR) smacks of double standards and hypocrisy" (info.gov.hk 2020).

We will start off with one video from the "Secure Homeland" category as a "base" text, before briefly looking at the "Bedrock of Community" category, that has eight consecutive videos (9 November to 18 November 2020) that deal with the security laws of a number of other places. For reasons of space these consecutive videos will not be quoted in full.

Secure Homeland: Episode 5, 3 July 2020

Scenes: Star Ferry terminal, Tsim Sha Tsui; crowds of upper-half of people; a blank world map; shots of the map with icons representing when/what law in the US, England, Canada, Australia, New Zealand, Japan with national security; Starry Lee Legislative Council member; US crowds walking on the street; US flags hanging off buildings; Americans walking in the street; Los Angeles county sheriff's office; location with a fence; a large wire fence with a large sign "Jail" behind it; blank outline world map with different places gradually appearing; Starry Lee; Hong Kong Island as seen from Kowloon.

English Subtitles: (male narrator): Countries around the world have national security laws in place. Some of them have enacted as early as the beginning of the twentieth century. The US passed the Espionage Act in 1917. It has been amended and repeated even since. The Counter-Terrorism and Security Act, the Emergency Act in Canada, the Defence Amendment Bill in Australia, the Intelligence and Security Act in New Zealand and Japan has laws in place against internal insurrection and external threats and crimes of disturbance. (Starry Lee now speaks): No sovereign state in the world will tolerate its own system to have *national security loopholes* and not manage to close them. For instance, the US now has many laws on national security, including the National Security Act, the Homeland Security Act and the US Patriot Act. *Anyone found guilty of treason in the US may be put to death,* not just the US, the UK, Canada, Australia, Japan and Singapore, all these places have different laws to ensure national security.

What has been said in the narration above is followed up in subsequent videos, given below followed up with analysis.

(Episode 6, 9 November 2020): In 2009 Macau implemented Article 23 of their Basic Law and in 2018 had a CSNC set up. There have been no problems, there has been wide acceptance of its NSL; the gaming industry likes it and has not affected it, and no foreign government has criticised Macau for it.

(Episode 7, 10 November 2020): Singapore ("another financial hub") has its its ISA—Internal Security Act, a colonial relic, and it's quite "draconian" according to the legal authority, and because people can be detained without trial for years; severe cases result in the death penalty.

(Episode 8, 11 November 2020): Malaysia has three sets of security laws; usual laws can be suspended in emergency situations. In addition, "confessions under duress" could still be used.

(Episode 9, 12 November 2020): The sarin gas attack in Tokyo in 1995 saw the death penalty imposed on the perpetrator.

(Episode 10, 13 November 2020): About a month after the 9/11 attacks, the US implemented the Patriot Act "to expand the ambit to homegrown terrorism"; refers to the US Government's ability to intercept communications.

(Episode 11, 16 November 2020): 2005 England Implementation of the Terrorism Act was introduced to impose "control orders" on terrorists; 2011 Terrorism Prevention and Implementation Measures Act allows a suspect to be detained before conviction.

(Episode 12, 17 November 2020): Catalonia independence referendums considered illegal; certain independence leaders were incarcerated.

(Episode 13, 18 November): Many countries around the world have laws and mechanisms concerning national security; they even set up security and intelligence agencies.

Analysis: As seen above, it is undeniable that many other places have quite draconian laws and Hong Kong does not have the death penalty, although Article 55 of the NSL which says that the Office for Safeguarding National Security could take over "complex cases" and the "Supreme People's Procuratorate can designate a prosecuting body to prosecute it (Article 56). This gives a degree of uncertainty about penalties. It is unclear if citizens watching the video would realize this without studying the text of the NSL carefully.

Certainly, aspects of security laws in liberal democracies can said to be problematic for civil liberties, for example The US's Homeland Security Act (2020) and Patriot Act which were a result of the traumatic events of 9/11. Ken Roach (Chapter 14) in Fu and Hor (2022), shows that "implicit practices and institutions to the rule of law which temper the effects of the often "overbroad security laws in liberal democracies may not be able mitigate some of the effects of the NSL" (2022, 308). Roach goes on to compare the NSL with institutional, cultural, and political factors of liberal democracies that gives mitigation to their national security laws,

Publishing

Secure Homeland Episode 13, 11 July 2020

Scenes: Hong Kong Island waterfront as seen from Kowloon; people passing stalls in Tsim Sha Tsui near the Star Ferry; newspaper stand; close up of newspapers; newspapers on edge; crowd crossing pedestrian crossing; crowd reflected in window as they pass by; crowd waiting to cross road at traffic lights; container shop passing by Hong Kong island; drone shot of tall buildings; Ma Fung Kwok Legislative Council member; another drone shot of skyscrapers; an even higher drone shot directly overhead looking down on tall buildings; a person taking a newspaper from a newsstand; Ma Fung Kuok.

English Subtitles: (male narrator): The publishing industry in Hong Kong is diversified and thriving. Books from around the world on any subject you want are basically available in Hong Kong. There has never been *any problem of the so-called "banned books"* [*only newspapers are shown, no books*]. Legislative Council member Ma Fung Kwok has pointed out the implementation of the National Security Law only targets four types of crimes that endanger national security. The majority of Hong Kong people enjoy the freedom stipulated in Article 27 of the Basic Law, including freedom of speech, freedom of the press and freedom to publish. *The industry has nothing to worry about.* (Ma Fung Kwok now speaks till the end of the video): With the National Security legislation in place, I believe our society is in a *lenient and relaxed* state. *Creativity, speech and publishing will enjoy more freedom with fewer restrictions and constraints* [*a brief glimpse of the Apple Daily newspaper's masthead can be seen*].

Analysis: Ma Fung Kwok, a pro-Beijing Legislative Council member is the authority figure here. The *Apple Daily* newspaper's masthead is near the word "publishing" towards the end of the video—this is before the demise of that newspaper which ceased publication on 24 June 2021. Ma does not say how the NSL would mean "fewer restrictions and constraints" under the new law, given the provisions discussed in Chap. 2 and the vagueness and ambiguity of language and the absence of "red lines" of what is legal or illegal. The use of the word "lenient" in the phrase "society is in a lenient and relaxed state" seems odd and not really reflective of a society undergoing massive change. Again, assurances are merely given that the NSL will not affect this area at all. In effect, this will not be the case (see Chap. 6).

Education

Bedrock of Community—Episode 21—30 November 2020

Scenes: Cover of National Security Law booklets (in Chinese); close up of building with "Middle School" sign on it; front of a primary school; group of people holding the Chinese flag and a long rectangular banner "support Hong Kong's National Security Law…."; close up of newspapers; fingers moving on a keyboard; Golden Bauhinia Square on National Day, line up of the disciplined services with a national security signboard; students on footbridge near Lion Rock; people on the Tsim Sha Tsui promenade; Hong Kong island waterfront; <u>Kevin Yeung Yun Hung Secretary for Education</u>; students walking passed a school; Kevin Yeung; fingers on keyboard; digital, images of plugs; vegetable stall; meat in supermarket freezer; Kevin Yeung.

English Subtitles: (male narrator): As stipulated in Article 10 of the National Security Law the HKSAR promotes national education in schools [*a group of people holding the Chinese flag and a long rectangular banner (in Chinese) "support Hong Kong's National Security Law"*], social organisations, the media, the internet and other means [*fingers on a computer keyboard*] to raise awareness of Hong Kong residents of national security and *the obligation to abide by the law* [*school children crossing a footbridge near Lion Rock*]. What progress has the government made it in this aspect? (Kevin Yeung now speaks till the end of the video): In the course and guidelines how to enhance students' sense of national identity is a crucial element. *The scope of national education is very broad—it's more than a nation's territorial security or regime security.* [*many different scenes follow*] Other aspects of security may include technology and food through different subjects we hope to institute our students with an awareness of national security and a sense of the *need to be law-abiding.*

Analysis: Kevin Yeung Yun Hung, Secretary for Education is the authority figure here. *The scope of national education is very broad—it's more than a nation's territorial security or regime security.* This fits in with the scope of the concept of holistic national security, where all kinds of security (e.g., food security, cyber security) could be discussed, and will be included in all subjects across the curriculum. This is a key area of the NSL (Articles 9 and 10) and its importance lies with the failure to introduce national education in 2012 and the rise of youth politics and localism after the 2014 OCLP/Umbrella Movement. Thus the "need to be law-abiding"; with a curriculum that has integrated national security issues within it, "law-abidingness" should naturally result.

Conclusion: Everything Is the Same but Better

This chapter has been all about persuading the public that Hong Kong society will continue much as before with all its usual and cherished systems intact. It must be remembered that these videos were put out in the first six months of the Law before it could have taken its full effect and much was unknown about how it impacted the Basic Law and Hong Kong's systems. To ease longstanding public fears about stability even before the text of the Law was published, so a sense of "trust" had to be invoked that all would be well. The "Hong Kong collocates" of "stability and prosperity" was often invoked at this time, and the blanketing of the city with National Security banners and posters emblazoned with "National Security Law" with the slogan "preserve one country, two systems, restore stability" at this time served, by repetition to inculcate the public that now order has been restored. Justification of the NSL's introduction was due to the violence arising out of the protests, shown in many scenes of violence that were depicted in the government videos; the many peaceful political marches and related activities were downplayed and not mentioned. The potential of even peaceful demonstrations turning violent was implied many times, thus invoking to a discourse of fear (of instability). Prominent voices in the commercial, academic, and political spheres in these videos served to legitimise the need for a national security law. From Chap. 2's analysis of the National Security Law, it is easy to see several problematic areas that would impact on Hong Kong's systems, but it is unlikely that the general public would know this early on in the Law's introduction. Chapter 6's focus on the NSL and civil society will show that the Law definitely had an all-compassing impact on how the local society functioned. The next chapter will deal with the reform of the electoral system, so that "patriots" would be elected, serving as a form of "insurance" that stability and prosperity of Hong Kong would be maintained.

References

Anderson, Neil. "How a Digital Revolution is Redefining the Way Property Owners Design, Operate and Manage Real Estate in Hong Kong". *South China Morning Post*, May 3, 2022. https://www.scmp.com/business/article/3176295/how-digital-revolution-redefining-way-property-owners-design-operate-and

BBC. "Hong Kong Leader Carrie Lam Won't Seek Second Term." *BBC*, April 4, 2022. https://www.bbc.com/news/world-asia-china-60978792

Bray, Chad, Georgina Lee, and Enoch Yiu. "A Silent Revolution is Underway in Hong Kong's Fintech Industry, Helping City Catch Up to Greater Bay Area Neighbours." *South China Morning Post*, November 6, 2021. https://www.scmp.com/business/banking-finance/article/3154984/silent-revolution-underway-hong-kongs-fintech-industry

Cao, Deborah. *Chinese Law: A Language Perspective*. Burlington, V.T.: Ashgate, 2004.

Denton, Robert. "The Rhetorical Functions of Slogans: Classifications and Characteristics." *Communication Quarterly* 28 (22 May, 1980): 10–18.

Dicks, Bella. "Multimodal Analysis." In Paul Atkinson, Sara Delamont, Alexandru Cernat, Joseph W. Sakshaug, and Richard A Williams, eds., *SAGE Research Methods Foundations*. London, Sage, 2019.

Eagleton, Jennifer. "The 'Ultimate Aim': Discourses of Future Democratization in Post-Handover Hong Kong." [Unpublished PhD thesis], Department of Linguistics, Macquarie University, Sydney, 2012.

Firth, John Rupert. *Studies in Linguistic Analysis*. Oxford: Blackwell, 1957. https://languagelog.ldc.upenn.edu/myl/Firth1957.pdf

Fu, Hualing, and Michael Hor. *The National Security Law of Hong Kong Restoration and Transformation*. Hong Kong: Hong Kong University Press, 2022.

Grundy, Tom. "Hong Kong's John Lee Chides Reporter for Referring to 2019 'Protests' Instead of 'the Black Violence'." *Hong Kong Free Press*, May 3, 2023. https://hongkongfp.com/2023/05/03/hong-kongs-john-lee-chides-reporter-for-referring-to-2019-protests-instead-of-the-black-violence/

Ho, Kelly. "Hong Kong Gov't spent HK$2.47 Million of Taxpayers Money on Anti-protest TV Ads." *Hong Kong Free Press*, April 9, 2020. https://hongkongfp.com/2020/04/09/hong-kong-govt-spent-hk2-47-million-of-taxpayers-money-on-anti-protest-tv-ads/

Hou, Wai Kai, Tsz Wai Li, Li Liang, Huinan Liu, Catherine K. Ettman, Stevan E. Hobfoll, Tatia Mei-Chun Lee, and Sandro Galea. "Trends of Depression and Anxiety During Massive Civil Unrest and COVID-19 in Hong Kong, 2019–2020." *Journal of Psychiatric Research* 145 (2021):77–84.

Hutton, Mecedes. "5 Years after First 2019 Protest Arrests, Fate of Over 7,300 Arrestees, 72% of Total, Remains Unclear". *Hong Kong Free Press,* June 9, 2024. https://hongkongfp.com/2024/06/09/5-years-after-first-2019-protest-arrests-over-7300-arrestees-72-of-total-have-yet-to-see-day-in-court/

ICDS. "Video Fake News Believed More, Shared More than Text and Audio Versions." Penn State Institute for Computer and Data Services, September 9, 2021. https://www.icds.psu.edu/video-fake-news-believed-more-shared-more-than-text-and-audio-versions/

Jones, Rodney. *Discourse Analysis, A Resource Book for Students.* 2nd edition. London, Routledge, 2009.

Kress, Gunther. *Multimodality: A social semiotic approach to contemporary communication.* Abingdon: Routledge, 2010.

Kress, Gunther, and Theo Van Leeuwen, T. "Colour as a Semiotic Mode: Notes for a Grammar of Colour." *Visual Communication* 1, no. 3 (2002): 343–368.

Lam, Carrie. "CE's letter to Hong Kong Citizens." Hong Kong Government, May 29, 2020. https://www.info.gov.hk/gia/general/202005/29/P2020052800745.htm

Lee, Ta-Ling. *Foundations of the Chinese Revolution, 1905-1922: An Historical Record of the T'ung-Meng Hui*. St. John's University Press, 1970.

Leung, Hillary. "Upholding National Security to Become 'Core Value' in Hong Kong's Updated Civil Service Code." December 14, 2023. https://hongkongfp.com/2023/12/14/upholding-national-security-to-become-core-value-in-hong-kongs-updated-civil-service-code/

Leung, Janny, H.C. "Sedition or Mere Dissent? Linguistic Analysis of a Political Slogan." *International Journal for Semiotics and the Law* 37 (2024): 647–675 (2024). https://doi.org/10.1007/s11196-023-10042-x

Maden, Chris. "In Carrie Lam's Letter, Hong Kong's Rule of Law is Sacrificed to State Paranoia." *Hong Kong Free Press*. June 6, 2020. https://hongkongfp.com/2020/06/06/in-carrie-lams-letter-hong-kongs-rule-of-law-is-sacrificed-to-state-paranoia/

Mahtani, Shibani, Timothy McLaughlin, Tiffany Liang and Ryan Ho Kilpatrick. In Hong Kong crackdown, police repeatedly broke their own rules—and faced no consequences. *Washington Post*, December 24, 2019. https://www.washingtonpost.com/graphics/2019/world/hong-kong-protests-excessive-force/

Song, Jianlin, and James Paul Gee "Slogans with Chinese Characteristics: The Political Functions of a Discourse Form." *Discourse & Society* 31, no. 2 (2019): 201–217.

Ting, Victor. "Black-clad Protesters United in Common Cause Insist: We are Not Rioters, We are Just Ordinary Citizens Who Love Hong Kong." *South China Morning Post,* June 16, 2019. https://www.scmp.com/news/hong-kong/politics/article/3014731/black-clad-protesters-united-common-cause-insist-we-are-not

Qiao, Xiaoqiao (喬小橋) Why Ivan Choy is Bitter" (蔡子強緣何痛心疾首). *Ta Kung Pao*, December 25, 2005. Accessed by WisersOne Database.

4

Ensuring Patriots Administer Hong Kong

This chapter will show how electoral changes in 2021 were seen by the Hong Kong authorities as a way to ensure that "patriots" ran Hong Kong by looking at the official justification for reforming the electoral system. The 2019 protests and earlier political turmoil were considered due to the lack of "patriots" in the Hong Kong government. The booklet, issued by the Hong Kong government's Constitutional and Mainland Affairs Bureau, *Improve Electoral System Ensure Patriots Administering Hong Kong* (CMAB 2021), will be extensively analysed in terms of this justification using CDA principles laid out in Chap. 1 of this book.

After studying this booklet, the chapter presents findings of a second study looking into the ways in which these electoral changes were reflected in the Hong Kong news discourse in the lead-up to the District Council Election on 19 December 2021. There will then be studies on two White Papers, one before the election and one after the election, the latter is particularly important as it was issued a day after the election and entitled: *Hong Kong Democratic Progress Under the Framework of "One Country, Two Systems"* (SCIO 2021b), issued by the mainland authorities a day after the election. This official text will also be analysed in terms of what was seen as Hong Kong's "democratic progress".

J. Eagleton, *Hong Kong's Second Return to China*,
https://doi.org/10.1007/978-3-031-84587-1_4

Situational Background

Two major events led to changes in the electoral system. The 2019 District Council election was won by the pan-democrats (this author's collective term for various democratic parties) and the unofficial pan-democrat "primaries" were organised in July 2020. The District Council election of 24 November 2019 saw a record high 71.2 percent turnout rate with around 2.94 million people casting their ballot, with pan-democrats winning a majority of the seats. The siege of the Polytechnic University (17–29 November) had not turned public sentiment against the protests, analysts seeing that voting was drawn from "localism" rather than "utilitarian pragmatism", due to lack of trust in Hong Kong's leaders and the Chinese political system over the extradition bill (Lam J.T.M 2021). Others saw "overall dissatisfaction in Hong Kong" as having led voters to "reward extremist tactics" (Ip 2019). The 2020 Hong Kong pro-democracy primaries were held on 11–12 July 2020 for selecting pro-democracy candidates for the subsequently postponed 2020 Legislative Council election (due to Covid-19) to maximise their electoral chances to be elected in the 70-seat Legislative Council under its proportional voting system. Over 600,000 Hongkongers voted in these unofficial primaries. The response to these primaries was harsh criticism from the Hong Kong and Central Chinese governments as an "act of opposition" to the new National Security Law (Davidson 2020; Ramzy et al. 2020). Seen as "illegal" by the authorities, these primaries resulted in charges being laid against those taking part, the trials of which are still ongoing in 2023.

In May 2021, Beijing radically overhauled Hong Kong's electoral system so that "patriots rule Hong Kong", seen as a "necessary condition" for implementing the governance framework of "One Country, Two Systems" (Ho 2021a). While the National Security Law (NSL) provided authorities with a "sword" to stabilise the system, the electoral changes served as a "shield" (Luo 2021). This idea is encapsulated in the verbs used in the phrases "Preserve 'One Country, Two Systems"—*Restore* Stability" and "Preserve "One Country, Two Systems"—*Enhance* Stability and Prosperity" (italics added) which appeared on public posters about the NSL and electoral changes respectively.

In the following sections, a number of official documents are critically analysed how show the arguments and reasons given to purport to justify and legitimise the changes to Hong Kong's electoral system and the course of its democratic progress. The chapter discusses three case studies examining official documents issued by the Hong Kong and Beijing governments. It highlights the interconnectedness of the discourse across texts and the need for having a deep understanding of history and the specific sociocultural context at a certain point in time.

Official Discursive Defence of Changing the Electoral System

The electoral changes were initiated by the National People's Congress (NPC) on 11 March 2021 to "amend electoral rules and improve the electoral system" in order to ensure a system in which only "patriots" govern Hong Kong (Shen 2021). The changes were widely criticised by both local and international sources as having a negative impact on democratic representation in Hong Kong.

The Improving Electoral System (Consolidated Amendments) Bill 2021 (Hong Kong Gov. 2021b) allows Beijing more power to vet, appoint, and remove lawmakers in Hong Kong's Legislative Council, while reducing the number of seats that could be elected by the public. What the authorities had to do was to convince the public that representation was not just essentially the same as before, but improved.

The Constitutional and Mainland Affairs Bureau of the Hong Kong Government (CMAB) published a booklet, entitled *Improve Electoral System Ensure Patriots Administering Hong Kong* (CMAB 2021) to explain and justify these electoral changes. Table 6.1 presents the Table of Contents alongside each part's discursive function.

The phrase "improving the election system" is repeated three times in different sections of the booklet. The communicative purpose of the discursive structure of the booklet is to provide a justified legal basis for the changes. In the next section, the foreword and the *Event Book of Chaos* is discussed in detail, followed by a more extensive analysis of the FAQs and their answers.

Table 6.1 Table of Contents of the Booklet

Content	Discursive Function
Foreword by Chief Executive Carrie Lam	To serve as a means to normalise the situation
Background	To argue that Hong Kong is an "inalienable part of China" To show the "success of 'One Country, Two Systems'"
The Recent Situation	To show events that "shamelessly obstruct and paralyse the action of the government" To give a "myriad of examples"
The Event Book of Chaos Involving Non-pro-establishment Members in the Sixth Term Legislative Council	To present a more specific timeline of events from October 2016 to November 2020 To label/categorise the "other" To bring up traditional Chinese tropes
The Legal Basis and Process of Improving the Electoral System	To legitimise the passage of the NPC's Decision ("The legal basis of the Decision is solid") To indicate authorisation to amend the law
Main Content of Improving the Electoral System	To briefly introduce the changes in the system
Timetable for Improving the Electoral System	To represent a timetable for the introduction of the amendment's Bill
Frequently Asked Questions	To refute arguments against the legislation

Foreword

This is addressed to "fellow Hong Kong citizens", the targeted readers of the booklet (the inclusive "we"). The "year-long social unrest" had "thrown citizens into great fear" and showing the need for patriots to administer Hong Kong is fundamental, referring to Deng Xiaoping whose "scope and criteria" was that Hong Kong should be managed by patriots. "These chaos [*sic*] have exposed the loopholes and deficiencies of Hong Kong's electoral system" as "opposing forces and radicals entered the political structure of the HKSAR through elections" and "advocating

Hong Kong independence". The National Security Law is seen as having "plugged the loophole" which endangered national security, but it is argued that more needs to be done. These changes are presented as showing that the "Mainland cares for Hong Kong". Couched in the discourse of fear, the use of emotional rhetoric such as this serves as a form of justification for the upcoming changes.

The Event Book of Chaos

The title *The Event Book of Chaos Involving Non-Pro-Establishment Members in the Sixth Term Legislative Council* (pp. 7–8), rather than the more concise "chronology of events", acts as a framing device. It indicates how we might ideologically read the incidents on the timeline. "Non-pro-establishment members" refers to the pan-democrats.[1] Individual names of these members are not given. The designation also implies that the pro-establishment members were not involved in any of the disturbances (the "chaos") mentioned in the timeline, a screenshot is given below. In labelling, there is a "lexicon of persuasion" (Sornig 1989, 104), which alongside tautology, paraphrase, euphemism, ambiguity, involves a movement from a concentrated to a more generic meaning/category. Semantic "vagueness" is perhaps one of the most useful of linguistic categories as this widens the scope of what can be contained in a label.

Frequently Asked Questions (FAQ)

When Hong Kong became a Special Administrative Region of China (HKSAR) on 1 July 1997, it became the only example of the "One Country, Two Systems" governance framework. This principle was to build a new political order that embodied a new hegemony of beliefs and ideology, but one that was partially in line with pre-1997 systems that were supposed to remain "unchanged", post-1997. A successful ruling

[1] From 1997 onwards, democrats were labelled and categorised as "Anti-China, Destabilising Hong Kong [反中亂港]", "Seeking Confrontation [搞對抗]", and "Espousing False Democracy [假民主]" (Eagleton 2012).

ideology "[…] must engage significantly with genuine wants, needs and desires; but this is also its Achilles heel, forcing it to recognise the "other" to itself and inscribing this otherness as a potentially disruptive force within its own forms" (Eagleton 1991, 45). For a governing ideology to be "convincing", that is, it must persuade others, it must also address its opposite and be "dialogical" in order to be "unifying". A dialogue is thus established between ideologies which have different meanings for certain "essentially contested" concepts like "democracy' and "elections" (Gallie 1956; Gray 1977, 344). Therefore, these 12 FAQs have to deal with what the opposition is saying about the electoral changes and justify the opposite.

The FAQ genre is characterised by a surface structure of question-answer adjacency pairs and the "substantial variability of their semantic macrostructure and microstructure and lexicosemantic realisation" (Tomaskova 2012, 124). Some FAQs start off with one or two statements, followed by a single question or questions, the statements acting as a frame for the subsequent answer by the use of certain subjective adjectives. The FAQs (given in italics) will be listed in full in order to better understand how they frame the scope of the answer to the FAQ.[2] There are 12 FAQs in total, but only seven will be analysed here. FAQs 1–4 focus on compatibility with the previous system and "One Country, Two Systems", the need for patriots and the criteria for their selection, while FAQs 10–12 deal with the legitimacy of who can run for election and why the Legislative Council will not be a "rubber stamp". These seven questions impact on why these changes are still within Hong Kong's governance framework, why "patriots" need to administer the region, and why citizen representation will fully remain.

FAQ 1: *The Central Authorities have taken action twice proactively in a year. Firstly, there was the National Security Law and the establishment of the Office for Safeguarding National Security of the Central People's Government in the HKSAR, and now the Central Authorities have substantially changed the electoral system of the HKSAR. Is it a departure from the*

[2] The booklet and FAQs can be found at https://www.cmab.gov.hk/improvement/filemanager/content/pdf/en/resource-centre/booklet.pdf

principles and policies of "One Country, Two Systems", "Hong Kong people administering Hong Kong" and a high degree of autonomy?

The answer to this FAQ begins with a negative as in "Absolutely not". This question deals with the three oft-quoted principles of "One Country, Two Systems", "Hong Kong people administering Hong Kong" and a high degree of autonomy. In the answer to the FAQ, only the first two principles are in quotation marks, perhaps indicating that the third one is not as strong as the former two. What these principles actually entail is not fully explained here. However, it is argued in the answer that they all would be threatened if no electoral changes were made. The phrase "Hong Kong people *ruling* Hong Kong" (italics added) was often used in the past and even appeared in the English version of the *Basic Law Factsheet* until just after the end of Occupy Central in December 2014 when it was changed to "administering" (Webb 2014).[3] The NSL would "plug the longstanding gaping hole" in national security while the new changes "plugged the loopholes" in the electoral system. Specific details about these actual "holes" were not mentioned, but well known, being the failure of Hong Kong to implement Article 23 of the Basic Law, which deals with national security, and the proportional voting system that allowed certain individuals to win elections (i.e., non-patriots).

A "small number of extremists" are said to have taken advantage of "inadequate national education and a weak sense of national identification" to spread "anti-Chinese sentiments". This implies that the Hong Kong people are cast as being easily exploited by this group, thus the need for more robust electoral laws. These extremists reportedly are "supported by external elements" (though never named in this FAQ), who talk about "mutual destruction" and incite violence to "seize power through election". The latter phrase "seize power through election" sounds odd, as elections are won by voting, while "seize power" implies a *coup d'état*. This refers to the plan by legal scholar Benny Tai and others from the pro-democracy camp to win a majority of seats in the Legislative Council for

[3] According to the *Oxford English Dictionary*, "ruling" as a transitive verb means to "direct, guide, manage (a thing); to have under one's control", while "administer" in the same dictionary is "[...] to carry out or oversee the tasks necessary for the running of (an organisation) [...] to manage the affairs of (an institution, community, etc.)." Arguably, "administering" could be taken as being less than "ruling".

2020–2022. By the so-called *laam chau* [攬炒] or "mutual destruction" route, which would see pro-democracy camps win a majority seats in the Legislative Council election, the chief executive would then be forced to resign due to the Budget bill being rejected twice. The plan first involved "democratic primaries" to increase the chance for candidates to be elected; this was simply an electoral strategy and not actually illegal as stated in Article 52 of the Basic Law, which came into force on 1 July 1997.

FAQ 2: *Is improving the electoral system contrary to the aim of selecting the chief executive and electing all the members of the LegCo by universal suffrage in accordance with the principle of gradual and orderly progress as enshrined in the Basic Law?*

In the answer to this FAQ, the central authorities have "generally and sincerely supported" this aim, which was to take place according to the "actual situation of the HKSAR and in accordance with the principle of gradual and orderly progress" (these words are from Articles 45 and 68 of the Basic Law). What the "actual situation" is, and what "gradual and orderly progress" means is not defined, and relies on "linguistic gatekeepers", who will decide a suitable time for the election by universal suffrage to take place.

In fact, it is the "opposition camp" that is cast as hindering democratic development on "three different occasions", which, again, are not stated in the text. The answer to the FAQ also mentions the "8.31 Decision" (of 2014), in which universal suffrage for 2017 was voted down by pan-democrats because it meant selection of a narrow pool of pre-Beijing-approved candidates for chief executive. The controversy about this 8.31 Decision directly led to the "Occupy Central/Umbrella Movement". This and other previous proposals for reforming the system towards universal suffrage were seen by many as being too limited in nature with little impact on the political status quo. However, the authorities framed these proposals as "progress" towards the ultimate aim of universal suffrage. The pan-democrats were constantly accused of "opposing for the sake of opposing" and presented as "hindering democracy", and were thus "anti-democratic" despite their use of democratic rhetoric. Because of the so-called exploitation of the electoral system by pan-democrats in the past, they were able to be elected, "paralysed" the operation of the Legislative Council, and "initiated the most severe social unrest" since the HKSAR's establishment. This stance by the authorities implies that the social unrest of the anti-extradition protests would not have occurred if not for the "opposition forces", which negates the very real public anger and fears over the proposed extradition bill as well as the popularity of the protests (PORI 2019; Tam and Jim 2020). If such unrest continues, it was said, "national security, social stability and people's livelihood cannot be safeguarded and the aim of universal suffrage will never be obtainable".

FAQ 3: *Why the steadfast and faithful implementation of "One Country, Two Systems" could only be guaranteed by "patriots administering Hong Kong"? Is there a higher patriotic standard for those who are involved in the administration of HKSAR?*

FAQ 3 consists of two questions emphasising the need for patriots to be elected members of the legislature. Being "steadfast and faithful" to the "One County, Two Systems" could only be done by patriots who understood that the "One Country, Two Systems" entails that Hong Kong is an "inalienable part of China" and that there would be no "Two Systems" without the "One Country". Acknowledging this sovereignty must involve loyalty to the nation, and thus patriots are needed to administer Hong Kong. However, how this loyalty is to be defined or exhibited is not clarified, but it is "a politician's most basic ethics". As such "patriots administering Hong Kong is natural and in line with justice, and allows no ambivalence". Since people in important positions were "in possession of important powers and shouldering important governing responsibilities", they "must be staunch patriots". They are expected to meet an "even higher standard of patriotism", including "having a deep understanding" of the "essence of the principle of 'One Country, Two Systems'", and "always being mindful of the fundamental interests of the Country and the overall interests of Hong Kong". However, it is unclear what this "deep understanding" and what this actual "higher standard" entail. The presupposition is that it is to be more firmly aligned with the Central People's Government.

FAQ 4: *Are there any detailed and objective criteria for patriots? Does loving our country mean loving the Chinese Communist Party?*

In the answer to this FAQ, criteria are discussed for defining the meaning of patriotism, meaning of taking the oath, as well as listing positive and negative criteria for taking public office. Deng Xiaoping's "criteria" are given in general and vague terms: "respect one's own nation, sincerely support the resumption of the exercise of sovereignty over Hong Kong by the Motherland, and not to impair Hong Kong's prosperity and stability". The booklet does not mention the following, also said by Deng: "Those who meet these requirements are patriots, whether they believe in capitalism or feudalism or even slavery. We don't demand that they be in favour of China's socialist system; we only ask them to love the Motherland and Hong Kong" (Deng 2004 [1984]). The words quoted in the FAQ, "respect", "sincerely support", and "not impair" need further clarification about what they mean in practice.

The criteria for defining the meaning of a "patriot" in China have undergone constant change (Qin 2012; Shu 2022). At the end of the Qing dynasty, patriots were opponents of the regime; under Sun Yat-sen those who embraced civic values were patriots. After World War II those against foreign invaders/threats to the nation were patriots, while after 1949 patriots were workers and peasants. After 1978, those who "served the people", e.g., patriotic businessmen, were patriots. Now patriots are those who are "for" the nation; this could be called "patriotism as nationalism" (Gustafsson 2014; Xinhua 2022).

The call for patriots to administer Hong Kong is not new. Another "patriot debate" about security took place in 2004 around the time of a major interpretation of the Basic Law. A senior government official questioned whether opponents of legislation against subversion (related to the abortive introduction of Article 23, 2003) could be considered patriotic. The *Xinhua News Agency* published an article emphasising the importance of "patriotism" among Hong Kong's leaders and declared that those who were not sufficiently patriotic were unfit to rule Hong Kong. On 16 February 2004, the pro-Beijing newspaper *Wen Wei Po* published an interview with an unnamed Chinese government official who warned that Beijing might be forced to act if pan-democrats won the Legislative Council in the upcoming elections (Eagleton 2012).

Being willing to "swear allegiance" in the form of oath-taking is seen as essential in designating a patriot since six legislators were unseated for taking the oath incorrectly in 2016 and 2017. Taking the oath wrongly as set out in the *Event Book of Chaos* could be seen as the catalyst for this focus on the meaning of "patriot". An earlier example of unorthodox oath-taking included Leung Kwok-hung ("Long Hair") in 2004, who took the oath in the "violent" style of the Red Guards (Ta Kung Pao 2004).

In the FAQ it is also said that the oath-taking requirement also comes with "a set of detailed and objective criteria with a positive list and a negative list" for assessing patriots to serve Hong Kong. However, neither the oath nor the full criteria are given in the actual answer to the FAQ. The oath can be found on the Civil Service Bureau website, while the lists are given in The Public Offices (Candidacy and Taking Up Offices) (Miscellaneous Amendments) 2021 Bill (Hong Kong Gov. 2021a) are mentioned but not elaborated on in the answer to the FAQ. Perhaps the reader is expected to take it at face value that these criteria are "detailed and objective" when in fact they are not. The current oath simply says that the civil servant will "uphold" the Basic Law of HKSAR, "bear allegiance" to the HKSAR, be "dedicated" to their duties and "be responsible" to the government of the HKSAR.

Referring to The Public Offices Bill positive list criteria must be satisfied, while the person must not "do or intend to do any of the things on the negative list". There are five "upholds" and one "loyalty" pledge in the positive criteria: (1) to uphold the constitutional order of Hong Kong; (2) to uphold national sovereignty; (3) to uphold that Hong Kong is an inalienable part of the PRC; (4) to uphold the implantation of the "One Country, Two Systems" and to safeguard the political structure of the HKSAR; (5) to uphold the objective to maintain the prosperity and stability of the HKSAR within the framework of the Basic Law. Lastly, one has to be "loyal to, and safeguard the interests of, the HKSAR". The reader is told that "the meaning of "uphold" should include genuinely and truthfully observe, support, maintain and embrace in words and deeds, as well as the intention to do so". The issue is that a Hong Kong public servant will have to assess this "intention", a subjective state, the assumption being that they would be evaluated by past political actions.

The nine negative criteria that oath-takers must not do are the following (in brief, italics added): (1) *commit* acts that endanger national security; (2) *refuse to recognise* the PRC's sovereignty over the HKSAR; (3) *refuse to recognise* the constitutional status of the HKSAR as a local administrative region of the PRC; (4) *advocate or support* Hong Kong independence; (5) *solicit* interference by foreign governments or organisations; (6) *commit* acts that undermine or have a tendency to undermine the order of the political structure; (7) *commit* acts that undermine or have a tendency to undermine the overall interests of the HKSAR; (8) *desecrate* the national flag or national emblem, or regional flag or regional emblem; and (9) *insult or disrespect* the national anthem or any other symbol and sign of national sovereignty. The next paragraph will briefly discuss the content of each of these criteria.

Acts that endanger national security (1) as listed in the National Security Law have often been seen as vague and ambiguous, with government authorities hedging about whether an act is illegal or not (HKFP 2023). In the author's experience, most pan-democrats have *not* directly "refused to recognise" China's sovereignty or Hong Kong's constitutional status as a Special Administrative Region of China (2 and 3), statements and acts by them could have been possibly seen by China as refusal of sovereignty or status. Few individuals/parties have "advocated" Hong Kong independence (4) in particular, so-called "localists" and the Hong Kong National Party in 2018. There has been a long history of Beijing and others accusing the pan-democrats of seeking foreign government intervention (5) for acts seen by pan-democrats as infringing on democratic promises and core freedoms. This was the case in the protests of 2019 as well as Democratic Party leader, Martin Lee, in 2004, when he went to the US Congress about the recent interpretation of the Basic Law. Negative criteria (6) concerns, "compels or overawes the chief executive by any unlawful means to change a policy, or a motion to be submitted to LegCo for consideration", and this also "indiscriminately objects to the government's motion, leaving it unable to perform its duties". This obviously refers to the plan to gain office and veto the budget and so the chief executive then has to resign (the democratic "primaries") and thus "seize power through election", which is mentioned in the answer to FAQ 1, or carry out elections seen as *de-facto* referendums. The negative criterion (7) "[C]ommits acts that undermine or have a tendency to undermine the overall interests of the HKSAR" is also vague about what "undermines" and what the "overall interests" entail.

Criteria 8 and 9 relate to the misuse of national symbols, often seen at political protests like the flag and anthem. Both the positive and negative criteria are neither "detailed" nor "objective" since they really need to be defined in specific detail about what actions are involved in either "upholding" certain things or "pursuing or committing" certain acts.

The second question in the FAQ 4 is not directly answered by either a "yes" or a "no", but by saying that "Leadership by the Communist Party of China is the defining feature of socialism with Chinese characteristics". This implies that one must respect the leadership given by the Party. However, President Xi Jinping recently stated that "In contemporary China, the essence of patriotism is loving the country, the Party and socialism all at the same time" (Xinhua 2022). The unstated answer is assumed to be a possible "yes". Readers would note the omission of a direct answer and read between the lines.

FAQ 10: *Is improving the electoral system tailor-made for the pro-establishment camp with the aim to exclude the opposition camp from the LegCo?*

The answer to this FAQ starts off with a simple "No". This question is a response to accusations that the pro-establishment camp is favoured by the new electoral changes. The answer suggests that some "radical candidates" may make use of "demagogical, extreme methods to appeal to a small proportion of votes and gain seats in the Legislative Council, making it challenging for the executive authorities to work with the legislature". This renders the "political ecology more radical, which is not conducive to the stability of Hong Kong". The proportional voting system, which encourages fragmentation, was partly a reason for the so-called "illegal" primary in 2021.[4]

We are told that "[i]n selecting which political system to adopt, protection of any political party has never been a deciding factor". Although the Chief Executive Election Ordinance stipulates that they are not to be a member of any political party, the chief executive and government officials were seen as being sympathetic towards certain political groups such as the Democratic Alliance for Betterment and Progress of Hong Kong

[4] "The type of proportional representation (PR) used in Hong Kong, known as Hare Quota with Largest Remainders (HQLR), encourages fragmentation. Rather than rewarding an electoral alliance for uniting as many votes as possible under one banner, HQLR punishes big winners and encourages political allies to divide. The effect of HQLR is to hinder the development of strong parties with encompassing platforms, limiting the LegCo's potential as a representative institution" (Carey 2017, 215–216). This causes fragmentation, undermining alliances.

(DAB, dab.org.hk), who had strong links with Beijing and the establishment. Despite saying that "Patriotism is not the monopoly of any specific groups", the vague criteria of what is a patriot, and the difficulty that democrats might have in fulfilling the criteria are obvious. Furthermore, saying "not all members of the opposition camp should be regarded as anti-China and destabilising forces" implies that "many" of the opposition camp practically are.

FAQ 11*: One of the objectives of improving the electoral system is to enhance the efficacy of the HKSAR Government's governance. Does it mean that the LegCo will become a rubber stamp in future?*

This is another FAQ that first answers with a simple "No". The LegCo is said to have a "checks and balances" function and to be "monitored by the government". Readers are told that "[a]s long as legislators love the country and Hong Kong, safeguard the national sovereignty, security and development interest, do not impair Hong Kong's stability and prosperity, they are allowed to be critical of the Government and fulfil their constitutional function and achieve good governance for the public good". However, these points are not further defined.

The list of things legislators is expected to adhere to is, once again, given as general principles. Strictly speaking, one could contest the validity of arguments about the executive authorities having been "always willing and able to exchange views and cooperate with legislators who had different political stances" before the LegCo "had deteriorated [...] with antagonistic politics". Improving the electoral system, according to the government, would help the LegCo restore its function as a platform for "rational interaction" between the executive authorities and the legislature, and would enhance efficacy of governance, and thus generate fewer disputes. The new composition of groups in the LegCo would make the legislative body "wider in coverage, more balanced, more diverse in views and more representative", despite citizens having fewer candidates to vote for, which is the very argument the authorities tackle in the next FAQ 12.

FAQ 12: *The establishment of the Candidate Eligibility Review Committee to "screen out" candidates will diminish electors' choices considerably. Also, it is stipulated that the Candidate Eligibility Review Committee's decision made pursuant to the opinion given by the Committee on National Security is not subject to any judicial proceedings. People who are not allowed to stand for election will then have no chance to appeal. Does this violate the principle of fair and just opportunities to stand for election?*

It is interesting that the first statement in the FAQ acknowledges that electors' choices will diminish, as this was one of the major criticisms of the election reform. The answer goes to state that, assessing the eligibility of candidates to stand for election is "the most basic ethical and legal requirement for politicians", equating the review committee to candidate vetting in overseas jurisdictions. According to the government, this does not "violate the principle of fair and just opportunities to stand for election". Candidates in elections have to "confirm in writing to uphold the Basic Law and swear allegiance to the HKSAR". It is added that in the past, the returning officers[5] would "decide whether the candidates meet the eligibility criteria", but that it is now the task of the new Candidate Eligibility Review Committee (CERC). This is positioned as simply an improved version of previous practice. The new committee is an "institutional safeguard" for ensuring "patriots administering Hong Kong", by excluding "anti-China and destabilising forces". However, the current committee is made up of past and present Hong Kong government officials, so one could presume that they would adhere to the official Beijing line.

Briefly, these FAQs all reiterate that the basic principles of Hong Kong remain the same, the problems of the original electoral system being "smoothed out" to ensure better running of the Legislative Council and the "One Country, Two Systems" because now only "patriots" could be elected. This repetition has the effect of being a "justification" as it makes certain claims memorable. However, criteria about who is a "patriot" are vague and subjective, with official "gatekeepers" (the Hong Kong government) needing to fill the role of definer of terms and arbiter of actions that were deemed appropriate or inappropriate to Hong Kong's legislators.

---

[5]A returning officer (in a parliamentary system) is responsible for overseeing elections in one or more constituencies. In Hong Kong, the returning officer is usually an administrative officer (a part of the Civil Service).

As a kind of aside before discussion of the December election, a brief foray into a White Paper released on December 4, 2021, entitled in English: “China: Democracy That Works”, but in Chinese “中国的民主”; lit. “China’s Democracy”). Issued by China’s State Council Information Office, the white paper lays out various aspects of the Chinese political system, which it claims constitute a “whole-process” people’s democracy.

China: Democracy that Works

This White Paper was considered a response to the US President Joe Biden’s December 9–10 Summit for Democracy, the Chinese White Paper’s title perhaps highlighting what many considered the chaotic nature of the US administration under President Donald Trump. However, it is still relevant to this discussion about election reform in Hong Kong as it could also be seen as ultimately the (ideal) basic structure of Hong Kong’s new electoral system, a system that now works because “patriots only” are administering Hong Kong, as indicated by some of the comments about the Legislative Council election. Beijing’s State Council Information Office which issued the White Paper argues that its system — in which all power is ultimately lies in the Chinese Communist Party — constitutes “a true democracy that works” (SCIO 2021a).

Before discussing such a democracy as outlined in this document, a discussion of the what democracy means is crucial as what is considered a democratic system is markedly different between mainland China and democrats in Hong Kong. For example, the *Cambridge Dictionary* defines “the belief in freedom and equality between people, or a system of government based on this belief, in which power is either held by elected representatives or directly by the people themselves”, showing the limitations of this word because of its lack of specificity. Democracy, then, as mentioned earlier, is an “essentially contested concept” (Gallie 1956), and a term that exhibits polysemy, a state which “characterizes the language of ideology”; essentially contested concepts involve widespread agreement on a concept (e.g., “fairness”) but not the best realisation of this concept. Essentially contested concepts are "concepts the proper use of which inevitably involves endless disputes about their proper uses on the part of their users", and these disputes "cannot be settled by appeal to empirical evidence, linguistic usage, or the canons of logic alone" (Gray 1977, 344).

Robert A. Dahl, a noted political scientist states: "yet a term that means anything means nothing. And so, it has become with 'democracy' which is not so much a term of restricted meaning as a vague endorsement of a popular idea" (Dahl 1989, 2). Accordingly, the wording in Hong Kong's Basic Law dealt with this contested concept in a vague and ambiguous manner and so different actors in the discourse conceived universal suffrage to be different. Thus, the concept of democracy can thus be "conceptually stretched" and can come "with adjectives"' (Collier and Levitsky 1996) and the minimal criteria for a regime to be denoted as "democratic" can be contested (Ibid).

The "democracy that works" as outlined in this White Paper is "whole-process democracy". This "integrates process-oriented democracy with results-oriented democracy, procedural democracy with substantive democracy, direct democracy with indirect democracy, and people's democracy with the will of the state". The white paper discusses its institutional framework and the "concrete and pragmatic principles" of "whole-process democracy" (still couched in rather abstract terms) and how to evaluate a democratic system that works under this system.

Since this is a democracy what "works" benchmarks (1) include "The best way to evaluate whether a country's political system is democratic and efficient is to observe whether the succession of its leaders is orderly and in line with the law," (p. 6) and (2) whether the "exercise of power can be kept under effective restraint and supervision" and "whether the exercise of power is genuinely subject to public scrutiny and checks" (p. 2). This latter benchmark appears to somewhat contradictory with the ruling party's growing efforts to regulate many aspects of daily life.

The White Paper says that democracy "is a concrete phenomenon that is constantly evolving. Rooted in history, culture and tradition, it takes diverse forms and develops along the paths chosen by different peoples based on their exploration and innovation" (p. 1). By emphasising democracy as "whole-process" and arguing that different systems should be able to co-exist, reflects its attempt to “redefine democracy as a weaker, more malleable concept” (Liu 2021).

Mao declared at that time that the political system run by the CCP was one of “people’s democratic dictatorship” following the Leninist model. The White Paper acknowledges that “Democracy and dictatorship appear to be a contradiction in terms” (p. 9) but state that “together they ensure the people’s status as masters of the country. A tiny minority is sanctioned in the interests of the great majority, and ‘dictatorship’ serves democracy” (p. 9). The document stresses the democracy element while downplaying the dictatorship element of its governing model what could be said to undermine the Western concept of democracy. In Hong Kong, the “executive-led” aspect of its system could be said to be the “One Country” (Sinocized) aspect of its governance framework, while the “Second System” could be its democratic (Western) aspect (Eagleton 2017). This relationship could be said to be rhetorically ambiguous, this ambiguity leading to polarisation between those who veer more towards arguments given by the “One Country” camp and those who veer more towards the “Second System”, that is, the democratic camp. These two aspects of Hong Kong’s political system obviously clash when discussions of political reform arise, with democrats in Hong Kong using Western concepts of democratic elections to push their ideas about a universal suffrage system for Hong Kong while balancing and making the case that these Western concepts are compatible with Chinese cultural concepts.

This “new model of democracy” proposed and implemented in China—emphasises the difficulty for a “country on the road to modernization to promote democracy while ensuring political stability and social progress” (p. 46), which was an argument constantly made by the Hong Kong Government, for example, Green Paper on Constitutional Development in July 2007 which contained antithetical statements like “How can a universal suffrage model be to comply with the principle of “meeting the interests of different sectors of society”, so as to attain the aim of preserving prosperity and stability?” (Legco.gov.hk, 6.04, 50), implying that stability and prosperity would indeed be threatened. The following quote by a Beijing official given around the time of the December Legislative Council election shows the connection to "whole-process democracy": "Whether Hong Kong's democratic electoral system is good or not depends on whether it helps the city maintain long-term stability" (Cheung 2021).

The December 2021 Legislative Council Election

The first "patriots only" Hong Kong Legislative Council election was held on 19 December 2021. Originally scheduled for September 2020, it was adjourned in July over Covid-19 health concerns. The day before the adjournment, 12 pro-democracy candidates were disqualified from running in the election. Ultimately, the pro-democracy parties did not send any candidates in the election, and only a dozen candidates who claimed to be "non-pro-establishment" took part.

Around 1.3 million voters cast ballots on Election Day, which was a 30.2 percent of the population, the lowest rate since before 1997. The authorities blamed the poor turnout on administrative factors and the effect of external (foreign) forces. However, the post-election coverage focused on the so-called "fact' that the new lawmakers come from different backgrounds and across the political spectrum" according to an (unnamed) government spokesman (Chau 2021), despite all but one coming from the pro-establishment camp. According to government officials and pro-Beijing political groups, those elected on 19 December show diversity and have "different opinions on the issues Hong Kong has to face". This also "showcases broad representation and political inclusiveness of the improved electoral system" (Ho 2021c).[6] This is despite the public being allowed to elect only 20 out of 90 seats in the legislature from a pool of candidates who had passed prior national security checks by the government.

[6] Said in a joint statement by the Government Employees Association, the Hong Kong Federation of Civil Service Unions, the Chinese Academy of Governance Hong Kong Alumni Association and the Federation of HKSARG Civil Servants.

For this analysis, accounts from the Hong Kong media are examined for their focus on topics as well as discursive practices, which was done by a qualitative content and discourse analysis. The articles were downloaded from the Factiva database from four Hong Kong newspapers (two Chinese-language and two English-language dailies), the *Ta Kung Pao* (a longstanding pro-Beijing newspaper, state-owned, and controlled by the Central Government Liaison Office in Hong Kong); the *Ming Pao* (emphasises objectivity and neutrality in order to avoid political risks); the *South China Morning Post* (once represented the interests of Hong Kong elites and the British government, and now more aligned with the establishment after its purchase by the Alibaba group), and the *Hong Kong Free Press* (online only, established in 2015). The period runs from 1 November to 20 December 2021 and the keywords "election" in English and its equivalent in Chinese "選舉" were used to select articles for the corpus (*Ta Kung Pao* 357 articles; *Ming Pao* 372 articles; *SCMP* 184 articles; *HKFP* 96 articles).

Before discussing the major election topics, we first take a look at the way the word "election" was described and how elections as a process were framed by the selected newspapers. Framing elections as races is a dominant trope (Goatly 1997) when discussing elections. It becomes difficult to conceive politics any other way, for such an activity or process as in an election can be considered a movement forward, that is, something that has a speed, where politicians are construed as racing along the campaign path towards a successful election outcome (Matlock 2013). In an earlier study, the author found that metaphors of BLOCKAGE, BARRIER, or expressions like "marking time on the spot" or "being at the crossroads" were frequently used to describe Hong Kong's political development, especially by pan-democratic parties (Eagleton 2022). The current electoral changes, which involve fewer directly-elected candidates with no real "opposition" parties standing, means that it seems likely that there would be fewer motion metaphors in the election coverage.

Generally, the *Hong Kong Free Press* does not overplay the word "race" (from the semantic field of a motion contest) but occasionally uses it, as in "running in the election", "stand for election", "swept into the legislature", "pro-Beijing sweep", and "barriers to the race", while "sitting out the election", implies non-movement. The other newspapers seem to use the usual election phraseology.

Topics

The major topics of the 2021 election gleaned from press coverage, more-or-less in order of prominence were as follows: (1) fears of a low voter turnout; (2) eligibility of candidates; (3) the legality of "inciting" people not to vote; (4) free transport on polling day and border arrangements to vote; (5) criticism about the lack of different views since "opposition" candidates were absent; and (6) focus of debate on livelihood rather than politics, which is cast as an improvement.

Fears of a Low Voter Turnout

A major topic was fear of a low voter turnout. An article in the *Hong Kong Free Press* implicitly refers to this fear as follows,

> Four civil service unions in Hong Kong have issued a joint statement to call on people to "vote enthusiastically" in the upcoming "patriots only" election, saying the revamped polls are of "great significance". (Ho 2021c)

Similar articles appeared in the other newspapers, especially in the *Ta Kung Po*, which stressed the importance of voting in "patriots" for good governance of Hong Kong. Referring to the new rules allowing only candidates deemed "patriots" by a vetting committee, one opposition supporter said: "They don't allow the people who they don't like to enter. So how do we vote for the people we want to choose?" (SCMP Reporters 2021). The thinking was if all the parties in the election have the same stance, why bother to vote. However, while one business figure saw the election as having "imperfections", he reportedly still believed that "the promise of better political discourse and a sense of normalcy at least provide a silver lining" (Hibberd 2021).

Eligibility of Candidates

Although the pan-democrats were in a dilemma about taking part in what they saw a restrictive poll and the near impossibility of being deemed "patriots", they were urged by commentators in the *Ta Kung Pao* to put up candidates, as that is what real political parties do: "People with breadth of vision in the Democratic Party should wake up as soon as possible, and rethink the position of the political group, and turn to the practical path of serving Hong Kong" (the *Ta Kung Pao* quoting a *China Daily* editorial). Even pro-establishment candidates were advised to find "running mates" of the same political persuasion to run against, to make the election seem more competitive. There were "emergency appeals" frequently heard on election day "as several pro-establishment candidates found themselves fighting an uphill battle for support even after Beijing overhauled the electoral system in their favour" (Lam et al. 2021). Officials also feared low voter participation, but put a positive spin on it by saying that it could mean that the public was satisfied with the administration:

> There is a saying from the government in the old days that when the administration is doing well and its credibility is high, the voter turnout will decrease because the people do not have a strong impetus to choose different lawmakers to supervise the government. (Lau 2021)

Furthermore, Chief Executive Carrie Lam had stated that "if the high voting rate is based on political deterioration, or based on some candidates who are fighting for authority to endanger national security, this is not a high voting rate we agree with" (a reference to the 2019 District Council elections). The low turnout is thus discursively framed as indicating a "quality" turnout.

The Legality of "Inciting" People Not to Vote

The Public Opinion Research Institute poll, showing that 34% would definitely vote "yes", 17% probably "yes", and 33% definitely "no" (PORI 2021), was criticised by the Beijing and Hong Kong authorities who said that the institute's surveys "incited and misled citizens and could abet those who intend to "disrupt Hong Kong" by trying to incite others not to vote or to cast blank ballots to undermine the election (Ho 2021b).

These arguments could be seen as yet another bid to manage expectations because of the lukewarm voter sentiment, especially among opposition supporters.

Free Transport on Polling Day and Border Arrangements to Vote

Free Election Day public transport was going to be provided as a "voluntary gesture" by Hong Kong bus and railway operators. Chief Executive Carrie Lam said the move was not aimed at boosting turnout (Cheung 2021). However, people vote in the same area where they live in. It could be argued there is no need for free transport. The Hong Kong government also set up polling stations at closed border checkpoints so that Hongkongers living in mainland China could vote in the legislative election. Despite comments to the contrary, these measures were seen as attempts to increase turnout on Election Day.

Criticism About the Lack of Different Views Since "Opposition" Candidates Were Absent

There were multiple articles in the *Ta Kung Pao* saying that there is a diversity of candidates from the grassroots and all walks of life. This reiterates what was said in the FAQs about "balanced participation" and that views would "not be a monotone" (一言堂) under the new system, but the new term of members representing different sectors will surely have multiple voices, and thus good governance will be achieved.

Focus of Debate on Livelihood Rather than Politics Is Cast as an Improvement

In previous elections, there were "anti-China disrupting Hong Kong" candidates, according to pro-government and pro-Beijing sources, so debates had centred on political stance rather than a serious discussion on political platforms and policy initiatives to improve people's livelihood.

The quality of discussion would, according to these sources, thus be improved. Furthermore, they reasoned "patriots" would not necessarily have the same views as other "patriots". Therefore, diversity of views would still be present.

Comparative Perspective

The *Ta Kung Pao*'s coverage appears similar to comments made by Hong Kong government officials. The newspaper also discussed how the new system would ensure stability and prosperity in Hong Kong, now and in the future. The *Hong Kong Free Press* tried to maintain neutrality when covering the election by adding explanatory detail to the official phrasing to ensure readers understand that, for example, the election was in fact one in which many would-be candidates were barred from participating. For example, articles often ended with variations of the following: "Most of Hong Kong's opposition are behind bars, have gone into self-exile, have quit politics or are banned". A paragraph detailing the electoral changes and the reaction to it in fairly balanced language was given on the HKFP's 2021 election webpage.[7] The *Ming Pao Daily News* and the *South China Morning Post* largely used "normal" political language of electoral "races" and "platforms" in their coverage of the election, although with occasional acknowledgement of the difference from previous polls and its less representative nature. To sum up, the following seems to illustrate the tenor of the election campaigning period:

> But, even though voting for the Legislative Council election is just days away, I don't feel excitement in the air. There aren't any heated discussions on the streets or in the media of the virtues of the various candidates and whether the platform of one is better than the other. (Kammerer 2021)

The assumption is that because only patriots are allowed to stand and that, regardless of who wins, a bright future had been promised for the city, there is perhaps a lack of incentive to vote in the election.

[7] See https://hongkongfp.com/2020-legislative-elections

We can see that the topics and coverage of the election were markedly different from the usual election discourse. The RACE metaphor and the usual MOTION metaphors related to elections were only employed to a limited extent (between the different pro-establishment groups, since there were few self-proclaimed democratic candidates taking part (Goatly 2007). Therefore, the election coverage mostly focused on the uniqueness of this particular ballot, speculation about who would take part, and the prediction of a poor turnout. The low turnout was then rhetorically "massaged" by the government and Beijing to see the result in a positive light. In other words, the government still "won".

A White Paper: *Democratic Progress Under the Framework of "One Country, Two Systems"*

The day after the first "patriots-only" Legislative Council election on 20 December 2021, the National People's Congress issued a White Paper entitled *Democratic Progress Under the Framework of "One Country, Two Systems"* (SCIO 2021b). This document laid out the central Chinese authorities' view of Hong Kong's development since 1997 as well as basic foundations and definitions for the central government's overhaul of Hong Kong's postcolonial political order. "White Papers" are informational documents that present government policies and legislation. In their traditional form, White Papers are written and used by policymakers to examine a policy problem and to consider an array of solutions. This particular White Paper is a kind of historical narrative of Hong Kong's development from pre-1997 to the present and the reasons why Hong Kong's democratic progress has its current form.

Briefly, the main arguments were the following: (1) under colonial rule there was no democracy in Hong Kong; (2) it was Hong Kong's return to Chinese rule that marked the beginning of Hong Kong's democratic development; (3) the central government remains committed to the pursuit of democracy in Hong Kong; (4) anti-China agitators disrupted that development; (5) the development has now been put back on the right course; (6) future prospects for democracy in Hong Kong are bright. Most of these topics were raised and discussed in the electoral reform booklet.

The White Paper mentions "three attempts" by the HKSAR Government, supported by the Central Government, to promote the development of democracy in the region. The content of these "attempts" is not described, just that they were "vetoed" by "self-proclaimed democrats" in the Legislative Council and "could not be taken forward". This makes the assumption that these "attempts" have always been positive and truly "democratic". Yet, this argument has been disputed by the pan-democrats. Democrats have always been accused of being "anti-democratic"; any "democratic" changes made by the British prior to 1 July 1997 have been framed as likely to cause problems, post-1997. The White Paper gives a timeline for when citizens of Chinese descent held government posts in the colonial government, using the anaphora, "it was not until [...] it was not until [...] it was not until [...]" (p. 5) to emphasise the "sudden" and "reactive" nature of democratic changes in Hong Kong. The British changes were not perceived to be in the nature of "true" democracy.

From the account detailed in the White Paper, one can clearly see that, according to the Central People's Government, since Hong Kong's return to the mainland, "anti-China forces" have not only disrupted the development of democracy in the HKSAR, but they have also been spreading false ideas with ulterior motives to undermine the relationship between the HKSAR and the Central Government. In a Hong Kong government press release, issued on the same day as the White Paper, it is also mentioned that "anti-China forces [...] even challenged the bottom line of national security as well as the authority of the Central Government and the Basic Law under the pretext of 'democracy', seriously threatening the prosperity and stability of the HKSAR and national security" (info.gov.hk 2021). The above arguments serve to legitimise the changes made to the electoral system.

The White Paper also says that there is no "one size fits all" democracy, nor is there a singular superior model. Western democracy cannot impose its own standards of democracy on others, making the point that Hong Kong's unique history and governance framework cannot fit the Western model of democracy. According to the White Paper, Hong Kong's "future is bright", "but only under the proper implementation of 'One Country, Two Systems', can this be realised". Therefore, their argument goes, far from sabotaging that goal, the revamped election system removes obstacles that blocked its progress. The trifecta of principles, designed to ease Hong Kong fears about life under Mainland rule, remain intact ("One Country, Two Systems", the rule of law, a high degree of autonomy). This has been done by reaffirming all the pledges that were officially made and written into law before 1997 (in the electoral changes document and the White Paper), while redefining the words the pledges contain. Hayek (1944, 161) earlier said that an effective method of persuading people to believe that the values are still the same, is "using the old words but changing their meaning", which is a common practice in political language. This also relates to Confucius's "rectification of names" [正名], something he said he would do if he were a governor, so that words would "correspond to reality".

The White Paper, which largely mimics aspects raised in the electoral changes booklet, generally expresses Mainland-style political standards, such as strict political vetting, indirect selection, and consultative procedures, indicating that the "White paper underlines Hong Kong's healthy shift away from Western-style democracy" (Wang 2021).

The following quote by a Beijing official given around the time of the December election shows the connection to the "whole-process democracy" described in this White Paper: "Whether Hong Kong's democratic electoral system is good or not depends on whether it helps the city maintain long-term stability" (Cheung 2021).

Conclusion: Ensuring the Election of Patriots

This chapter shows that the main reason given by the authorities for changing the electoral system in Hong Kong was that the "wrong" people had been able to stand for and be elected to the legislature. These "people" were the pan-democrats who the government and Beijing saw as having instigated the protests of 2019 and earlier "chaos", thus preventing "smooth governance" and the running of "One Country, Two

Systems". It was thought by the authorities that the election of "patriots" would minimise further trouble and ensure the stability and prosperity of Hong Kong. The vagueness and ambiguity involved in the criteria for selecting "patriots" to administer Hong Kong meant that certain "gatekeepers" were positioned to define terms as they saw fit.

The changes were also legitimised and justified by the failure of the local introduction of Article 23 of the Basic Law, and the scope and length as well as the nature of the 2019 protests, which touched on sensitive mainland issues such as separatism and independence. Although Hong Kong residents had real fears about the extradition bill that caused them to take to the streets, the authorities "othered" the pan-democrats by grouping them in general categories and labelling them "radical extremists" who led the ordinary people (who had insufficient national education) astray with their inflammatory rhetoric.

Despite the more restrictive nature of voting under the new system, the Hong Kong and Beijing authorities had to make the case that the principles of the system as originally envisioned still remained in place, but were now enhanced. The arguments about the changes indicate a high level of awareness among the Hong Kong authorities, as with the mainland officials, about the power of language in generating meaning. This chapter has shown proof of the various strategies in which the official documents construct and legitimate their ideological perspective on Hong Kong reality and how concepts such as "democracy" can be (re)defined. That the term has become an "essentially contested concept" (Collier and Levitsky 1996), is painfully clear in the discourses about the Hong Kong case.

References

Carey, John M., "Electoral Formula and Fragmentation in Hong Kong." *Journal of East Asian Studies* 17, no. 2 (2017): 215–231.

Chau, Candice. "Hong Kong Gov't Condemns Criticism of 'Patriots' Election, as China Media Hails 'High' turnout." *Hong Kong Free Press*, December 22, 2021. https://hongkongfp.com/2021/12/22/hong-kong-govt-condemns-criticism-of-patriots-election-as-china-media-hails-high-turnout/

Cheung, Tony. "Hong Kong Elections: Beijing Diplomat Ramps Up Warnings Against Foreign interference in Legislative Council poll', *South China Morning Post,* December 15, 2021. https://www.scmp.com/news/hong-kong/politics/article/3159831/hong-kong-elections-beijing-diplomat-ramps-warnings-against

CMAB. "Improve Electoral System, Ensure Patriots Administering Hong Kong." Constitutional and Mainland Affairs Bureau, 2021. https://www.cmab.gov.hk/improvement/filemanager/content/pdf/en/resource-centre/booklet.pdf

Collier, David and Steven Levitsky. "Democracy 'with Adjectives': Conceptual Innovation in Comparative Research." Working Paper, no. 230, Kellogg Institute for International Studies. August 1996. http://kellogg.nd.edu/publications/workingpapers/WPS/230.pdf

Dahl, Robert. *Democracy and Its Critics*. New Haven/London: Yale University Press, 1989.

Davidson, Helen. "Hong Kong Primaries: China Declares Pro-Democracy Polls 'illegal'." *The Guardian,* July 14, 2020. https://www.theguardian.com/world/2020/jul/14/hong-kong-primaries-china-declares-pro-democracy-polls-illegal

Deng, Xiaoping. "Deng Xiaoping on "One Country, Two Systems." *China Daily*. February 19, 2004 [1984]. https://www.chinadaily.com.cn/english/doc/2004-02/19/content_307590.htm

Eagleton, Jennifer. "The 'Ultimate Aim': Discourses of Future Democratization in Post-Handover Hong Kong." [Unpublished PhD thesis], Department of Linguistics, Macquarie University, Sydney, 2012.

Eagleton, Jennifer. "Rhetorical Ambiguity, Democracy and Political Change: The Contradictions of the Hong Kong political system." *Contrastes Revista Internacional de Filosofía* 20, no. 3 (2017): 77–93.

Eagleton, Jennifer. *Discursive Change in Hong Kong: Sociopolitical Dynamics, Metaphor, and One Country, Two Systems*, Maryland: Lexington Books, 2022.

Eagleton, Terry. *Ideology: An Introduction.* London, New York: Verso, 1991.

Gallie, William B. "Essentially contested concepts." *Proceedings of the Aristotelian Society* 56 (1956): 167–198.

Goatly, Andrew. *The Language of Metaphors*, 2nd edition, London: Routledge, 1997.

Goatly, Andrew. *Washing the Brain—Metaphor and Hidden Ideology.* Netherlands: John Benjamins, 2007.

Gray, John N. "On the Contestability of Social and Political Concepts." *Political Theory* 5, no. 3 (1977): 331–348.

Gustafsson, Karl. "Is Patriotism Distinct from Nationalism? The Meaning of 'Patriotism' in China in the 2000s." Working Papers in Contemporary Asian Studies, no. 42, Centre for East and South-East Asian Studies, Lund University, 2014. https://lucris.lub.lu.se/ws/portalfiles/portal/3452180/4530041

Hayek, F.A. (1944). *The Road to Serfdom*, 1944. https://ctheory.sitehost.iu.edu/img/Hayek_The_Road_to_Serfdom.pdf

Hibberd, Robin. "Flawed Legislative Council Election Still the Best Way to get Hong Kong Back on Track." *South China Morning Post*, December 20, 2021. https://www.scmp.com/comment/opinion/article/3160379/flawed-legislative-council-election-still-best-way-get-hong-kong

Ho, Kelly. "Hong Kong's Lam says China's Patriots-only Rule is not Meant to Exclude Democrats from Politics." *Hong Kong Free Press*, February 23, 2021a. https://hongkongfp.com/2021/02/23/hong-kongs-lam-says-chinas-patriots-only-rule-is-not-meant-to-exclude-democrats-from-politics/

Ho, Kelly. "Some Opinion Survey Questions Could Breach Hong Kong Law, Anti-graft Chief Warns." *Hong Kong Free Press*, November 30, 2021b. https://hongkongfp.com/2021/11/30/some-opinion-survey-questions-could-breach-hong-kong-law-anti-graft-chief-warns/

Ho, Kelly. '"Elect the Virtuous": Civil Servants Call on Hongkongers to Vote in "Patriots Only" Election', *Hong Kong Free Press*, December 1, 2021c. https://hongkongfp.com/2021/12/01/elect-the-virtuous-civil-servants-call-on-hongkongers-to-vote-in-patriots-only-election/

HKFP. "Explainer: Is It Legal for People in Hong Kong to Commemorate the Tiananmen Crackdown?" *Hong Kong Free Press*, June 4, 2023. https://hongkongfp.com/2023/06/04/explainer-is-it-legal-for-hongkongers-to-commemorate-tiananmen-crackdown/

Hong Kong Gov. Public Offices (Candidacy and Taking Up Offices) (Miscellaneous Amendments) Ordinance 2021a. (Ordinance passed 21 May 2021). https://www.elegislation.gov.hk/hk/2021/13!en

Hong Kong Gov. Improving Electoral System (Consolidated Amendments) Ordinance 2021b. (Ordinance passed 27 May). https://www.gld.gov.hk/egazette/pdf/20212598e/es32021259817.pdf.

Info.gov.hk. "CE Welcomes Publication of White Paper on "Hong Kong: Democratic Progress Under the Framework of One Country, Two Systems." Hong Kong Government. December, 20, 2021. https://www.info.gov.hk/gia/general/202112/20/P2021122000637.htm

Ip, Regina. "Anti-government Victory in District Council Elections will not Bring Peace', *The South China Morning Post*, December 3, 2019. https://

www.scmp.com/comment/opinion/article/3039891/anti-government-victory-hong-kongs-district-council-elections-wont

Kammerer, Peter. "Even with lacklustre Legislative Council Election, a Huge To-do List Awaits the Winners. *South China Morning Post.* December 14, 2021. https://www.scmp.com/comment/opinion/article/3159402/even-lacklustre-legislative-council-election-huge-do-list-awaits.

Lam, Jermain T.M., "The 2019 District Council Election in Hong Kong: A Localism Perspective." *Asian Affairs: An American Review* 48, no. 2 (2021): 113–132.

Lam, Jeffie, Sammy Heung, and Nadia Lam. "Hong Kong Legco Election: Once Confident Pro-Establishment Candidates Make Emergency Appeals for Votes, Claiming Shaky Support." *South China Morning* Post, December 20, 2021. https://www.scmp.com/news/hong-kong/politics/article/3160333/hong-kong-legco-election-once-confident-pro-establishment

Lau, Chris. "Hong Kong Elections: City Leader Carrie Lam says Low Voter Turnout 'Does Not Mean Anything', May Indicate Good Governance." *South China Morning Post*, December 8, 2021. https://www.scmp.com/news/hong-kong/politics/article/3158944/hong-kong-elections-city-leader-carrie-lam-says-low-voter/

Legco.gov.hk *Green Paper on Constitutional Development.* Hong Kong Government, July 11, 2007 https://www.legco.gov.hk/yr06-07/english/panels/ca/papers/ca0716-gppr200707-e.pdf

Liu, Natalie. "Chinese White Paper Seeks to Redefine Democracy." Voice of America, December 24, 2021. https://www.voanews.com/a/chinese-white-paper-seeks-to-redefine-democracy-/6369108.html

Luo, Huining. "Reinforce Foundations of National Security, Safeguard Peace and Prosperity of Hong Kong." Speech at the Hong Kong 'National Security Education Day' 2021 Opening Ceremony, 15 April 15, 2021. https://www.chinadailyhk.com/hk/article/163176#Full-text-of-Luo's-speech-on-National-Security-Education-Day

Matlock, Teenie. "Motion Metaphors in Political Races." In Mike Borkent, Barbara Dancygier, and Jennifer, Hinnell, eds., *Language and the Creative Mind*, Stanford, CA: CSLI Publications (2013), 193–202.

PORI. "Survey on Hong Kong People's Views Regarding the Anti-Extradition Bill Movement (Round 1).". Research Report, Hong Kong Public Opinion Research Institute, December 27, 2019. https://www.pori.hk/research-reports-en/hong-kong-peoples-views-regarding-the-anti-extradition-bill-movement.html?lang=en

PORI. "Telephone survey #1 (15/11/2021–18/11/2021) People's Voting Propensity, Awareness of Candidates and the New Geographical Constituencies." Hong Kong Public Research Institute, November 23. 2021. https://www.pori.hk/wpcontent/uploads/2021/11/PORI_PC_20211123_tp_lc_ggpi_eng.pdf#page=21

Qin, Amy. "In China, What Does it Mean to be a Patriot?" Asia Blog, The Asia Society, May 31, 2012. https://asiasociety.org/blog/asia/china-what-does-it-mean-be-patriot.

Ramzy, Austin, Elaine Yu, and Tiffany May. "Hong Kong Voters Defy Beijing, Endorsing Protest Leaders in Primary." *The New York Times*, July 13, 2020. https://www.nytimes.com/2020/07/13/world/asia/hong-kong-elections-security.html.

SCIO. "China: Democracy That Works." State Council Information Office, December 4, 2021a. http://english.scio.gov.cn/whitepapers/2021-12/04/content_77908921.htm.

SCIO. "Democratic Progress Under the Framework of One Country Two Systems." State Council Information Office, December 20, 2021b. http://english.scio.gov.cn/whitepapers/2021-12/20/content_77941455.htm.

SCMP Reporters. "Hong Kong Legco Election: city splits into "parallel universes" as some residents vote while others shop or go sightseeing." *South China Morning Post*, December 19, 2021. https://www.scmp.com/news/hong-kong/politics/article/3160321/hong-kong-legco-election-city-splits-parallel-universes.

Shen, Du. "Improving Hong Kong's Electoral System Important for Developing High-quality Democracy." *China Today*, 7 March 7, 2021. http://www.chinatoday.com.cn/ctenglish/2018/zdtj/202103/t20210307_800238930.html.

Shu, Dongxin. "Evolution of Chinese Patriotism from Past to Present." *Chinese Studies* 11, no. 2 (2022): 79–89.

Sornig, Karl. "Some Remarks on Linguistic Strategies of Persuasion." In Ruth Wodak, ed., *Language, Power and Ideology: Studies in Political Discourse*, Amsterdam; Philadelphia: J. Benjamins Pub. Co., 1989, 95–114.

Ta Kung Pao. "A 58-person Constitutional Affairs Committee is Nonsense (58人的政制事務委員會是胡鬧). *Ta Kung Pao*, October 12, 2004. Accessed by WiseNews Database.

Tam, Felix, and Jim, Clare. "Exclusive: Support for Hong Kong Protesters' Demands Rises even as Coronavirus Halts Rallies: Poll." *Reuters*, March 27, 2020. https://www.reuters.com/article/us-hongkong-protests-poll-exclusive-idUSKBN21E11L

Tomaskova, Renata. "'Frequently Asked Questions': A Genre between Centre and Periphery." *Journal of English Philology* 4 (2012): 117–132.

Wang, Zemin. "White Paper Underlines Hong Kong's Healthy Shift away from Western-style Democracy." *South China Morning Post*, December 23, 2021. https://www.scmp.com/comment/opinion/article/3160657/white-paper-underlines-hong-kongs-healthy-shift-away-western-style

Webb, David. "Government Changes Basic Law Facts." Webb-site.com, December 18, 2014. https://webb-site.com/articles/lowerautonomy.asp

Xinhua. "Xi Jinping on Patriotism." State Council Information Office, June 4, 2022. http://english.scio.gov.cn/topnews/2022-06/04/content_78252995.htm

5

Education Under the National Security Law

The Hong Kong Government has frequently pointed out that national security education is a part of, and inseparable from, national education (EDB 2021b). National security education is to "develop in students a sense of belonging to the country, an affection for the Chinese people, a sense of national identity, as well as an awareness of and a sense of responsibility for safeguarding national security" (ibid.). Subsequently, there have been changes in the curriculum of both primary and secondary schools that aim to give students this sense of belonging as well the need to uphold National Security. This chapter will first focus on one course in the new curriculum under the NSL, then how the Code of Ethics of Teachers reflects the NSL, and how they deal with incidents by students involving possible breaches of the NSL. This will be followed by an analysis of national security education in tertiary educational institutions.

J. Eagleton, *Hong Kong's Second Return to China*,
https://doi.org/10.1007/978-3-031-84587-1_5

Attempts at National Education Before the National Security Law

You could say that, after 1997, political education was somewhat contradictory. It wanted to promote critical thinking, but on the other hand it wanted to enhance uncritical acceptance of the new administration including the official stance on the Chinese nation. Students were supposed to "learn" that they belong to China based on ethnicity and race. However, students did not easily accept this message as events in 2012 have shown with the attempted introduction of Moral and National Education (MNE) (CDC 2011), a school curriculum proposed by the Education Bureau of Hong Kong. This curriculum was controversial for its stance on the Chinese Communist Party and criticism of the US's two-party system.

As the Beijing Central Government's thinking goes, 15 years after Hong Kong's return to China, residents in Hong Kong should have a stronger Chinese identity. According to the Beijing-affiliated press, the Hong Kong people need such a curriculum because they have been brainwashed by colonialism. The editorial argued that the new curriculum would "expand the vision" of Hong Kong people, enabling them to adapt more smoothly to the new post-handover environment.

Students, teachers, and residents of Hong Kong saw the adoption of national-education classes as a way of "brainwashing" students and speeding up the integration of Hong Kong, and an inroad into its promised "high degree of autonomy" (Pomfret and Yip 2012). The proposed curriculum (which was similar to one used in mainland China) included a book called *The China Model* that described the Chinese Communist Party as "progressive, selfless, and united" and criticized Western multiparty systems. The book also glosses over the topics of the Tiananmen protests and the Cultural Revolution (GNAD 2012).

In July 2012, the "Civil Alliance Against the National Education" (民間反對國民教育科大聯), which included a number organisations (including Scholarism, Parents' Concern Group, Hong Kong Federation of Students, Alliance Youth, Civil Human Rights Front and others), On 29 July 2012, 30 organisations protested in a march.

Scholarism (a student group initially formed against the new national education and helmed by Joshua Wong) occupied Hong Kong Government Offices on 30 August 2012 and began a hunger strike in their attempt to overturn the proposed curriculum. Others joined in and occupation of the area continued for some time. On 7 September, around 120,000 attendees, including *Apple Daily* proprietor Jimmy Lai, alongside other senior democracy leaders participated in the protest. On 8 September 2012, then Chief Executive Leung Chun-ying announced the temporary withdrawal of the curriculum, until the revising of the Moral, Civil and National Education guidelines of the new subject was addressed (Bradsher 2012). The subject then seems to have been put on hold.

With disaffection with the pace of democratic reform, many young people became involved in "localist" causes, participants in the civil disobedience action of the Occupy Central/Umbrella Movement and become members of political activist groups. It was the younger generation who would form the greater part of the 2019 anti-extradition bill protests, particularly in the more radical (and violent) acts of the protests.

The following quotation from a 15 December 2019 *Guardian* article entitled "Children of the Revolution: The Hong Kong Youths Ready to 'Sacrifice Everything'" proved to the authorities in Beijing of the need for national education:

> "I really want to give all I have to Hong Kong," the 13-year-old said, his eyes welling up in tears. "When you pursue freedom, sacrifices are unavoidable. "We are halfway into the gate of hell. We've put our future and career on a line, but it is worth it." (Guardian 2019)

Sentiments like this would not have gone down well with the Beijing authorities.

Numerous government officials, pro-Beijing figures blamed the 2019 protests not only on a lack of national education, but on Liberal Studies, which had been introduced in 2009 as a compulsory subject. This subject sought to advance critical thinking rather than only rote memorisation, and it was "regarded as an interdisciplinary subject that nurtures critical thinking through issue-inquiry learning approach as one of its learning objectives" (Ip 2010, 1). Hong Kong's first Chief Executive, Tung

Chee-hwa said of the course: "The liberal studies curriculum is a failure. It is one of the reasons behind the youth problems today" (Liu et al. 2019). Wong Kam-leung, chairman of the Education Workers Union: "it instilled in students the desire to criticise a lot of things" (Chan and Magramo 2021); Priscilla Leung, pro-Beijing politician, barrister, and academic: teachers "fail to offer an objective view" (Hung 2021); Education Bureau stated that: too much emphasis on current affairs for which students lacked "systematic knowledge"; There was also "a readiness to challenge authority and criticise and object indiscriminately at the expense of the principle of adopting facts as the basis of careful thinking and judgement" (EDB 2021a).

The Education Bureau released National Security: Specific Measures for Schools in early February 2021 (updated in 2023) with the following mandate:

> The objective is to deepen students' understanding of the country's development and national security, enhance students' sense of national identity, nurture students as good law-abiding citizens, and create a peaceful and orderly school environment and atmosphere. (p. 1)

One of the ways to do this was to scrap liberal studies in favour of a new course "Citizenship and Social Development". We will discuss what this new course wants to theoretically achieve before discussing the course in depth. This concerns the legitimation of ideology.

Legitimation of Ideology: Why It Is Important

A recent Chinese Communist Party document "Resolutely Claim Victory in Ideological Struggle" noted the importance of education into the ruling ideology: "Schools are not ivory towers, nor some type of Shangri-La, but the frontline positions of the ideological battlefield" (学校是意识形态工作的前沿阵地，可不是 一个象牙之塔，也不是一个桃花源) (OCNSC 2022).

To provide legitimacy for Hong Kong systems was to be through the contents of the course. Legitimation refers to the "process whereby an act, process, or ideology becomes legitimate by its attachment to norms and values within a given society. It is the process of making something acceptable and normative to a group or audience".[1] As Lipset has stated, legitimation is "the capacity of a political regime to engender and maintain the belief that existing political institutions are the most appropriate or proper ones for the society" (1983, 64). Research into the process of legitimation has mostly focused on legitimacy claims or whether regimes are legitimate (i.e., enjoy public support), but it makes sense that it could be used to show that any, action or concept is valid under a particular set of circumstances.

There are six claims of legitimacy: foundational myth, ideology, personalism, procedures, performance, and international engagement (Von Soest and Grauvogel 2017) and four legitimation mechanisms (Duklaskis and Gerschewski 2017): indoctrination, passivity, performance, and democratic-procedural mechanisms. Four mechanisms that exist simultaneously and interact with each other: *Indoctrination* (education, media, etc.); *Ideology* (for example, nationalism, communism, pragmatism, etc.); *Performance in institutions* (elections, courts, parliaments, etc.). Indoctrination is the foundational legitimation mechanism for authoritarian regimes. In the case of a new course, this can be defined as teaching students to uncritically accept ideas raised in that course. In the following, how the course's textbooks will show the "legality" of Hong Kong's governance framework, performance legitimation, and procedural legitimation.[2]

Citizenship and Social Development: A Post-National Security Law Course

The Citizenship and Social Development Curriculum and Assessment Guide (Secondary 4–6) was endorsed on 1 June 2021 (EDB 2021c). The implementation of the course commenced at Secondary 4 in September 2021.

---

[1] DBMedia. "About: Legitimation". https://dbpedia.org/page/Legitimation

[2] Thanks to Dr Stephan Ortmann of the Department of Social Sciences, Hong Kong Metropolitan University, for sharing of data and insights about legitimation of educational textbooks in Hong Kong at a 2024 Hong Kong Studies conference held in the city.

Sources	Mainland Chinese media, leftist papers, government officials
Themes	(1) Hong Kong under "One Country, Two Systems" (2) Our Country since Reform and Opening-up (3) Interconnectedness and Interdependence of the Contemporary World Each theme 45–50 hours (half of Liberal Studies) Mandatory Mainland Study Tour (10 hours) Independent Enquiry Study (IES) is removed
Assessment	2 hr examination of data response questions
Grading	Grading: "Attained" or "Unattained"

We will only look at Theme 1: Hong Kong under "One Country, Two Systems" in this analysis through examples from three publishers with government approved textbooks *Modern Educational Research Society* (Modern); *Hong Kong Educational Publishing Company* (New Horizon) *Marshall Cavendish* (New Focus).

The topics of Theme 1 are (1) The meaning and implementation of "One Country, Two Systems"; (2) Situation of the country and sense of national identity; and (3) Characteristics of cultural diversity of the Hong Kong society. Only the first two topics will be dealt with.

The Ideology of Legality

The main legitimation strategy is drawn from the assertion that Hong Kong is legally Chinese territory as the People's Republic of China had asserted sovereignty over Hong Kong, and that "unequal treaties"' are considered illegal, therefore, by inference, they need not be adhered to:

a. Vienna Convention on the Law of Treaties

In 1969, the Vienna Convention on the Law of Treaties was passed by the United Nations (UN) and was open for signature by countries The Vienna Convention on the Law of Treaties is an international convention related to international treaties, and is the most frequently cited source of law in interpreting international law in modern times. It affirms disputes and in conformity with the principles of justice and international law. It defines a coerced treaty as invalid. *New Horizon.* p. 11

However, this Convention does not apply to treaties before 1969. Historical "legal" claims are used to determine politics, not one-sided treaties. For this reason, the Chinese government grants Hong Kong its "high degree" of autonomy (CPG below refers to the Central People's Government):

> 2.2.4 Powers vested in the HKSAR by the Central Authorities
> Under the *Basic Law,* the Central Authorities vested in the HKSAR these power to ensure it enjoys a high degree of autonomy.
> Powers vested in the HKSAR to ensure a high degree of autonomy (is central) with Executive power, judicial power including the power of final adjudication, legislative power, other powers granted, power to conduct external affairs on its own through CPG authorisation. *New Focus;* p. 32

This legality is further framed in the textbook with a "Knowledge enrichment box" on the same page as above which states: "High degree of autonomy—The Central Authorities' authorisation is the prerequisite for the high degree of autonomy enjoyed by the HKSAR".

For "One Country, Two Systems", the definition is that socialism is the main ideology; capitalism is just allowed to be practised (which acts like an appendix). In the textbook the governance framework is depicted as a circle, the "One Country" being the outer circle, with the "Two Systems" forming the inner circle. Two text boxes point to the different circles (bold in the original):

> 1.1 The Constitution established the basic policy of "one country, two systems"
> Basic essence of "one country, two systems"
>
> **One country** (outer circle)—"One country": within the People's Republic of China, the HKSAR is an inseparable part and a local administrative region directly under the Central People's Government.
>
> "**Two systems**" (inner circle: within the "one country" (inner circle), the main body of the country practises socialism, while Hong Kong and Macau can retain the previous capitalist system and way of life for a long period of time.
>
> *New Horizon,* p. 43

The textbooks stress the "overall jurisdiction" of the Central Authorities over Hong Kong: "The Central authorities have complete jurisdiction over HKSAR" which "does not have any inherent power" (*Modern*, p. 21) and "As the Basic Law is an "authorization law" of the Chinese constitution, it gives the Chinese government the right to allow HK to maintain the "previous capitalist system and way of life for a long period of time" (*New Horizon*, p. 43)

Legality is also used to justify the executive-led system. The role of Chief Executive as "dual head" and intermediary between Hong Kong government and Chinese government provides a "legal status that is above the executive authorities, legislature and judiciary" (*New Focus*, p. 79), while in *New Horizon*: "Any agenda or proposal for the future development of Hong Kong must reinforce the executive-led system headed by the Chief Executive and must not deviate from this design principle" (p. 75).

While textbooks seek to strengthen national identity, they heavily emphasize this is a duty of everyone; many laws are mentioned in regard to national symbols are contained in the textbooks as well as the general curriculum under the National Security Law:

> *New Horizon*: "Developing a sense of belonging to the country and adhering to the principle of 'one country' are the core requirements for the implementation of the Basic Law" (p. 43)
>
> *Modern*: "Other duties of Hong Kongers are respecting and complying with the Constitution, caring about national development and participating in public affairs" (p. 114)

Performance Legitimization

Focus of the textbooks are the many achievements of China, emphasizing the role of the Chinese government in achieving this success. This gives legitimacy to its project and governance overall. There is a very limited discussion of problems, China is idealized and there seems to no discussion of problems. Any problems that exist are being solved by the government. The Chinese government and its policies (Five-Year Plans) are portrayed as the primary reason for the achievements; this provides "regime legitimacy", because it can get the job done (see the 2021 White Paper, "China: Democracy that Works" that is discussed in Chap. 5 of this book)"

> 3.1 Reasons for China's achievements in different fields
> 3.1.1 Political stability and appropriate policies
> Since reform and opening up, China has been working towards developing the economy and building a moderately prosperous society. In a series of Five-Year Plans, economic development plans have been set and implemented. Though establishing special economic zones, opening up coastal cities, and promoting the development of the western part of the country and inland areas, China has developed steadily in different areas and fields. Its economy has also transitioned from a phase of rapid growth to a stage of high-quality development.
> 3.12 Favourable economic conditions
> *New Focus*, p. 152

Hong Kong's executive-led system is also justified based on both nationalistic terms and the need for performance (bold in original):

> 6 Achievement of the country and sense of national identity
> The brilliant achievements of the country in different areas make Hong Kong residents feel proud of their identity as Chinese. This enhances the identity among Hong Kong residents.
> **High technology....**Hong Kong residents **feel optimistic and take pride in the country's long-term scientific and technological development.** They also **benefit from them.**
> ....Hong Kong residents **have first-hand experiences of the country's rapid development of science and technology;** their sense of superiority as Chinese is enhanced.
> *Modern,* p. 199

> F. Achievements of the country and the sense of national identity
> In recent years, our country has made tremendous achievements in various fields: new high-end technologies have entered the forefront of the world; the healthcare level continues to improve; the cultural and educational development is rapid; infrastructure is laying the foundation for national development; and absolute poverty has been successfully eradicated. **These**

achievements have a significant impact on the country as well as the world, and help strengthen the sense of belonging, recognition and pride in the country among citizens, thereby enhancing their sense of national identity.

New Horizon, p. 208

Interestingly, the *New Focus* textbook skips this section.

Hong Kong's executive-led system (which is at rhetorical odds with a semi-democratic system—see Eagleton 2017) is also justified based on both nationalistic terms and the need for performance. In the *New Focus* textbook on page 70, there is an outline map of China in the upper left-hand corner of the page with the words "Safeguarding sovereignty and territorial integrity" written inside the map. The map of China is linked to a large circle containing the phrase "significance of an executive-led system", this is joined by a drawing in the lower right-hand corner of Hong Kong's skyscrapers under which are the phrased "maintaining prosperity and stability of Hong Kong".

Economic performance ("prosperity") is used to justify Hong Kong's governance framework in which patriots administer the region:

New Horizon: "patriots administering Hong Kong" then "respect their own nation, support the resumption of the exercise of sovereignty over Hong Kong by China, and do not impair the Hong Kong's *prosperity and stability*" (p. 36, emphasis added):

The textbook cites a government source that says the system is "conducive to the long-term prosperity, order and stability" (p. 35), and so is therefore valid. The National Security Law is similarly justified because the situation is now under control:

New Horizon: "By cracking down on illegal and criminal acts endangering national security, the National Security Law safeguards national security, the prosperity and stability of Hong Kong, as well as the legitimate rights and interests of Hong Kong residents" (p. 66)

New Focus: "National security is not only the foundation of China's prosperity and stability, it is also the prerequisite for its survival and development" (p. 48)

Modern: National security "prerequisite for the well-being of the people" so their "lives and property is protected" and a "safe and stable environment for her development" (p. 42)

Procedural Legitimization

The reduction of directly elected seats and restrictions on participation in elections have made elections less representative; despite reducing the legitimacy of the system, elections are promoted as "improved". Readers can compare the way this is portrayed in school textbooks and the way FAQs answer those opposing election reform in the previous chapter.

Source B

On 19 September 2021, the Election Committee Subsector Ordinary Elections was held in Hong Kong. This election is the first election under the new electoral system. Nearly 90% of registered voters participated in the vote, and 1,448 new members of the Election Committee were elected finally. The pictures show the staff counting the votes at the central counting station in the Hong Kong Convention and Exhibition Centre.

Note: The Election Committee is responsible for electing the Chief Executive and some members of the Legislative Council.

(Source: adapted from the website of the Mainland and Constitutional Affairs Bureau.)

New Horizon, p. 74

The small-circle Election Committee (the elects the Chief Executive of Hong Kong) and "patriots-only elections" are promoted as "important" and useful for "good governance":

Conclusion I Summarise the arguments and reiterate the role.

In conclusion, under the new electoral system, the Election Committee is responsible for nominating the candidates in LegCo Election and electing 40 LegCo members, as well as nominating and electing the Chief Elective. It plays an important role in implementing the principle of "patriots administering Hong Kong" in the political system and promoting good governance in Hong Kong. *New Focus*, p. 81

The answer construction exercise in the *New Focus* textbook given below lets students determine the function of the Election Committee but the actual argument is added without discussion or empirical support. The *Wen Wei Bao* mentioned below is a pro-Beijing newspaper (bold in original).

> Q&A Drill
> 1. Analyze the question
> Based on the sources, state and explain ***Two*** reasons for the possible improvement in governance due to "patriots administering Hong Kong". Circle the keywords.
>
> Hong Kong Government in 2021:
> - Conducive to long-term prosperity, order and stability
> - Effective resolution of deep-seated problems
>
> *Wen Wei Po* in 2021:
> - Direct attention to developing economy and improving livelihoods
> - Can inject innovation, vigour and vitality in fields such as science, regime and culture
>
> *New Focus*, pp. 33–34

The *Modern* textbook also claims procedural legitimation for the Chinese government (based on a speech by Xi Jinping). This emphasizes the role of small parties and consultation led by the Chinese Communist Party. The result is "people's broad participation". Page 135 of the *Modern* textbook, has a vertical box labelled "guidelines on thinking". Under the word "point" there are arrows downwards indicating the end result of the process of what China's "system of multiparty cooperation and political consultation" can achieve:

> Point: The political system of China can effectively ensure people's broad participation in national affairs
> China Implements the system of multiparty cooperation and political consultation
> Formation of the CPPCC National Committee and its functions
> Ensuring people's broad participation in national governance

"Broad participation" does not mean "full participation". This reminds one of the uses of the phrase "broadly representative" in the Basic Law to refer to the membership of the Election Committee for the Chief Executive as well as discussions of a possible a universal suffrage system for Hong Kong where some were arguing against "one person, one vote" and for indirect rather than direct elections.[3] So, in some respects that arguments before the 2019 National Security Law about the Hong Kong system are merely continuations of what has been said before, but made more forcefully.

The definition of the "rule of law" in the textbooks still follows the liberal tradition; it is "highly regarded internationally" (citing the Hong Kong government), and there is an emphasis on "law-abidingness", the end result of the "self-reflection" process:

> Self-reflection
> Safeguarding the spirit of the rule of law
> Abiding by the laws and upholding the rule of law are common values in Hong Kong society. They are among the cornerstones of Hong Kong's prosperity and stability. Therefore, Hong Kong residents should fulfil their obligations of abiding by the law and safeguarding the spirit of the rule of law in Hong Kong.
> Law-abidingness

Aside of promoting the "improved" elections, there is also an emphasis on the rule of law (an entire chapter is devoted to this topic. However, it comes after National Security which also has a whole chapter devoted to it.

The textbooks also defend Hong Kong's judicial independence. A question fails to explain why NPCSC interpretations can be problematic (NPCSC is not a court, can be used to override political decisions in Hong Kong). It also used an uncontroversial foreign policy case to support the claim:

[3] The author's unpublished PhD thesis "The 'Ultimate Aim': Discourses of Democratization in Post-handover Hong Kong" done through Macquarie University Sydney in 2012 dealt with how "universal suffrage" and "democracy was talked about till the end of 2007 (its first 10 years as a Special Administrative Region).

> Why wouldn't the NPCSC's Interpretation of the Basic Law affect judicial independence?
>
> With the power to interpret the Basic Law, the Standing Committee of the National People's Congress (NPCSC) has successively made interpretation of the Basic Law five times. It is said that the interpretation undermines judicial independence. Do you think that this statement in correct? Let's take a look at the following case:
>
> *New Horizon*, p. 105

The superiority of Chinese law is emphasized. "The Basic Law is the constitutional document for the HKSAR. It enshrines within a legal document the important concepts of One Country, Two Systems" (see https://www.basiclaw.gov.hk/en/basiclaw/facts.html), but of course comes under the People's Republic's constitution. The Executive-dominant system is mandated by the Central Government, its constitution and therefore cannot be reformed. In Theme 2 of *New Horizon*, p. 141, there is a diagram showing the "advantages of Hong Kong" as a central hexagon shape with six hexagons surrounding it with a small image related to the HKSAR's "advantages": trade information network; excellent international transportation; the freest and most open economy; and advantageous business environment; advantage in talents; and financial advantages. It is odd that rule of law is not mentioned as one advantage as it often been in the past.

Aside of the rule of law, the textbooks emphasize the existence of rights and freedoms. The last chapter on Hong Kong's political system in the textbooks (Chap. 6) is dedicated to it, and mentions that "according to Chapter III of the Basic Law, the rights enjoyed by Hong Kong residents the aspects of "freedom of the person", "political rights", and "economic, social and cultural rights". The listed freedoms are all freedoms also given in the United Nations Covenants and in Article 4 of the National Security Law.

Limits on rights are generally justified in terms of societal interests (the greater good) and legality but remain very vague; in *New Focus* the law is "the boundary that balances individual rights and community interests" (p. 97); in *New Horizon*: The Basic Law "stipulates conditions for restricting fundamental rights to protect the human rights of Hong Kong residents and the overall social interests" (p. 121). The *Modern* textbook omits this aspect altogether.

Hong Kong's administration after the introduction of the National Security Law is legitimated through the ideology of legality, (promised) performance, and the claim that procedural legitimation remains effective (mainly: rule of law, rights unchanged and elections "improved"). The critical thinking aspect seems to have been removed, and the official views are presented uncritically. There is almost a complete lack of discussion questions. Students are taught how to get to a predetermined answer by framing words like "thinking path", and "guidelines on thinking"; Students are only asked to find reasons in favour but not possible counter-arguments. The contents of the texts seem to veer towards a positive outlook.

The Education Bureau had issued FAQs on the Citizenship and Social Development (EDB, n.d.) course in which this aspect was noted, which was different from the Liberal Studies curriculum (LS) (italics added in both excerpts below:

> FAQ 10: The curriculum framework of Citizenship and Social Development inclines to teach *contents with positive connotations*. Is it not in line with the "arguments for and against" approach as emphasised in the existing LS curriculum? (Italics added):
>
> Answer: The existing Liberal Studies Curriculum and Assessment Guide requires students to grasp relevant knowledge, explore contemporary issues from multiple perspectives, and make reasonable judgements basing on evidence in an objective and impartial manner. The so-called "arguments for and against" is one of the inference processes only before students express their opinions and make judgements. *In fact, not all the issues could be rigidly polarised by the "arguments for and against"*. Moreover, teachers have to help students understand the development background and conditions of the issues.

The text seems to be justifying the changes by saying that all issues cannot be discussed with "arguments for and against", but does not give an example of what such an issue would be. Just listing the "positive" aspects of an issue downplays and marginalizes discussion of any "negative" aspects of an issue that you need for a full discussion. "Arguments for and against" enables a more comprehensive knowledge of an issue. Apparently, it is up to teachers to guide students on the "development background" which put stress on teachers who have to make sure that they don't breach national security guidelines while teaching the course.

In other words, teachers have to perform a policing function. Before a discussion of teachers' code of ethics and how they are supposed to handle national security issues, taking a look at how teachers view this course is useful. Teachers are confused over the teaching materials to use, and that these materials are "structured so as to ensure there is little room for free discussion and debate in the classroom". Unlike Liberal Studies, no contemporary news reports are used as examples to illustrate points being made in the textbooks. Teachers are also unwilling to share their concerns with fellow teachers amid a "growing culture of informing on teachers for having the wrong political opinions in schools" (Cheng et al. 2021).

One teacher who had taught Liberal Studies for over 10 years, said all of the topics in the new Values Education curriculum (of which Citizenship and Social Development is one) must be taught in the order specified by the education bureau, using approved textbooks. "The textbooks and syllabus materials define the three treaties [that led to the founding of a British colony in Hong Kong] as unequal treaties, and Hong Kong as an 'issue', and as an inseparable part of China". "The biggest difference compared with Liberal Studies is that you could debate the good or bad on both sides of any topic, whereas now … there's very little room for discussion because Hong Kong is defined as an inseparable part [of China]" (Cheng et al. 2021).

Teachers are now far less likely to discuss their work with colleagues, or share teaching materials. "If we share our teaching materials, and then they are deemed problematic, they could be used to label us", so they are cut off from their peer support and so "we get more and more isolated and powerless" (Cheng et al. 2021). "Liberal Studies used to be a core subject that would help students qualify for university', but their "role has been reduced to just getting the students through the course, with a pass or fail."

The pass-fail system may also impact on how serious the course is treated by students. While a binary grading system reduces pressure on students, without "meaningful academic pressure, the subject may not be treated "seriously". Hong Kong's education system is highly exam-oriented, and universities' admission policy determines how much effort students allocate for different subjects, and spend massive amounts on tuition. A letter to the editor in 2020 (Wong 2020) before the course began noted that a pass-or-fail system would likely mean less incentive for grade-conscious students to study hard and excel at knowledge of the motherland and patriotic values. If the subject is expected to include topics like the constitutional order of China, to deepen students' sense of belonging to the China, such a grading system will not help.

The first Diploma of Secondary Education examination for Citizenship and Social Development was held in April 2024. According to a source, candidates before the exam did not seem to do much preparation. From social media posts, "it's apparent that many believed that a superficial display of patriotism, such as echoing slogans like 'I love China' or quoting figures like Mao Zedong or Chinese President Xi Jinping, would suffice" (Wong 2024 in a letter to the editor—the same person who had written the letter to the editor in 2020).

One Form 4 student said that many of his peers were reluctant to make much of an effort to craft thoughtful responses to questions during assessments and assignments. Additionally, teachers seemed hesitant to address instances of disengagement, such as students dozing off in class, as long as the students did not overtly challenge the curriculum (Wong 2024). The Beijing-aligned *Global Times* said it was "HKDSE first Citizenship and Social Development exam "sets reassuring precedent', the new subject allowing "Hong Kong students to understand China's contemporary development and the historical context of Hong Kong issues more systematically, and has raised their awareness of matters related to national security" (Yang and Qingqing 2024).

Guidelines on Teachers' Professional Conduct

As noted above, teachers have to perform a policing function in ensuring that they can ably help in the development of a sense of national identity in students. However, in a sense, they are also "policed", since they are seen as occasional enablers of political thinking if they pass on their views to students. Just a few days after the introduction of the law, pro-establishment lawmakers began calling for the installation of video cameras in classrooms to monitor teachers' speech (Wong 2021). Former Chief Executive Leung Chun-ying has urged people to report school teacher misconduct and said public interest overrides personal privacy (Wong 2020). Leung had previously published the name and personal details of teachers facing protested-related charges on Facebook. Leung was accused of imposing "Cultural Revolution-style conflict and criticism", on teachers.

The Guidelines of Teachers' Professional Conduct (EDB 2022) contains points likely to exist in teachers' codes elsewhere, including things upholding "professional beliefs", "being a role model", upholding "probity and integrity", "be committed and responsible", "care for students", "respect privacy", safeguard professionalism". (pp. 4–5) However, number two on the list is "honor the rule of law"—here teachers have to be "law-abiding" and "observe rules and regulations"; they also have to have a "correct understanding" of the Chinese constitution, the Basic Law, and the National Security Law (problematic because of the abstract and ambiguous nature of language used in those documents). They have to:

> Consciously safeguard national security, social order and public interest; fulfil social responsibility and civic obligations; support and promote national education actively; cultivate in students a sense of belonging towards the country.

"Dos" and "don'ts" of teachers' behaviour are given for each of the eight codes listed (a footnote in the guidelines state that the "dos" and "don'ts" of teachers' behaviour, while quite thorough in nature these "are by no means exhaustive" (p. 2). The "dos" and "don'ts about "honouring the rule of law" (pp. 8–9) are particularly important and directly relate to the content of the Citizenship and Social Development course that they are supposed to teach. Comments will be made under each of the following that pertain to these "dos" and how they generally relate to the wider sociocultural situation that teachers find themselves in.

- Uphold the spirit of the rule of law, observe laws and relevant regulations; consciously safeguard national security, social order and public interest; fulfil social responsibility and civic obligations.

Phrases like "upholding the rule of law" or "rule of law is one of Hong Kong's core values" are frequently seen in various texts promoting Hong Kong as a place to do business, for example. However, just what the "rule of law" means is never given. Often it is equated with just "obeying" the law rather than discussing equality before the law or consistency in application of the law. The list of things like "social order" that have to be "consciously safeguarded" are not elaborated. They have to be contextualized with other texts given to teachers—for example, the "social order" would be about "loving the Motherland" and protecting national security, according to what the authorities have deemed acceptable.

- Grasp the basic knowledge of national history and development; *acquire a correct understanding* of the Constitution, the Basic Law, the Hong Kong National Security Law and relevant legislation; respect the fundamental regime of the nation.

To fully understand what these texts fully mean, a significant amount of time needs to be spent. Teachers in government schools have to take an oath of allegiance and even some native English teachers may have to do so working in such (government) schools (Leung 2022). It is mandatory for all teachers to take a Basic Law test before taking up a position in schools.

- Acquire a correct understanding of the National Flag and National Emblem Ordinance, the Regional Flag and Regional Emblem Ordinance, as well as the National Anthem Ordinance; respect the symbols and signs representing the country and the Hong Kong Special Administrative Region;

Schools have to display the flag each day, and have a weekly flag-raising ceremony. Schools are encouraged to procure a movable flagpole to be able to conduct the national flag raising ceremony indoors under inclement weather condition quite detailed guidelines and FAQ in a 16-page booklet. The seriousness of the outward forms of nationalism is apparent in

China's flag-raising ceremonies. There is a 16-page booklet of "FAQs" concerning use of flag and national emblems reflecting the solemnity that they must be held (EDB 2024): "All participants in a national flag raising ceremony must stand solemnly facing the national flag, look at the national flag with respectful attention, and sing the national anthem" (Q3, p. 2). The outward form of how you show loyalty to the state is important. One school was found to be "singing the national anthem softly" during a flag-raising ceremony as noted in a recent Education Bureau Annual Report on schools' implementation of the National Security Law. Teachers were recommended to: "give reminders and help students develop a habit of singing the national anthem loudly" (Leung 2024). The students however were praised for their "solemn" behaviour; but most schools did exhibit "solemn" behaviour at most flag-raising ceremonies (Yiu 2023a).

- Develop in students a sense of belonging to the country, a sense of national identity and an affection for the nation.

Teachers can attempt to develop this sense of belonging, but how can they be assessed that they have achieved this? An end of course exam? Teachers will probably adhere to the course materials quite closely in order not to be accused of teaching illegal content or their own opinions. From the positivity shown in the textbooks, it would seem having as not having any major criticisms of the country.

- In the event of receiving information on matters that involve a breach of laws and regulations or deviation from the *moral standards generally acceptable to society*, or identifying any potential illegalities or irregularities on campus, handle the matters and report to the school management, police and/or the departments concerned as appropriate according to the law, relevant regulations and guidelines as well as actual circumstances.

It is unstated what the acceptable moral standards are; these can be assumed to be traditional Chinese values and so on. Here the teacher's policing function is apparent. There seem to be so many laws, regulations, and guidelines, that teachers will tend to be conservative in their behaviour in order to avoid accidently doing something they should not.

- Report immediately, or as soon as reasonably practicable thereafter, to the school upon being charged with or convicted of any offence in Hong Kong or elsewhere, or any known personal involvement in ongoing criminal proceedings or investigation, including but not limited to arrest by the police or other law enforcement agencies.

While informing your employer if you have been charged or convicted with an offence has to be done, being involved in criminal proceedings or investigation at all even not under arrest could be problematic if later not charged with any wrongdoing—could have impacts on their teaching career merely by association.

Don'ts of "honouring the rule of law" seem to be common sense and just the opposite of the above, which makes one wonder if these are really necessary to put down, perhaps for the purposes of emphasis (italics added):

- *Organise*, plan, commit, or participate in any acts that violate the Basic Law, the Hong Kong National Security Law or any Hong Kong legislation.
- *Advocate* the disruption of social order.
- *Disseminate* to students and promote messages that breach laws and regulations and disrupt social order; directly or indirectly encourage them to engage in activities that violate laws and regulations and disrupt social order.
- *Condone* any potentially illegal activities on campus.

The Teacher's Law of China in many respects is similar to the Hong Kong teachers' code.[4] In Article 3 of China's law, teachers are tasked with "training builders and successors to the socialist cause and enhancing the quality of the nation". Article 4 People's governments at various levels shall adopt measures to strengthen ideological and political education and professional training of teachers…" Further, under Article 8 (3) of the Law, teachers have the obligation (italics added) "to conduct

[4] (Adopted at the Fourth Meeting of the Standing Committee of the Eighth National People's Congress on October 31, 1993, promulgated by Order No. 15 of the President of the People's Republic of China and effective as of January 1, 1994). https://www.chinaeducenter.com/en/cedu/tlc.php

education among students in the basic principles defined in the Constitution, *education in patriotism, national unity and the legal system, and education in ideology, morality*, culture, science and technology, and to organise and lead students to engage in beneficial social activities." The contents of the Citizenship and Social Development course reflect these words.

Looking at codes of ethics, guidance for conduct for teachers in some democratic states, the codes are more of an abstract rendering of what teachers are supposed to impart to their students unlike in Hong Kong that is rather specific in nature. In South Australia, the Code of Ethics for the Teaching Profession[5] discusses the concepts of "integrity" and "respect" and by fostering "critical thinking and action, valuing the contributions of our educational communities, to influence positive futures" as well as to:

- Build learners' capabilities to participate as knowledgeable members of and contributors to, a socially just, responsible and democratic society
- Develop professional relationships with learners, parents/caregivers, colleagues and the broader community
- Act ethically in decision making, acknowledging and accepting the diversity of interest groups and perspectives

The Code of Ethics for Educators of the Association of American Educators[6] focuses on the building up of the individual: "The professional educator does not intentionally expose the student to disparagement". And while facts need to be given in an objective manner, "The professional educator endeavors to present facts without distortion, bias, or personal prejudice" the "professional educator endeavors to maintain the dignity of the profession by respecting and obeying the law, and by demonstrating personal integrity." "The professional educator does not intentionally misrepresent official policies of the school or educational organizations, and clearly distinguishes those views from his or her own

[5] Teacher's Registration Board of South Australia; https://www.trb.sa.edu.au/__data/assets/pdf_file/0011/922457/Code-of-Ethics.pdf

[6] Association of American Educators, Code of Ethics for Educators; https://www.aaeteachers.org/index.php/about-us/aae-code-of-ethics

personal opinions"—this indicates that teachers are allowed to express their own personal opinions as long as they make it clear that it is their own opinions, unlike Hong Kong.

These codes naturally relate to the places and the different attitude to education and the individualistic rather than the collective nature of Western societies. Hong Kong with its very detailed guidelines for teachers makes it hard for them to deviate from.

Mechanism of Handling Suspected Professional Misconduct of Teachers

Teachers are given examples of teachers' misconduct after the introduction of the NSL in the form of case studies. In this section, the focus is on examples of cases related to teaching materials and "facts" rather than cases involving handling sexual and other misconduct cases which can be found in most schools everywhere.

> Using biased and Incorrect Teaching Materials
>
> A teacher persistently used a large quantity of biased materials for teaching the senior secondary subject Liberal Studies. These teaching materials illustrated viewpoints from a single-sided angle, lacked justification or evidence, and even distorted the facts. In addition, the materials contained untrue remarks about others, spread hatred and radical views and presented a defamatory stance against the nation, which easily aroused readers' hostility towards the nation and its people. (p. 5)

While there have been a few cases of teacher dismissal since the introduction of the National Security Law. It is uncertain what particular case the above example refers to. Needless to say, the "biased materials" might have had to do with matters about freedom and independence, since the tone of the language such as "defamatory stance against the nation" which "easily aroused readers' hostility towards the nation and its people" would seemingly refer to sensitive topics relating to the Chinese nation as colonialism and independence. A primary school teacher had been dismissed over the use of materials promoting independence (BBC 2020).

> Teaching Untrue Contents Persistently
>
> A teacher of General Studies repeatedly presented untrue information about Chinese historical events in junior primary classes. The panel head was also held responsible for not having properly reviewed the teaching materials prepared by the teacher. (p. 5)
>
> In this case, the teacher neither fulfilled his/her primary duty of lesson preparation nor had a correct understanding of the teaching contents. He/she made personal wild guesses with his/her casual thoughts when teaching history and failed to teach students correct historical facts, which seriously affected students' learning and hindered their development of a sense of national identity. Such incompetent and irresponsible attitude constituted serious professional misconduct and fell short of parents' and society's expectations of teachers.

This case could be the where a Hong Kong primary school teacher who gave pupils a factually incorrect account of the Sino-British Opium War has been barred from the profession, the second educator to incur such a punishment. The teacher involved taught told Primary Two students in an online class that Britain waged the First Opium War of 1839–1842 in an attempt to destroy opium in China's territories. The opposite was the case: Britain sought to sell massive amounts of opium in China while Qing dynasty officials tried to ban it. The war led to the foundation of Hong Kong as a British colony and the start of what China calls a century of humiliation at the hands of foreign powers.

Although the facts were "wrong" it was felt that the punishment of dismissal was disproportionate; The Education Bureau said the teacher was "seriously wrong and thus lacked competence as a teacher". It said the teacher did not mislead students on purpose, but should be deregistered due to the seriousness of the matter. The punishment was seen as excessive and it was thought that pressure came from pro-Beijing lawmakers for this punishment. The Education Bureau was accused of choosing "capital [most extreme] punishment". I believe many teachers are concerned about the serious consequences simply for saying a word or two wrong" (Wong 2020a). Because of the sensitivities involving certain topics in Hong Kong' and mainland China's history, and the dismissal or deregistration of teachers for touching on these sensitivities, it is understandable as mentioned before that teachers would adhere closely to textbook materials in order not to draw attention to themselves.

A teacher was also de-registered for "serious professional misconduct" as the syllabus, teaching materials, and worksheet designed by the teacher had contained pro-independence messages. It was the first time Hong Kong had de-registered a teacher for professional misconduct unrelated to sexual and criminal offences. Chief Executive Carrie Lam noted that casting out "bad apples" in the teaching profession would continue. "If there is a very tiny faction of teachers who are using their teaching responsibilities to convey wrong messages to promote misunderstanding about the nation, to smear the country and the Hong Kong SAR government without basis, then that becomes a very serious matter" Wong (2020b).

National Security: Specific Measures for Schools

The Education Bureau released these measures in early February 2021 (updated in 2023) with the following mandate:

> The objective is to deepen students' understanding of the country's development and national security, enhance students' sense of national identity, nurture students as good law-abiding citizens, and create a peaceful and orderly school environment and atmosphere. (p. 1)

In the section "Creating a Peaceful and Orderly School Environment and Atmosphere" in this document (p. 6), Schools have to ensure actions that what had occurred in 2019 do no longer occur. This is why certain actions below have been prohibited (italics added).

> Schools should watch out for political propaganda or disturbances caused to teachers and students in the vicinity, such as the *chanting of slogans, distribution of leaflets and setting up of street counters,* etc. Schools should dissuade their staff and students from joining those activities. If suspected illegal acts are involved, schools should consider seeking assistance from

the Police Community Relations Officer/School Liaison Officer of the Police district concerned.

In Appendix 3 of the "Specific Measures", how to handle the behaviour and conduct of school staff is given, noting (italics added):

> A school is a place for students to learn. *No one should use it for expressing political aspirations, not to mention inciting students to indicate their stance on political issues or even take part in political activities.* The entire staff of our school will remain committed and strive to *prevent political interference* in school. Together, we will safeguard the well-being of our students and help them discern right from wrong by rational thinking.

A sample template statement is provided for schools' reference in Appendix 4 of the Specific Measures, see below:

> It has come to our knowledge that an organisation known as [*name of the organisation established in the name of the school*] has recently emerged to call on our teachers and students to express their support for a particular stance on the political issue of [*e.g., political declaration and/ or activities*] by means of [*form of action/ activity*]. We hereby declare that the remarks, stance and acts of this organisation are not related to our school and do not represent the stance of our school or our teachers/ students. We are very much concerned that the activities that our students are asked by this organisation to join may be illegal.

Further, teachers are given specific examples of the types of incidents "involving political propaganda in schools" contained in Appendix 5 of the Specific Measures such as wearing anything that carries a political message on campus, "chanting slogans, forming human chains, posting slogans/ publicity materials or singing songs" that carry political message on school grounds—all of which occurred in the 2019 protests. Damaging school facilities (e.g., graffiti) for political propaganda or expressing certain political views or demands are also prohibited.

Possessing or displaying items that are allegedly advocating "Hong Kong independence", promoting/expressing hatred or violence—Students are advised to stop doing so, reminding them "the likelihood of contravening the National Security Law or other laws applicable to Hong Kong". "If illegal acts are involved" the school may consult the Police Community Relations Officer/ School Liaison Officer of the Police district concerned. However, in "case of a grave/emergency situation, the school should report to the Police immediately". "Grave" is not defined, leaving it up the teacher or more likely school management, putting the burden on the individual teacher or institution. In order to attempt to follow guidelines, more robust punishment may occur to minimize criticism of their actions.

Requesting peers/others to express their political stance or coercing peers into supporting their own political stance by means of bullying—schools should indicate they have a "zero tolerance" for such actions. "Requesting" others to express their views in of itself seems problematic. School is not a place for expressing one's "political aspirations".

Initiating, organising or participating in class boycotts in contravention of the rules outside the campus, including assemblies and processions not brought to the attention of or not approved by the Police—Students are to be told that boycotts are "detrimental to their learning" and they are again told that should be told that "school is not a place for expressing political aspirations".

Schools also have to supply an annual report on measures they are doing as regards to national security.

A number of schools have posted these measures online and they include such things as "The school arranges staff meetings and talks for staff to understand and familiarize themselves with the legislative background provisions, significance, etc., of the National Security Law, as well as circulating relevant information disseminated by the government" or they might have had a "staff development day" in which a talk on the National Education Law was arranged, or "explaining the implementation of national security education—the success of these fairly general measures in fully understanding the National Security Law is uncertain.

National Security Education in Tertiary Institutions

All of Hong Kong's publicly funded universities are obliged to introduce National Security Law courses as a requirement for graduation from the start of the 2022 academic year. Unlike schools, where National Security Law education and textbooks are prescribed by Hong Kong's Education Department, universities draw up their own courses which are then reviewed by the department. As research it is difficult to obtain access to materials related to the content of the course unless being a student oneself, the author made many attempts to obtain different tertiary institution courses' materials but failed to do so. However, some materials (a number of lecture transcripts and the examination) for the course at the University of Hong Kong have been obtained through a personal contact at the *Hong Kong Free Press*.

The content of the University of Hong Kong course "UG5E1001—Introduction to the Constitution, the Basic Law and the National Security Law", which was devised by the Faculty of Law" is a non-credit bearing online, pass/fail course required for all undergraduates to pass prior to graduation, and is based on a series of pre-recorded lectures and study materials followed by a 20-question multiple-choice test, that is accessible once all of the videos have been watched. which can be attempted multiple times. Fast forward has been disabled on the videos. The course involves a "basic introduction of the Constitution, the Basic Law and the National Security Law. The supplementary materials provide students with an opportunity to examine the international perspective on the topics under study."[7] Students are allowed to consult course materials during the test, which will last no longer than an hour (Lee 2022). Like the Citizenship and Social Development course for secondary students it is a pass/fail course, which would likely result in similar student attitudes to the course as mentioned earlier even though it is a mandatory course in order to graduate (Chau 2022).

[7] For a brief description of UG5E1001 Introduction to the Constitution, the Basic Law and the National Security Law, please see https://www.cedars.hku.hk/ge/ug5e1001.html—Cedars

The Lecture Transcripts

Albert Chen, a University of Hong Kong law professor (and also a member of the Basic Law Committee) gives most of the lectures in the course. After a very basic sharing of what "law" is in a general sense, Professor Chan explains the reason for the NSL's introduction. Chen emphasises that mainland China's supreme law, the Constitution of the People's Republic of China, applies in Hong Kong. Although, he says, there are instances where the differences between the mainland's "socialist system" and Hong Kong's "capitalist system" make certain provisions unsuitable. Professor Chen also notes that since Hong Kong is not a state, legally, there is "no concept of (being) citizens of Hong Kong". In international agreements and cultural activities, the name "Hong Kong, China" can be used.

As background to the introduction of the national security law, Chen introduces Article 23 of the Basic Law, which mandates that the city pass its own security law, acknowledging that it was "very controversial, as some people expressed concerns that it may curtail civil liberties in Hong Kong", after the massive protest against Article 23 in 2003 and the withdrawal of the potential legislation. In one lecture transcript, Chen says that Article 23 was not enacted several years later because the policy of the central government towards Hong Kong was "liberal at the time." The "watershed moment", were "the riots of 2019" which convinced Beijing that there was an "extremely serious loophole in Hong Kong law that needed to be plugged urgently". The loophole, according to Chen, was the lack of a law to protect China's national security in the city, which allowed political activists to openly advocate for Hong Kong independence. This is the standard view of the Hong Kong Government and the Beijing Authorities.

There is a lack of real-life cases contained in the lecture transcripts, but a number of hypothetical scenarios. The lectures give students, for example, a hypothetical situation of someone promoting Hong Kong independence in the United Kingdom, concluding that that individual would be subject to the national security law by explaining the legal elements of the relevant provisions, but not the prosecution principle involved that would be in handling the case in the courtroom. As a student commented

"In my opinion, this course fails to contextualize real-life scenarios… which roots its ambiguity" (Fung 2022). Without "real-life scenarios" it may be difficult to contextualize whether the law is applicable or not, or to know when "red lines" are being crossed or not. According to one student who had taken the test:

> The examples used by Professor Chen are confusing. The NSL does not have a retroactive period, but Chen is referencing something that happened in 2019 or 2020 when there was no NSL. He also mentioned Tong's case, but for me, it's just like reading the news. It would be better if he could explain more about what kind of behaviour or wording threatened national security. (Fung 2022)

Professor Chen mentioned Tong's case just briefly in the lecture about criminal procedure to explain that in NSL cases, jury trial is not guaranteed, but by specially appointed judges. Tong Ying-Kit was the first person convicted under the new legislation and imprisoned for nine years. He was found guilty of inciting secession and terrorist activities after driving his motorbike with a flag reading "Liberate Hong Kong, revolution of our times" into three police officers during a demonstration in Wan Chai a day after the Law came into force. Jury trials are an important feature of Hong Kong's common law system, so it would have been worthwhile discussing this change further—as no national security case so far has had a jury, only a specially designated NSL judge adjudicating national security cases.

The Examination

In the 20-question multiple-choice test (1–10 are True or False questions and 11–20 are pick the right answer), students are asked to identify security law violations. One question is pretty basic "Constitutional law deals with the structure and powers of government and the basic rights and duties of citizens". The answer is "true". Another question describes a group of protesters with a political agenda disrupting the operations of the MTR (Mass Transit Railway) and throwing petrol bombs. This is one of the few "hypothetical" questions given in the examination—arguably this type of question would prove more useful for students so the theoretical aspects of the law can have real-life application.

Perhaps this question could also be considered "hypothetical":

> Under the common law, if doing "X" is a criminal offence, then attempting to do "X" or inciting someone else to do "X" are also criminal offences. But aiding and abetting someone to do "X" or conspiring with others to do "X", although unadvisable, are not in themselves criminal offences.

The answer is "false". While the answer makes sense, but what if "X" that someone is doing does not fall neatly within what was considered a "criminal act" (taking into consideration the unclarity in what is a potential crime under the National Security Law), would "intent" be taken into consideration?

Students are asked to determine whether the following statement is true or false: "Unless detailed planning to cause terror in the community can be proved, such behaviour will not give rise to a charge of terrorism under the National Security Law". The answer is "false". Presumably planning that is "not detailed" is liable for prosecution.

Presumably other tertiary institutions would likely to have a similar format to the University of Hong Kong. Like the school system in Hong Kong with Citizenship and Social Development, the "must pass" nature of the course is in the pass/fail mode, and the nature of examination questions means that likely a majority of students would pass the course with a minimum of effort.

Conclusion: National Security Through Education

The effect of National Security on Education can be clearly seen in statistics: A total of 6,748 teachers left Hong Kong schools in the academic year of 2022/2023, a 25 percent increase (The Standard 2024). The worst turnover rate at 19 percent was recorded for kindergarten teachers with under 10 years of experience, followed by veteran teachers with over 15 years of experience at 16.1 percent. It is hard to argue that this is not the result of the introduction of the National Security Law, which government officials never cite as a possible reason for the exodus, saying "There are various reasons for teacher loss, which mainly includes retirement, pursuing further studies, changing types of schools, taking up employment outside the teaching profession, or leaving the post due to other personal reasons" (Yiu 2023b). Teachers seem to have a large role to play to not only to instil national identity in students but also to ensure that no sensitive topic is raised in the classroom that could possibly be deemed "political" in nature. Constant surveillance of their conduct in this area, what they can or cannot talk about it might prove a strain on their mental and physical health.

Students have also left the Hong Kong educational system. According to official figures, more than 64,000 students from kindergartens to secondary schools withdrew from the local education system in the past two years. In the academic year of 2021–2022, over 33,600 students, or 4 percent of the total student population, left Hong Kong schools, a 10 percent increase from 2022 (Yiu 2023a). Students may feel that they can no longer freely discuss issues relevant to their lives in Hong Kong, which makes the learning experience limited and does not equip them with critical thinking skills they might need in the future.

References

BBC. "Hong Kong Teacher Struck Off for Allegedly Promoting Independence as Lam Vows More Action Against 'Bad Apples'." BBC, October 6, 2020. https://www.bbc.com/news/world-asia-54431729

Bradsher, Keith. "Hong Kong Retreats on 'National Education' Plan." *New York Times*. September 9, 2012. http://www.nytimes.com/2012/09/09/world/asia/amid-protest-hong-kong-backs-down-on-moral-education-plan.html

CDC. *Moral and National Education Curriculum Guide (Primary 1 to Secondary 6) Consultation Draft*. Curriculum Development Council, May 2011. https://www.legco.gov.hk/yr10-11/english/panels/ed/papers/ed0509cb2-1748-2-e.pdf

Chan, Ho-him and Kathleen Magramo. "Hong Kong's Liberal Studies to be Renamed 'Citizenship and Social Development' as Part of Massive Overhaul." *South China Morning Post,* March 31, 2021. https://www.scmp.com/news/

hong-kong/education/article/3127778/hong-kongs-liberal-studies-expected-be-renamed-citizenship

Chau, Candice. "University of Hong Kong Makes National Security Law Course a Mandatory Graduation Requirement." *Hong Kong Free Press,* July 25, 2022. https://hongkongfp.com/2022/07/25/university-of-hong-kong-makes-national-security-law-course-a-mandatory-graduation-requirement/

Cheng, Yut Yiu, Lu, Xi, and Man, Hoi Yan. "Scant Room for Classroom Debate After Death of Hong Kong's Liberal Studies: Teachers, Radio Free Asia. September 13, 2021. https://www.rfa.org/english/news/china/hongkong-education-09132021154441.html

Duklaskis, Alexander, and Johannes Gerschewski. "What Autocracies Say (and What Citizens Hear). Proposing Four Mechanisms of Autocratic Legitimation." *Contemporary Politics* 23, no. 3 (2017): 251–268.

Eagleton, Jennifer. "Rhetorical Ambiguity, Democracy and Political Change: The Contradictions of the Hong Kong Political System." *Contrastes.* Revista Internacional de Filosofía. Suplemento 20, (2017): 77–93. Departamento de Filosofía, Universidad de Málaga.

EDB. FAQs on Citizenship and Social Development." Education Bureau, n.d. https://www.edb.gov.hk/attachment/en/curriculum-development/renewal/Optimising_SS/FAQs_Optimisng_SS_CS_Eng_2023.pdfs

EDB. National Security: Specific Measures for Schools (Enhanced Version dated June 2023). Education Bureau. https://www.edb.gov.hk/attachment/en/sch-admin/national-security/specific-measures.pdf

EDB. "Reform of Liberal Studies (Part 1)." Education Bureau, February 9, 2021a. https://www.edb.gov.hk/en/about-edb/press/cleartheair/20210209.html

EDB. "Debunking Myths About Implementing National Security Education in Hong Kong Schools." Education Bureau, February 22, 2021b. https://www.edb.gov.hk/en/about-edb/press/cleartheair/20210222.html

EDB. Citizenship and Social Development Curriculum and Assessment Guide (Secondary 4–6), 2021c. Education Bureau, June. https://cs.edb.edcity.hk/file/C_and_A_guide/202106/CS_CAG_S4-6_Eng_2021.pdf

EDB. "Guidelines on Teachers' Professional Conduct." Education Bureau, 2022. https://www.edb.gov.hk/attachment/en/teacher/guidelines_tpc/guidelines_en.pdf

EDB. National Security: Specific Measures for Schools (Enhanced Version dated June 2023). Education Bureau. https://www.edb.gov.hk/attachment/en/sch-admin/national-security/specific-measures.pdf

EDB. "National Flag, National Emblem, National Anthem, Regional Flag and Regional Emblem Frequently Asked Questions and Answers." Education

Bureau, February 2024. https://www.edb.gov.hk/attachment/en/sch-admin/admin/about-sch/national-flag-emblem-anthem-regional-flag/FAQ_EN.pdf

Fung, Dawna. "HKU's National Security Course Explains the Law but Fails to Answer Where the Red Line is Drawn, Students Say." *Hong Kong Free Press*, October 4, 2022. https://hongkongfp.com/2022/10/04/hkus-national-security-course-explains-the-law-but-fails-to-answer-where-the-red-line-is-drawn-students-say/

GNAD. "Hong Kong Students and Residents Reject National-education Classes, 2012." Global Nonviolent Action Database, November 8, 2012. https://nvdatabase.swarthmore.edu/content/hong-kong-students-and-residents-reject-national-education-classes-2012

Guardian. "Children of the Revolution: The Hong Kong Youths Ready to 'Sacrifice Everything'". *The Guardian,* December 15, 2019. https://www.theguardian.com/world/2019/dec/15/children-of-the-revolution-the-hong-kong-youths-ready-to-sacrifice-everything

Hung, Jason. "The Climate of Civil Disobedience: Liberal Studies as a Political Instrument under Hong Kong's Secondary Education Curriculum." "Pacific Forum, Issues and Insights", Working Paper 21, no. 1, February 2021. https://pacforum.org/publications/issues-insights-vol-21-wp-1-the-climate-of-civil-disobedience-liberal-studies-as-a-political-instrument-under-hong-kongs-secondary-education-curriculum/

Ip. Christy Wai-hung. "Promoting Critical Thinking: Discussing the Capacity of Issue Inquiry Approach in Liberal Studies." (Education Policy Studies Series), The Chinese University of Hong Kong, 2010. https://hkier.cuhk.edu.hk/en/publications/op73

Lee, Peter. "HKU National Security Course: 10 Hours of Video Viewing and a Multiple-choice Test to Pass, and to Graduate." *Hong Kong Free Press,* August 19, 2022. https://hongkongfp.com/2022/08/19/hku-national-security-course-10-hours-of-video-viewing-and-a-multiple-choice-test-to-pass-and-to-graduate/

Leung, Hillary. "Exclusive Some Foreign English Teachers Employed by Govt must Swear Allegiance to Hong Kong or Risk Their Job." *Hong Kong Free Press,* June 10, 2022. https://hongkongfp.com/2022/06/10/exlcusive-some-foreign-english-teachers-employed-by-govt-must-swear-allegiance-to-hong-kong-or-risk-their-job/

Leung, Hillary. "Students at 2 Hong Kong Schools Not Singing China's National Anthem Loudly Enough, Inspections Find." Hong Kong Free Press, June 26, 2024. https://hongkongfp.com/2024/06/26/students-at-2-hong-kong-schools-not-singing-chinas-national-anthem-loudly-enough-inspections-find/

Lai, Ying Kit, and Johnny Tam. "CE Shelves National Education Guidelines after Panel Report." *South China Morning Post,* October 8, 2012. https://www.scmp.com/news/hong-kong/article/1056353/ce-shelves-national-education-guidelines-after-panel-report

Lipset, Seymour Martin: *Political Man: The Social Bases of Politics*. 2nd edn London: Heinemann, 1983.

Liu, Luis, He Shusi, Li Bingcun, and Gu Mengyan. "Education Flaws Linked to HK Unrest." *China Daily,* September 2, 2019. https://www.chinadaily.com.cn/global/2019-09/02/content_37507007.htm

OCNSC. "Resolutely Claim Victory in Ideological Struggle; Office of the Central National Security Commission" (中央国家安全委员会办公室). *The Total National Security Paradigm: A Study Outline* (总体国家安全观学习纲要), April 14, 2022. https://www.strategictranslation.org/articles/chapter-six-persevere-in-placing-political-security-in-the-predominant-position

Pomfret, James, and Bobby Yip. "Hong Kong protests grow against China "brainwashing" in schools." Reuters, Alert Net. September 3, Web. October 13, 2012. https://news.trust.org/item/20120903162900-qxhdt/

The Standard. "Over 6,700 Teachers Leave School in 2022/23 Academic Year: Data." *The Standard,* January 10, 2024. https://www.thestandard.com.hk/breaking-news/section/4/212265/Over-6,700-teachers-leave-school-in-2022/23-academic-year

Von Soest, Christian, and Julia Grauvogel. "Identity, Procedures and Performance: How Authoritarian Regimes Legitimize their Rule." *Contemporary Politics* 23, no. 3 (2017): 287–305.

Wong, Henry. "Hong Kong Schools: Why Pass-fail System is No Way to Deepen Patriotic Feelings." Letter to the Editor, *South China Morning Post,* December 8, 2020. https://www.scmp.com/comment/letters/article/3112868/hong-kong-schools-why-pass-fail-system-no-way-deepen-patriotic?module=inline&pgtype=article

Wong, Henry. "Why Citizenship Subject Will Fail to Cultivate Patriotism in Hong Kong Students. Letter to the Editor, *South China Morning Post,* May 6, 2024. https://www.scmp.com/opinion/letters/article/3261284/why-citizenship-subject-will-fail-cultivate-patriotism-hong-kong-students

Wong, Natalie. "Hong Kong's Pro-Establishment Lawmakers Push for Surveillance Cameras in Classrooms to Monitor Teachers' Speech." *South China Morning Post,* January 22, 2021. https://www.scmp.com/news/hong-kong/politics/article/3118789/hong-kongs-pro-establishment-lawmakers-make-case

Wong, Rachel. "Hong Kong Ex-leader CY Leung Urges Public to Report Teacher Misconduct." *Hong Kong Free Press,* October 19, 2020a. https://hongkongfp.com/2020/10/19/hong-kong-ex-leader-cy-leung-urges-public-to-report-teacher-misconduct/

Wong, Rachel. "Second Hong Kong Teacher Sacked, this Time for Opium War Blunder as Lawmaker Says Punishment Too Harsh." *Hong Kong Free Press,* November 13, 2020b. https://hongkongfp.com/2020/11/13/second-hong-kong-teacher-sacked-this-time-for-opium-war-blunder-as-lawmaker-says-punishment-too-harsh/

Yang, Weimin, and Chen Qingqing. "HK DSE First Citizenship and Social Development Exam 'Sets Reassuring Precedent'." *Global Times,* April 18, 2024. https://www.globaltimes.cn/page/202404/1310855.shtml

Yiu, William. "Hong Kong Schools Lost 33,600 Students in Last Academic Year Amid Emigration Wave, 10 Per Cent More than in 2020-21." *South China Morning Post,* May 2, 2023a. https://www.scmp.com/news/hong-kong/education/article/3219042/hong-kong-schools-lost-33600-students-last-academic-year-amid-emigration-wave-10-cent-more-2020-21

Yiu, William. "Hong Kong Schools Need to Pump Up the Volume on 'a Little Soft' National Anthem Singing, Annual Inspection Report Says." *South China Morning Post,* December 30, 2023b.

6

Civil Society Under the National Security Law

Some have said that Hong Kong is experiencing a "Cultural Revolution 2.0" after the introduction of the National Security Law in 2019—a reference to the decade-long campaign by the late Chinese leader Mao Zedong in 1966 to purge society of the perceived enemies of communism and to consolidate his grip on power (Hui 2020). That campaign relied on a pervasive culture of spying and informing on friends, family, and colleagues, controlling art, literature, theatre, and music as well as education and the media. While the current situation in Hong Kong cannot be compared to that decade, the NSL has affected most aspects of society in the areas mentioned above. In this chapter, small case studies of government texts and other texts on education, publishing, and the media as well as the arts, will show these effects, and provide comments on them in light of Article 27 of the Basic Law and Article 4 of the NSL which states that Hongkongers have "The rights and freedoms, including the freedoms of speech, of the press, of publication, of association, of assembly, of procession and of demonstration…shall be protected in accordance with the law". First, there will be overview of media changes as this "sets the scene" or the scope of "what can be talked about" in civil society, followed by developments in publication and free speech as well as the arts and of freedom of procession and assembly.

J. Eagleton, *Hong Kong's Second Return to China*,
https://doi.org/10.1007/978-3-031-84587-1_6

Freedom of the Press and of Publication

According to Beijing and Hong Kong officials, freedom of the press has survived intact since the National Security Law came into force, still remaining "in the pocket of the people of Hong Kong" (info.gov.hk 2022), although noting that this freedom is "not absolute", particularly for journalists (italics added):

> Hong Kong people enjoy freedom of the press and freedom of speech .... Nonetheless, freedom of the press and freedom of speech are not absolute. The exercise of them may be subject to restrictions that are provided by law and are necessary for pursuing legitimate aims such as protection of national security or public order. *Journalists, like everyone else, have an obligation to abide by all the laws.* (info.gov.hk 2023)

There have been legal threats, smear campaigns, and intimidation of sources against journalists. The Hong Kong Journalist Association (HKJA) has been pressured to release lists of its member lists and funding sources. There has talk about the need for "fake news laws" for use against information seen as targeting the police, such as the widely circulating rumours that police killed protesters at the Prince Edward subway station during the 2019 protests. However, Chief Executive John Lee has said that there would be no need for a "fake news" law "as long as media industry practices self-discipline". Media outlets had "improved compared to the past", and that he hoped the industry could "enhance the credibility of news information" (Chan 2024). There have been many closures of news outlets since 2020, and the ones that remain are careful about what they print, so this is probably a true statement.

The Hong Kong Journalist Association (HKJA) has long been labelled as a threat to national security, members not being "real" journalists. In a recent article in the Beijing-affiliated *Global Times,* The Association is seen as "failing to represent Hong Kong media". Its foreign connections "raises eyebrows" (Huang and Chen 2024).

> Indeed, the HKJA, with its spotty history of colluding with separatist politicians and instigating riots in Hong Kong, is by no means a professional organization representing the Hong Kong media. It instead serves as a base

for anti-China separatist forces to disrupt Hong Kong, and a malignant tumor that harms the city's safety and stability, said analysts.

From the above, the implication is that the believability of reporting by members of the Association is likely to be biased against Hong Kong and the mainland, and harms the stability of the city.

For the HKJA, pro-China media also raised questions about its membership, whether it had "student members" on its board, whether it was "infiltrating" schools, and whether it was accepting foreign funding. The Beijing controlled *Ta Kung Pao* newspaper took "old, shredded documents taken from HKJA's garbage to carry out an "expose" on the group (IFJ 2022). Chris Tang, the Secretary for Security, demanded that HKJA "clear its name" by releasing information about its membership and source of funds. In January 2021, the Registry of Trade Unions asked the HKJA to justify its activities, such as its social media posts during the 2019 anti-extradition protests, and to provide additional financial information, in response to the allegation that some of its activities may be inconsistent with the Trade Union Ordinance.

There have been legal threats, smear campaigns, and intimidation of sources of journalists; privacy being given as a reason to limit access to information needed for investigative reporting; refusal of issuing of visas to foreign journalists and so on. For a full detailing of what has happened to the media since the introduction of the National Security Law as that could deserve a chapter all its own, please consult the International Federation of Journalists Report *Lights Out Is this the End for Hong Kong Media? An IFJ Report on Press Freedom in Hong Kong 2022* (IFJ 2022).

For example, after a mid-term review of RTHK (Radio Television Hong Kong) and broadcast licenses in 2023, the Broadcast Authority issued 11 suggestions for a month-long public consultation. One major proposal was to state that the impartiality requirement should not apply to programs on national education, national identity, or the NSL. It is unclear whether this is currently in effect. Other suggestions included outsourced programs or channels acquired from "reputable sources" on the mainland for direct re-transmission exempt from complying with the Code of Practice. Regular, critical programming has been seriously curtailed (The Standard 2023).

Books Under the National Security Law

Since the National Security Law was imposed in 2020, politically sensitive titles have gradually been taken off the shelves of public libraries. The authorities will not release the titles of books that have been removed for "reasons of national security". The ones remain in public circulation must serve the "interests of Hong Kong". "Any library material which was suspected of breaching the National Security Law or other laws would be suspended from library services," an Audit Commission's report read. "Upon careful examination, if it was thought that the content of the material concerned posed a risk of violating the law, it would be withdrawn from the library collections permanently and disposed of". This would be of course, an "ongoing exercise" (Leung 2023). Furthermore, the general public have been actively encouraged by police to inform on any words or deeds that could be deemed subversive under the National Security Law (Chen 2023; Ho 2023b).

In addition to public libraries, authorities have also called on schools to ensure that the titles stocked in their libraries do not endanger national security. Educators fearful of crossing red lines have also removed certain books from schools, such as George Orwell's classic works of political satire, *Animal Farm* and *1984*. Local media has reported that hundreds of books touching on topics such as the protests in 2019 and the Tiananmen crackdown in 1989 have been removed from these libraries. However, the author has found that there are still books on this topic in the University of Hong Kong Library; journal articles can also still be accessed online and the effect on academic freedom and exchange is still limited to a certain extent. We are told that book removal from public libraries could still be bought from bookstores (Chau 2023b); however, people would see that still holding on to these books would be problematic. A *Ming Pao Daily* investigation found that since 2020, around 40 percent of books and recordings about political topics or figures had been removed from public libraries. Of 468 political books and recordings identified by the newspaper, at least 195 had been removed—96 of them in the past year (Ho 2023b).

Publishers thus would become wary of anything that touches on political issues if they wanted their publication to be stored in libraries. A publication that was accused of and found guilty of "sedition" in a court of law will be our first case study of relating to free speech that crossed the government's "red lines".

Seditious Sheep: Weaponisation of Metaphor in Children's Books

Several members of the Speech Therapists' Union in Hong Kong were jailed in 2022 under a colonial ordinance for "sedition" in a judge-only trial for producing three children's picture books depicting sheep that the authorities said showed support for the 2019 protest movement and "incited hatred" towards the Hong Kong government and China.

The books suggested that the wolves, who were taken to be the Central Government and the HKSAR Government, were wicked and evil. The sheep were kind and being oppressed by wolves. The wolves, under their tyrannical leader, were the aggressors trying to ruin the peaceful and happy life of the sheep. These were books of cartoons with accompanying commentary. Although presented as children's stories, the books undeniably had a political agenda. The foreword of the first book referred to the mass street protests in early 2019 against the Extradition Bill followed by subsequent events.[1] At the end of the books, there was a timeline matching real life events with the events in the books.

"Seditious intention" is defined in the Hong Kong Crimes Ordinance, "is an intention—(a) to bring into hatred or contempt or to excite disaffection against the person of Her Majesty, or Her Heirs or Successors, or against the Government of the Colony…"[2] This is considered an "archaic"

[1] (1) Guardians of Sheep Village (羊村守衛者) showed sheep resisting the wolves' attempts to take over their village. (2) Twelve Warriors of Sheep Village (羊村十二勇士) is a tale of 12 sheep who tried to escape the wolves, in apparent reference to 12 people who were captured at sea by Chinese authorities in August 2020 while trying to flee Hong Kong; and (3) The Street Cleaners of Sheep Village (羊村清道夫) alluded to the Hong Kong government's initial reluctance to close the border with China at the start of the coronavirus outbreak. The books were printed and distributed in Cantonese (also Taiwanese & English online versions).

[2] "SEDITION ORDINANCE," Historical Laws of Hong Kong Online, 2024, https://oelawhk.lib.hku.hk/items/show/2043.

crime that had been frequently used to target political speech (Smith et al. 2022). Sedition laws share some commonalities (italics added):

> Notably, *most do not require any evidence that allegedly seditious speech would be likely to incite violence*, and most are *vague and overbroad*, allowing them to be misused and manipulated to suppress free speech. For instance, in the last ten years, sedition laws have been used by governments to prosecute a student activist for protesting an election, a government official for a critical Facebook post, and a journalist for a satirical cartoon. In 1951, the Supreme Court of Canada noted that "probably no crime has been left in such vagueness of definition" as the offense of sedition. (p. 2)

A growing number of States have either repealed or reformed their sedition laws. Others have brought them back (Lai 2021; Chau 2022a). In several Commonwealth States, domestic courts have ruled the sedition offense unconstitutional. And in others, parliaments or courts have significantly narrowed vague or overbroad sedition laws, limiting their application to situations where speech is likely to incite violence and seeking to clarify ambiguities. Finally, based on public records, it appears that a large number of Commonwealth States have not prosecuted the offense in at least the last decade.

Method of Analysis

The judge's "Reasons for Verdict" (67 pages) and "Reasons for Sentence" (16 pages) were downloaded from the Hong Kong Judiciary's website (DoJ 2022a,b). Themes were analysed according to the charges in the case. The speech therapists were found guilty of the following (a) to bring into hatred or contempt or to excite disaffection against the Central Authorities and/or the Government of the Hong Kong Special Administrative Region; (b) to bring into hatred or contempt or to excite disaffection against the administration of justice in Hong Kong; (c) to raise discontent or disaffection amongst inhabitants of Hong Kong; (d) to incite persons to violence; and/or (e) to counsel disobedience to law or to any lawful order.

Some of the following is based on an analysis provided by former Dean of the Faculty of Law or the University of Hong Kong and other sources (Chan 2022). The verdict (a legal genre) will be analysed from three main aspects: (a) the statutory construction of wording; (b) legal certainty, and (b) proportionality.

What are "Discontent", "Disaffection", "Hatred", and "Contempt"?

Firstly, there is "Statutory construction" (or statutory interpretation) is the process of determining what a particular statute means so that a court may apply it accurately. Although sometimes the words of a statute may have a plain meaning, in many cases there is some ambiguity in the words of the statute that must be resolved by the judge. To find the true meanings of statutes, judges look at "traditional canons of construction, legislative history, and purpose".

It would have to be determined to what extent would criticism against the state amount to "disaffection", "discontent", "hatred", or contempt". As something that would impact freedom of speech, this criticism would have to reach a certain level of intensity before this would be so. One of the defence counsels submitted to the court (which agreed) "that it should not read the books through the eyes of an extremely radical or cynical reader, but it must consider the likely effect of the books on ordinary people and on the audience to which the books are addressed" (119).

Any criticism against the state could not amount to "disaffection", "discontent", "hatred" or "contempt" unless *there is a real risk* that national security is threatened or compromised. It is not the emotion per se, but actual harm created by such emotion that justifies criminal sanction. The court made two assumptions without any evidential basis. First, merely saying that the state was wicked or unfair in treating its citizens did not necessarily lead to a conclusion that the readers of the books would feel contempt for the state, or a mere suggestion that the immigration arrangement between the PRC and the HKSAR Government was abused would lead the readers to feel discontent with new immigrants. This is an issue of *threshold or intensity*. *Secondly*, even if this inference could be made, it does not automatically mean that national security was endangered. The children may be misled, but this does not mean that national security would be threatened.

Legal Certainty

Legal certainty is "The principle requires that the law must be clear, precise and unambiguous, and its legal implications foreseeable" (LexisNexis Definition). The law must be such that it is clearly understandable by those who must abide by it. The court rejected the argument that the words "disaffection", "discontent", "hatred", and "contempt" in Section 9 are too vague so that an ordinary person will not be able to regulate his conduct to avoid criminal liability. The judge gave three reasons. *First*, these are ordinary words with ordinary meaning, which may vary with time, place, and circumstances of the conduct in question and are best left to the trial judge or jury:

> 94. [these] are just words with ordinary meaning, and these concepts are best left to the trial judge or jury to be applied in their ordinary meaning to the time, place and circumstances of the conduct in question. …From these experiences and observations, it is clear that while the feelings or emotions are subjective, some objective facts will have to exist first in order to bring about that kind of subjective feelings or emotions… (DoJ 2022a)

Secondly, although these words are descriptive of a person's subjective feelings or emotions, some objective facts will have to exist to allow the ascertainment of subjective feelings or emotions. *Thirdly*, Section 9(2) sets out some conduct which will not be regarded as seditious; hence, there are objective guidelines to allow a defendant to delineate the area of risk.

First, the fact that the matter is best resolved by the trial judge or jury does not absolve the state from defining what the prohibited act is. Section 9(2) is helpful in identifying what does not constitute seditious intention, but as pointed out above, the absence of a negative does not prove the existence of a positive. Once the conduct in question does not fall within Section 9(2), it still begs the question what constitutes "hatred", "contempt", "disaffection" and "discontent". *Secondly*, these are general terms. Even if some objective facts exist, the standard or intensity required may vary from person to person. The same words may be perfectly acceptable by one person but regarded as offensive by another person. In a plural society, there could hardly be any objective standard to determine these subjective feelings save in the most obvious situations.

Different people may have different standards in what constitutes "hatred", "contempt", "disaffection", and "discontent" and in assessing what is acceptable or not. The courts did not consider international and comparative materials on the basis that "their political background, social condition, culture and the availability of alternative legislations to deal with seditious situations to safeguard their national security are different to those in the HKSAR" (HKDC 981, [103]). Therefore, the focus "should be on the unique political and social conditions of the Region, and the other laws in force in HKSAR" (ibid.)—the same argument used to justify a different kind of universal suffrage (as promised in the Basic Law) that was different from the Western forms of democracy.

Proportionality

In criminal law, the principle of proportional justice is used to describe the idea that the punishment fits the crime; that is, it should be in proportion to the severity of the crime itself. The concept of proportionality is "You must not use a steam hammer to crack a nut, if a nutcracker would do."[3] That is, the concept is used as a criterion of fairness and justice in statutory interpretation processes. In this case, there are two aspects to this.

The *first* is that there needs to be a rational connection between the restriction and the objective to be achieved. The court has identified the objective as the protection of national security. The means to achieve this

[3] "The proportionality test may require the reviewing court to assess the balance that the decision maker has struck, not merely whether it is within the range of rational or reasonable decisions. It may also require attention to be directed to the relative weight accorded to the competing interests and considerations." "The principle of proportionality and the concept of margin of appreciation in human rights law" - *Basic Law Bulletin*, December 2013. https://www.doj.gov.hk/en/publications/pdf/basiclaw/basic15_2.pdf

objective is to punish any publication with a seditious intention (as defined earlier). The *second aspect* of the proportionality test is that the offence should not go further than necessary to protect national security. Thus, the social impact of the offence needs to be considered as well its impact possible freedom of expression and balance the risk against national security.

These books were published between June and July 2021. The 2019 protests after the university sieges of November that year, Covid-19's emergence in January 2020, and the National Security Law that came into effect on 30 June 2020 caused immediate changes to civil society. However, the judge stated that (italics added):

> Although the situation in the HKSAR has more or less calmed down after the promulgation of the NSL, it is clear that these people have little change in their attitude. They just go underground and the *seeds of unrest are still there*. The political situation appears to be calm on the surface but very volatile underneath. HKDC 981, [104] (2022)

The above sounds rather like a political opinion.[4] There is a preoccupation of the potential for political unrest in the future (this was also mentioned in videos discussed in Chap. 3)."[5] Next we have to look at the "intent" and the "act" of these speech therapists.

The Defendants' Intent (*Mens Rea*)

Intent of committing a criminal act of intent is key here. *Mens rea* is the "'guilty mind', the term, according to LexisNexis, means "'criminal intention', or an intention to do the act which is made penal by statute or the

[4] This means that a person charged with these offences is unlikely to be able to obtain bail. A number of defendants charged with these offences have been detained before trial for over a year. At the end of their trial, they were immediately released, as the sentence was equal to the time served while they were detained (a period of 19 months).

[5] For example, in "Bedrock of Community—Episode 31—Date: 14 December 2020 (https://www.isd.gov.hk/nationalsecurity/eng/videos-Bedrock-31.html); "Yet, we have some worries—the notion of Hong Kong independence still remains, as well as the notion of violence. We must not let our guard down again if we want to return to what it was like before June last year, before the violence broke out, so we can go back to work as usual and people can live normal life again."

common law", although it can also include mental states like *knowledge* (without intent) or *recklessness* (also without intent). This term is really the "mental element of an offence". There is no doubt the speech therapists intended the books to carry their own political message (given the circumstances and the timeline at the end of each of the books). In para 124 of the Reasons for Verdict, for instance, the judge said that Hong Kong's Chief Executive was depicted in the books as a wolf masquerading as a sheep "at the direction of the wolf-chairman":

> By identifying (the People's Republic of China) government as the wolves, and the Chief Executive of HKSAR as the wolves masqueraded as a sheep at the direction of the Wolf-chairman, along the story line told in Book 1, the children will be led into belief that (the PRC government) is coming to Hong Kong with the wicked intention of taking away their home and ruining their happy life with no right to do so at all. p. 54, *Reasons for Verdict*

Assuming that the intent as revealed in the books, wherein lies the criminal mind? The commentaries going with the cartoons expressed one view of the political situation facing Hong Kong in the second half of 2019 and early 2020. Looking at the media coverage of the 2019 anti-extradition law protests, there were different views of what it was for: (change the following). The defendants might be totally wrong; they might have turned a blind eye to the mayhem in the streets and ignored the danger facing the community as the insurgency threatened the total collapse of law and order. But there is no suggestion that they had in any way taken part in the insurgency or had given support to those taking part in it. They clearly thought the imposition of the national security law by the Central Government was unjustified. This was disputed by others.

The crime lies in the pictures and words in the books and their promotion. Were they doing anything more than to say, in effect: the Hong Kong government, together with the Central Government were wrong, or even oppressively wrong? If a jury said: "We're not sure, maybe that was their intent" then this leaves a doubt regarding their likely intent and they should be acquitted as a result.

The Criminal Act (*Actus Reus*)

The criminal act or *actus reus* is "All the elements of a criminal offence except the accused's mental element".[6] As the judge himself said, section 10(1)(c) "qualified as an offence endangering national security" (para 61). Sedition is not an offence against an individual or property; rather it is a crime against the state. It is unclear if the prosecution had shown beyond a reasonable doubt, that the state was harmed by these books when it said that that the defendants *intended* to excite disaffection against the government. This has to be balanced with the right to free speech in the common law system.

In paragraph 122 of the Reasons for Verdict the judge noted defence counsel as saying that the books "just represent the perspective of a section of the public, and the events may be exaggerated, but this form of writing is acceptable in all broadminded democratic societies, and that is so even if some readers may find the contents disturbing, shocking or even offensive". The judge agreed, saying "but still, it depends on what has really been depicted". Still, it is unclear what harm to the state has occurred. The books were published between June 2020 and the middle of March 2021, when the NSL was supposed to have restored social stability and harmony. There is an implication that the Hong Kong government was harmed by a children's allegorical story. The judge discussed the "unconstitutionality" of what the defendant had done in the following (paragraph 104, p. 46, italics added):

> Since the start of the Anti-Extradition Movement in mid-2019, HKSAR went through a lengthy period of mass riots and civil unrest, some of them were extremely violent and weapons and petrol bombs were used. While the exact number of people participating in these riotous activities will never be known, it can be said with certainty that there were over tens of thousands of them. What these people had demonstrated during this

[6] "The term comes from a mistranslation of the Latin Actus non facit reum, nisi mens sit rea, which properly translated means "an act does not make a man guilty of a crime unless his mind be also guilty". It is used to refer to the act, conduct, omission, or state of affairs which the offence in question prohibits. The mental and other elements of a criminal offence can, however, on occasions be difficult to distinguish, e.g., "possessing", "keeping", permitting". These terms import both physical and mental elements." https://www.lexisnexis.co.uk/legal/glossary/actus-reus

> period of time was that they *did not recognise the sovereignty of the PRC over HKSAR, and they did not support the policy of One Country Two Systems.* There were calls for Hong Kong independence or self-determination. Although the situation in HKSAR had more or less calmed down after the promulgation of the national security law, it is clear that these people have little change in their attitude. They just go underground and the *seeds of unrest* are still there. The political situation appears to be calm on the surface *but very volatile underneath.*

Had the rioters gone "underground"? Did "seeds of unrest" exist? Did volatility lurk "underneath" when public order had been clearly restored when these books appeared? These again seemed to be subjective opinions.

The summing up of the arguments:

Defence Argument	Judge's Reason for Verdict
The books are simply children's fables	A fable will not identify real characters; the book points to actual happenings.
The books were promoting universal values	They will be told they are sheep and that the wolves trying to harm them are the central government
Mere criticism of the government/criticism of a political nature although strongly worded.	Children were asked what they would do in a media interview—they said they would either escape or fight.
Not inciting or causing public disorders by acts of violence.	They [children] would be guided to violence.
Did not incite or propose any negative thoughts to the readers	The seditious intention stems not merely from the words, but from words intended to cause certain effects in a child's mind.
Ended with an open-ended question, leaving it to readers to decide what was best for them.	Intended to arouse public hatred especially among young children.
The books were to explain social events in Hong Kong.	It is patently clear from the structure of each book that the thinking of the children is to be guided in a particular way when the story is being told, e.g., by parents.
The books are also an aid for parents/educational workers to help their children understand social happenings.	A brainwashing exercise with a view to guiding the very young children to accept their views and values, i.e., Beijing has no sovereignty over Hong Kong.

The Sentencing

At paragraph 7 of his Reasons for Sentence he said that "the targets of these books are children, including those as young as 4 years old". Then in paragraphs 29–30 he said this: "...the sentence to be imposed must depend on the defendants' culpabilities in the offence and the harm caused by them,"

> First, the harm caused by the defendants as a result of their offence must be identified at the outset. The defendants are to be punished not because of the publications or for their words, but because of the harm or the risk of harm that was or would be resulted to the mind of children. (DOJ 2022b, paragraph 30)

The approach to sentencing adopted by the judge seems to admit that the state had necessarily been harmed or that national security has been endangered by the books), but that the minds of children would be harmed. Section 10 of the Crimes Ordinance does not seem to focus on children's welfare. Its sole purpose is to protect the state from harm.

> What the defendants had done, with children aged 4 and above to be their target, was in effect a brainwashing exercise with a view to guiding the very young children to accept their views and values, i.e., PRC has no sovereignty over HKSAR which is not part of PRC. It was said that there was no evidence that the children had been so affected. This is incorrect because one of the defendants had said in one of the media interviews that she had asked the children how they would respond to the wolves, and one said he would escape and the other said he would fight. (Paragraph 30)

Summing Up of This Section

These convictions have attracted worldwide publicity. The explanation for the offence of sedition is still rather subjective and vague, making many assumptions on what was the "subjective intention" of the books. The indeterminacy of these words and others that are in the NSL means that people can inadvertently cross legal "red lines" and thus risk prosecution. Another major point is what is an "objective fact". According to the judge, there seems to be only a certain "truth", and that seems to be the one that the Hong Kong Government is promoting. The judge accuses the speech therapists of refusing to acknowledge the of Hong Kong's situation (this was a common criticism of democrats). If one has studied Hong Kong history, many of the points/feelings in the books. The judge and others also stressed that authorities were willing to accept criticism, but that criticism had to be based on what was true—but it was not everyone's "truth". The discursive reconstruction of history in Hong Kong is an ongoing process about what is the "acceptable truth" by the gatekeeping authorities.

Furthermore, children's books simplify and perhaps exaggerate a story to more forcefully get their point across. The wolves (the PRC) will not, literally "eat the sheep". i.e., have more control over them or that "sheep would not act like this". In some respects, these books also act like satire. "Harming the children"—youth and later adults, leads on to education about national security.

Case Study 2: Tiananmen Commemorations and the Pillar of Shame

Yearly stories about the annual commemorations of June Fourth 1989 always mentioned versions of the phrase "Hong Kong as "the only place on Chinese soil" where this could be done. This occasion came to be seen as a symbol of Hong Kong as remaining a "Second System" exhibiting the continuing separation of systems apart from the "One Country", thus acting like a benchmark for freedom of association after the NSL's introduction.

In recent years, the authorities cited anti-epidemic measures as the reason to ban the annual candlelight commemoration in Victoria Park. Hong Kong lifted Covid-19 social distancing measures in early 2023 (HKFP 2023). Victoria Park was occupied by a "patriotic carnival" (as it had been for the last few years), so the regular assembly venue was unavailable. There was no official word on whether a public vigil or commemoration would be legal in the wake of the Beijing-imposed national security law (this is still the case). However, early in 2019, Chief Executive Carrie Lam said the following implying the go ahead of the event. Interesting to note that this was said just before acceleration of the anti-extradition protests.

> Chief Executive Carrie Lam: "A lot of people have memories about today's date, and for the gov't, it is also proof that Hong Kong is a free place…We respect the public's freedom of speech and assembly, which are protected under the Basic Law." (HKFP 2019)

Chief Executive John Lee however warned in May 2023 that police would take action against any lawbreakers, though he was unable to give a yes/no answer as to whether publicly mourning the Tiananmen crackdown was illegal:

> Chief Executive John Lee: "Everybody should act in accordance with the law and think of what they do, so as to be ready to face the consequences…any activity that contradictions the law, of course, the police will have to take action. Police will take action resolutely, particularly in regard to public order activities." (Ho 2023a)

His ambiguous answer echoed the secretary for security and other government officials, rather than saying definitively whether those commemorating victims of June Fourth would risk legal consequences, he warned that "unidentified individuals" intended to harm national security: "Authorities will take action against people who plan to harm national security on "a special occasion in a few days' time," (Chau 2023b), not specifying what this "special occasion" was, although it was obvious to all. Lee went on to say: "However, I want to tell these people that if you commit these acts, we will definitely take decisive action and arrest you, and will prosecute you if there is evidence. You will not get lucky" (ibid.). Interesting is the use of the third pronoun "you". "You" is used to refer to an indeterminate person, as a more common alternative to the very formal indefinite pronoun one. Though this may be semantically third person, for agreement purposes, you is always second person. Whether someone violated the law depended on "many factors" including their intentions and actions, and said that the authorities would gather sufficient evidence ahead of any prosecutions.

Such is the sensitivity of June Fourth 1989, that even the name cannot specifically be given. Hong Kong activist Chow Hang-tung was barred from using the phrase "Tiananmen massacre" during a national security trial, with a magistrate told her to use "proper terminology", which in this case was "Tiananmen incident", obviously a more neutral term (Chau 2022). The way you describe the evens of June 1989 categorises you politically, especially in the Hong Kong context.

The Pillar of Shame

A more fixed (and year-long reminder) memorial to June Fourth 1989 was the statue of writhing figures by Danish sculptor Jens Galschiøt, the "Pillar of Shame" (1996), which was erected by students on the campus of the University of Hong Kong. This sculpture and other democracy-related memorials at other universities in Hong Kong were removed from campuses in December 2021 while students and faculty were at university recess, the former late at night. Following the images of the Pillar of Shame and what replaced it (Figs. 6.1 and 6.2) are the reasons given for the statue's removal.

> The Council of the University of Hong Kong (HKU Council) made a decision at its meeting on December 22 (Wednesday) to remove a statue, widely known as the Pillar of Shame, from campus (italics added).
>
> The decision on the *aged statue* was based on external legal advice and risk assessment for the best interest of the University.
>
> No party *has ever obtained any approval from the University to display* the statue on campus, and the University has the right to take appropriate actions to handle it at any time. The University is also very concerned about the *potential safety issues* resulting from the fragile statue. Latest legal advice given to the University cautioned that the continued display of the statue would pose legal risks to the University based on the *Crimes Ordinance enacted under the Hong Kong colonial government.*

Fig. 6.1 Pillar of Shame (6 October 2021) University of Hong Kong ((author photograph)

> The HKU Council has requested that the statue be put in storage, and that the University should continue to seek legal advice on any appropriate follow up action. (HKU Council 23 December 2021)

The letter implies that they are concerned about the safety issue of the "aged statue" and "potential safety issues"—trying to foreground this rather than the probably more important reason of "legal risks" based on the colonial Crimes Ordinance.

Fig. 6.2 Replacement structures after removal (8 February 2022), University of Hong Kong (author photograph)

Students said the removal of the Pillar of Shame and other memorials ("goddesses of democracies") that had been on campus for more than a decade—24 years in the case of the HKU Pillar of Shame—violated freedom of expression, artistic freedom, and university autonomy. But it was also an attempt by the authorities, "to obliterate history" and censor memories and debate surrounding 4 June 1989 (Leung and Sharma, 5 January 2020) (Figs. 6.3, 6.4 and 6.5).

Fig. 6.3 "Goddess of Democracy" at the Chinese University of Hong Kong (author photograph)

The "Martyr's Slogan" as it was known reads: "The souls of the martyrs shall forever linger despite the cold-blooded massacre. The spark of democracy shall forever glow for the demise of evil". Asked why the university, which took down a "pillar of shame" Tiananmen statue in December, had covered the 20-character slogan, a HKU spokesperson said by email: "The University of Hong Kong regularly conducts maintenance works at various locations and facilities, with the above site being

Fig. 6.4 A Goddess of Democracy Polytechnic University of Hong Kong (right) taken years before the NSL (author photograph)

one such project". For more than three decades it had been a tradition for HKU students to repaint the slogan on the bridge each year before June Fourth.

In May 2023, the Pillar of Shame was seized from storage at the Kadoorie Centre by Hong Kong's National Security Department, reportedly to be used as a "piece of evidence" in an "incitement to subversion case" (Lee 2024) Secretary for Security, Chris Tang Ping-keung, defended

Fig. 6.5 University of Hong Kong bridge: "Martyr's Slogan" before removal (author photograph)

the decision, saying that the removal was unrelated to the upcoming June Fourth anniversary. This case might be related to the organiser of Hong Kong's annual Tiananmen vigil—the Hong Kong Alliance in Support of Patriotic Democratic Movements of China (now defunct)—together with three of its leading members, Lee Cheuk-yan, Albert Ho, and Chow Hang-tung had been charged with inciting subversion under the National Security Law (the case was heard in November 2024) (Lee 2024).

The Arts: "Projects in Engineering Souls"

In October 2014, Xi Jinping delivered a speech at the Beijing Forum on Literature and Art encouraging those in China's creative industries to promote Party ideology and patriotism with their work, seeing literature and art as "projects to engineer souls, literature and art workers are engineers of the soul":

> In the Socialist core value view, the most profound, fundamental and eternal matter is patriotism. *Patriotism is a topic that is often written about and often is renewed.* Works that contain the feelings of a country are most able to call the sons and daughters of China to unite in struggle. (Xi 2014)

A tenet was also "strengthening and improving Party leadership over literature and art". This speech attracted Xi yet more comparison to his Mao Zedong, who in 1942 outlined similar responsibilities for artists and intellectuals in Communist China at the Yan'an Forum on Literature and Art. In the context of holistic national security, one of 20 major areas was cultural security:

> Cultural security refers to a state in which a country's cultural characteristics and cultural sovereignty in relation to a country's ideology including national spirit, ideals, beliefs, mainstream value system are relatively not in danger and free from internal and external threats, and the capability to maintain a sustained state of security.
>
> Culture is the soul of a country and a nation. Cultural security is related to national stability, national unity, and spiritual inheritance. It is an important guarantee for building a socialist cultural power, fully and accurately implementing the "one country, two systems" policy, and safeguarding national security.[7]

This appears on the Hong Kong Government's national education website. We can see from this that most likely "traditional" cultural values would be promoted as well as the "ideology" of the government that

[7] https://www.nsed.gov.hk/national_security/index.php?l=en&a=national_security_main_focus&d=cultural_security

would be officially approved. Certain "gatekeepers' would likely need to "approve" would be acceptable and not threaten national security.

The Hong Kong Arts Development Council (HKADC) is the main body in supporting and funding a wide range of local arts groups. In early 2021, the council was accused by the *Ta Kung Pao* that it had been funding subversive organisations in the past, giving $1.9 million to projects that it said violated China's national security law. Hours after this accusation, Chief Executive Carrie Lam said the following:

> With the national security law in place, we have to safeguard national security," she said during a Legislative Council question and answer session. "We have to respect the freedom of artistic expression but I'm sure staff [at art and cultural centres] are able to tell… whether pieces are meant to incite hatred or to destroy relations between two places and undermine national security. (Lai 2021)

Apart from funding, leases of arts and culture venues have been affected. NGOs have been invited to submit proposals to operate and maintain a historic listed building, which has been home to arts and cultural venue Fringe Club for 40 years. In a 35-page project brief, the Culture, Sports and Tourism Bureau said the potential operator should safeguard national security. The term "national security" appears 22 times in the document.[8] The bureau also said that whoever runs the arts space should be able to terminate contracts with anyone they engage if their contractors acted "contrary to the interest of national security":

> The Operator should exercise its professional judgement, highest degree of sensitivity and prudence in assessing any potential national security risks or issues that may be involved in the operation, management, maintenance and development of the Premises. (13.1, p. 28)

[8] https://www.cstb.gov.hk/file_manager/ifp/IFP000projectbriefeng.pdf - Project Brief - Culture, Sports and Tourism Bureau Invitation for proposals for operating, managing, maintaining and developing for arts and culture use the Premises situated on portions of the Basement and the whole of all the Ground Floor, the First Floor and the Roof of No. 2 Lower Albert Road, South Block, Central, Hong Kong.

The arts space also has to "put in place effective mechanism" to ensure that the use of the Premises for any events, operation, procurement and any other activities, etc. is strictly in compliance with the NSL and other laws in Hong Kong.

By leaving the definitions about what is a "national security risk" to the organisation, caution to the extreme would result in who they might hire/support. The Foreign Correspondents' Club (FCC) that occupies a part of the Fringe Club premises had been worried about its lease renewal ever since the controversial lunch talk by the head of the Hong Kong independence-advocating National Party in 2018. They did renew their lease, but it included a national security clause. When asked about the new national security clause, the head of the FCC Keith Richburg said that the lease could be terminated "on national security grounds". However, "Since we don't plan on violating national security or any other Hong Kong law, that [provision] does not seem problematic" (Chau 2022b). This sounds like a "politically correct" attitude/diplomatic answer. This could mean that potentially controversial topics would not be entertained in the club. The government's view was "I think it is very sensible that if a location is being used to act against the national interests of our country, why we should allow them to use the premises. I think this is a very simple question." The FCC was accused of using freedom of speech as an excuse and that the club "betrayed the ethics of a journalists' organization."

M+ Museum of Visual Culture

Self-described as "Asia's first global museum of contemporary visual culture", M+ Museum in West Kowloon Cultural District (WKCD), a Hong Kong government-initiated project is an interesting case study of the NSL's effect on the arts. While there has been much debate and controversies about the planning, building, and running of WKCD, and M+ in particular, the most current controversy was about work it shows in its galleries.

The M+ Museum focus is on modern and contemporary art, particularly China and its diaspora. Whereas in China museums face difficulties showing certain kinds of contemporary art that authorities deem too critical of the country's government, institutions and galleries in Hong Kong could, theoretically present more explicitly political art as part of its role as the "Second System" of the "One Country". Before its official opening on 12 November 2021, there was a discussion about what works the Museum would show. It has a sizeable collection of works by artists critical of Beijing in its signature collection, and founding collection, the Sigg Collection of Contemporary Chinese Art, includes dissident artist Ai Weiwei. After a media preview of the recently completed museum building on 12 March 2021, Director Suhanya Raffel was asked if works by Ai Weiwei and others referencing Tiananmen would be shown (italics added):

> Ai Weiwei works have never been censored in Hong Kong, says Suhanya Raffel—the woman at the helm of M+. She then adds a *nuance t*o her answer—censorship is a question that applies to museums around the world. "When we talk about issues of censorship it needs to be more thoughtful and calibrated about how public institutions are responding to very local pressures as well." (Smith 2021)

While Raffel says she has "never been censored" in the city, her last sentence acts as a kind of disclaimer, hinting at possible institutional oversight beyond the museum's control. One of the most controversial of Ai's artworks is his "Study of Perspective—Tian'anmen" (1997). The photograph shows the artist's upturned middle finger aimed at the Gate of Heavenly Peace in Beijing. Other photographs in Ai's "Study of Perspective" series shows Ai's finger upturned at other famous political landmarks (such as the White House).

On 26 March 2021, Bernard Chan, of the Executive Council and a WKCD Authority board member, wrote an opinion piece in the *South China Morning Post* entitled "Art Censorship: Why the Hong Kong Government has no Business Playing Cultural Gatekeeper" (Chan 2021). He highlighted that Beijing had designated Hong Kong a hub for arts and cultural exchange between China and the rest of the world in the recent 14th Five-year Plan, adding that the role would depend on the city's "image as an open, tolerant and cosmopolitan city" (ibid.):

> The opening of the West Kowloon Cultural District should secure Hong Kong's status as one of the world's key art centres. The central government supports this; Beijing has designated Hong Kong as a hub for arts and cultural exchange between China and the rest of the world in the 14th Five-year Plan announced recently.
>
> But if Hong Kong's image as an open, tolerant and cosmopolitan city is damaged, the hard work we have put in to build its art infrastructure will be wasted as well. That's why I'm surprised to hear calls for the Hong Kong government to take charge of supervising and even censoring the art shown in our museums and galleries.
>
> Such a move would put us at risk of losing our global reputation—we would be imperiling an economic sector in which we have invested years of effort and billions of dollars. (Chan 2021)

This shows the ideological "battle" between Hong Kong and the Mainland to meet the expectations of being a part of China and how it views the purpose of art as a means to guard public behaviour and uphold certain social values and the pushing of creative barriers that is celebrated in the international art world.

A museum's shift in its agenda was suggested in a M+ members' newsletter on 28 March, 2021 where executive director Suhanya Raffel announced that M+ would be "an important cultural institution to promote cultural exchanges among Mainland China, Asia and beyond… as laid down in the National 14th Five-Year Plan"—The first public statement in which the museum aligned its curatorial policy with China's national strategic goals.

Henry Tang, the government official in charge of WKCD where the museum is located had said that no artwork deemed to breach the law would be displayed. "If there are any works that the national security department thinks… (have) violated the law, we will act according to the law," he told reporters (AFP 2021). Tang confirmed that Ai Weiwei's photograph would not be displayed when M+ opened but denied any censorship. "We have never planned for that photograph to be included in the opening exhibition, so there is no question that we have retracted it or we have succumbed to pressures and have changed it" (ibid.).

During the Covid-19 pandemic, M+ closed; on reopening a number of artworks were removed. One was Wang Xingwei's 2001 painting *New*

Beijing, depicting two penguins with gunshot wounds to the heart, were widely believed to represent the pair of injured Tiananmen Square protesters shown in a 1989 photograph by Liu Heung Shing; Zhou Tiehai's 1996 *Press Conference III*, referring to the Cold War (depicting the artist in a press conference discussing the commodification of Chinese contemporary art within the global art market) was also removed as was Wang Guangyi's 1989 *Mao Zedong: Red Grid No. 2*, which deploys the grid as a distancing lens through which to consider the Communist leader (however all these two works can also be viewed in the M+ Collections Online).

The replaced paintings were substituted with noticeably less political artworks by the same artists—rather than presenting artists whose works were not initially on view, New Beijing was replaced by Wang Xingwei's *St. Thomas* (1997), a postmodernist pastiche of European Baroque painting that features two police officers resembling artists Andy Warhol and Joseph Beuys watching a crouching figure break through a wooden door—the latter a reference to Marcel Duchamp's final installation, Étant Données (1946–1966). Mao Zedong: Red Grid No. 2 was substituted with a painting featuring a similar overlaid grid structure and the letters "A" and "O," Rationality in Common Behaviours (1988), which depicts an ambiguous human figure and a urinal (another Duchamp reference) rather than the face of Mao from official portraits.

As mentioned, the removed artworks had images visible in the online collection, although Ai's "Study of Perspective: Tian'anmen (1997) does not. In this case, the M+ logo on a grey background replaces the image of the artwork. This may be because: "The object has not yet been photographed or we only have a low-quality image online publication of the object is under copyright restrictions; An image may be considered inappropriate for online publication (private email to the author from M+, on 19 April, 2024). The latter explanation seems to be the case, "inappropriate" meaning not politically correct. The online collection however shows other works in Ai's "Study of Perspective" series.[9]

[9] M+ opened with Sigg Collection: From Revolution to Globalisation Ai's "Whitewash" was shown. This was a series of earthenware storage jars dating to the Chinese Neolithic period. White paint was used to thoroughly coat about one quarter of the jars, removing the distinctive colour and marks of the clay, giving a "sense of newness". In the 1990s, Ai Weiwei began using Chinese historical artefacts in his work, e.g., he dropped a Han-dynasty urn so that it would break into pieces. "By

Given local realities in Hong Kong the curators of M+ have to avoid being seen as challenging the Central Government too directly, so there is likely to be less blatant criticism of China in its future acquisitions. In the author's experience of visiting M+ many times, commentary by Chinese artists on social and cultural issues can be quite creative in how they criticise the society they live in. Criticism of Hong Kong's new situation is also problematic, but critical artworks can still be found in private galleries.[10]

Film Censorship Guidelines for Censors

Hong Kong's film censorship law was amended in 2021 to include national security clauses which targeted content deemed to "endorse, support, glorify, encourage and incite activities that might endanger national security." (OFNAA 2021 para. 52). The law empowers Hong Kong's chief secretary, to revoke a film's licence if it is "found to be contrary to national security interests." The authority can request changes such as the removal of certain scenes from a film. Violating the law included up to three years imprisonment and fines of up to HK$1 million ($128,400). "National security" is mentioned 53 times in this document.

At the Fresh Wave Film Festival in 2023, rather than pull censored films from the line-up, the filmmakers decided to feature blacked out sections and muted sound during scenes that the Office for Film, Newspaper and Article Administration (OFNAA) found problematic,

displaying, adapting, and destroying historical artefacts, Ai reinstates, transforms, and also questions the value placed on objects, in a criticism of both politics and tradition"—adapted and quoted from the online collection—Ai Weiwei | Objects | M+ (mplus.org.hk).

[10] The author noticed the following artwork by Wai Pong-yu in Hong Kong's Galerie du Monde's "Living Paper Exhibition" (19.01–9.03, 2024) when she attended the gallery on 10 January 2024. In "Rhythm of Landscape 55", Wai "selected pages of the Apple Daily, which he sanded down, allowing the colours to fade and tears and holes to appear. Then, using a ruler, he drew lines with co-loured inks across the surface, the shape and fast strokes of the pen further eroding the paper. "The stories that were once part of the city's intellectual terrain have now gone", he writes. The work lies on a sheet of mesh, engendering an uneven surface. It is set on a low pedestal which is lit from below, inviting visitors to view the piece as a relic and symbol of the past", from Galerie Du Monde's notes.

apparently because the films contained "characters that struggle with the past and appear to reference the 2019 pro-democracy social movement" (Wong 2023). The festival organisers released a statement that the black images and mute sound in the film were not technical errors.

In another controversial example of censorship, the M+ Museum of Visual Culture was "ordered" to censor the name of the 1993 film *Beijing Bastards* by Chinese director Zhang Yuan (Tsui 2024; Lawson-Tancred 2024), with no specific reason given as they never detail the reasons for their decision. The film, which "was highly improvised" concerns a rock musician and his friends the 1990s and the disillusionment generally felt among young people at that time. The movie was instead screened under the title "A film by Zhang Yuan" and any mention of the original name was removed from the film's credits. Apparently, some pronunciations of "bastard" in Cantonese, sound similar to the phrase "Chief Xi" (possibly referring to Chinese leader Xi Jinping). The reason for the title change was to "highlight the filmmaker's presence in [the programme]" (Lawson-Tancred 2024). Other Chinese films in the programme were unaffected. The name thus was considered "unsuitable" rather than the contents, otherwise the entire film would have been not approved for screening. Perhaps the original title "Beijing Bastards" would suggest or perhaps "incite hatred" for government figures. However, for marketing purposes How can you sell tickets for a film without disclosing its name?" (Tsui 2024).

Funding would likely to become more problematic with the NSL, and that actors and others in "Hong Kong film companies are very afraid, and this fear shadows everything." People involved in the industry are naturally more "apprehensive about crossing unclear "red lines" concerning national security. It is not "direct suppression", but it would more or less likely make the filmmaker avoid sensitive topics (particularly political ones) (The Standard 2023). Brief glimpses of the 2019 protests in a documentary have had to be deleted. As of 2023, 21 movies and short films have had scenes cut or their release blocked since October 2021 till June 2023 (Pang 2023). The film censorship law does not apply to any films put out by the government (Chau 2023c).

Freedom of Association, Procession, and of Demonstration

Under the Basic Law of the HKSAR, the Hong Kong Bill of Rights Ordinance, as well as the National Security Law, citizens have the freedom or right to peaceful assembly and public processions in Hong Kong. Protests were banned during the Covid-19 pandemic for health reasons.

The first protest in three years authorised by the Hong Kong police took place on 26 March 2023, in Tseung Kwan O. About 80 Hongkongers marched to protest against a plan to build six public facilities on a new patch of reclaimed land southwest of the residential district. According to the Public Order Ordinance (Cap. 245), any group who wants to hold a public meeting of over 50 persons or public procession of more than 30 persons is required to notify the Commissioner of Police. Groups had to give details on their meetings or processions when they submitted their notification form. Groups also had to observe the guidelines attached to the form to ensure "good order and public safety":

> Impose Conditions/Prohibit/Object a Notified event
> The Commissioner may impose conditions upon the conduct of the public/meeting procession in the interests of national security or public safety, public order or the protection of the rights and freedoms of others, and if the commissioner chooses to do so, such conditions, together with the reason, will be communicated in writing to the organizer.[11]

The required letter of no objection[12] was issued by the police commissioner; however, this came with a long list of conditions (italics added):

> The Commissioner of Police may impose conditions upon the conduct of the public meeting/procession *in the interest of national security or public safety, public order or the protection of the rights and freedoms of others*, and if

[11] Guidance Note on Notification of a Public Meeting/Public Procession A Guide to the Public Order Ordinance, Cap 245 (https://www.police.gov.hk/info/doc/licensing/general/en/gnnp_en.pdf).

[12] These were always given during the annual 1st July processions/protests since 2003.

> the Commissioner of Police chooses to do so, such conditions, together with the reason, will be communicated in writing to the organiser;[13]

In the current case, numbers were capped at 100 and all participants were required to wear a numbered tag. Marshals were also required to march alongside the protesters in a wide circle carrying "crime scene tape". This was the designated a "protest zone" which moved as the march progressed. After the march began nobody was allowed into the zone, and reporters were also excluded from joining the march. If the tape was too loose marchers were instructed to pick it up. In addition, all posters, banners, and online materials were vetted in advance by police (showing the sensitivity of slogans as noted Chap. 3). Marchers were forbidden to wear black clothes, or yellow raincoats. Black was often worn during the 2019, the government later calling the protests "black violence", while "yellow" was the colour of 2014's OCLP/Umbrella Movement, but more specifically was a kind of intertextual reference to Marco Leung who was wearing a yellow raincoat when he fell from scaffolding at Pacific Place Mall in Admiralty in June 2019 after hanging a protest sign on top of the mall (Wong 2021).

The wearing of "number plates" seems to have been regarded as particularly controversial. A retired civil servant commented that "I am here to join a march, not a shame parade." The organiser said the arrangements were "strict", but "better than being banned from expressing our views"—this latter statement reflects the "better than nothing" acceptance that will likely to become normalised over time in such circumstances. He did not say whether he had, like other recent organisers, been warned that if any condition was breached the letter of no objection would be instantaneously voided, and the whole event would become an unlawful assembly (Hamlett 2023).

There have been warnings to organisers that they may be criminally liable if anyone breaks the law during their event. This does not seem to be the case after the author consulted a local legal scholar in a private

[13] Voter and Registration Office, n.d., p. 5. See also Notification of the Intention to hold a Public Meeting/Procession under the Public Order Ordinance, Cap. 245 (https://www.reo.gov.hk/pdf/2016lc/Public_Meeting_or_Procession(Eng).pdf).

correspondence. This similar to "real-name" requirements typically used to track people's activities in mainland China, and will likely inhibit some marches taking place, fearing official reprisals. [14] "The Hong Kong government will definitely be retaliating against participants," he said. "They may or may not prosecute them, or they could investigate them, or confiscate their travel documents" (Gao 2023).

Protests are physical actions of public concern. The greater number of participants, the greater the scope of public concern, so numbers are an important indication of this concern (after every protest march in the past "police figures" and "organizer figures" given of the number of participants. The police figures would be on the low side, while the organizers' figures would be on the high side. The reality would be somewhere in the middle). The government-run Independent Police Complaints Council (IPCC) said the conditions placed on protesters were "understandable", and said not every demonstration would necessarily be subject to the same restrictions in future. Whether badge-wearing would be mandatory for all demonstrations in future was uncertain. "After every action, the police will consider the whole process, and then they will come up with some good ideas about how things should proceed" (news.gov.hk 2023).

> We have to be careful that any public gathering will not be either hijacked or turned into troubles that will cause not just inconvenience, but risk to public order, public safety, and also national security," Lee said. "We also have to respect the rights of other people who are not involved in the public gathering, whether it is a procession or whether it is a public meeting. (RTHK 2023)

Police also defended their decision to ask participants to hang a number card around their necks.

---

[14] China has implemented comprehensive online real-name registration rules since 2012 which require Internet users to disclose their identities (real names, ID numbers and other information). Only a few countries in the world, such as South Korea, have implemented a real-name system on the Internet. (Lee and Liu 2016). In Hong Kong, the Regulation requires that, users should complete real-name registration for their SIM cards with their telecommunications service providers from 1 March 2022. This measure was to reduce the incidence of scams, although people did criticise this action. "Real-name Registration Programme for Subscriber Identification Module (SIM) Cards" Office of the Communications Authority, see: https://www.ofca.gov.hk/en/consumer_focus/guide/hot_topics/sim_registration/index.html

They further explained that the move can ensure the demonstration will proceed peacefully and orderly, citing past experiences that "outlaws" may take this opportunity to infiltrate the demonstration, disrupt public order, or even engage in violent activities. During the demonstration against the extradition bill in 2019, police deployed "raptors" (its Special Tactical Squad)—but many of them did not display any identification numbers on their uniforms (Cheng 2019). During, according to a report by the Independent Police Complaints Council, in 2019 "the Police have had to make exceptions to normal practice, to deal with what they believed to be exceptional circumstances" (IPCC, Vol. 4, Chapter 13, 1). The police explained that the "tactical outfit did not have space for display of their identification numbers" (p. 105) and provided other justifications for the practice.[15]

The top court in Hong Kong said in a 2005 case that the right to demonstrate was a fundamental right, and one of those which lay at the foundations of a democratic society. Like freedom of expression, it could be curtailed for a number of important purposes, which included public order. However, any restrictions imposed should, the court said, be "necessary in a democratic society" and "proportionate" to the danger being averted.[16]

Thus, the right to freedom of association and procession after the NSL's introduction exists in a way that extra conditions need to be met despite "letters of no objection" being issued by police. All public processions have been approved since the procession mention above, but only a few have actually taken place. For example, a Hong Kong women's group cancelled a rally night before the scheduled event ("after balancing the interests of all parties") because police said that "violent groups" sought to attend, according to the police's "risk assessment" (Chau 2023a).

[15] "Meanwhile, complaints came from the public and the press that certain plain-clothes officers had refused to show their warrant cards when requested or questioned, especially during stop and search operations. Police spokesman clarified that such practice should apply only where it was not feasible to show the warrant card. As the public expect police officers to wear identification and it is a well-known police practice (required under Police General Orders) that plain-clothes police officers in the discharge of duty do need to show their warrant cards to identify themselves, this recent departure from normal practice sparked widespread continuing concern and criticism, drawing persistent queries from the media, Legislative Council (LegCo)", p. 105.

[16] Court of Final Appeal (CFA) in a 2005 case: Leung Kwok-hung and others v HKSA. https://www.legco.gov.hk/yr06-07/english/bc/bc58/papers/bc580511cb2-1975-2-e.pdf

These serve to act as discouragements to go ahead with a protest because of worst-case scenarios posed to organisers that might affect national security and thus possible prosecution. The effect of this potential of liability serves as a disincentive to carry out mass public action. Being a place of frequent mass actions in the past, the lack of these in the present day would be likely seen and discussed by those in authority that Hong Kong is indeed now peaceful and stable.

Conclusion: Everything Endangers

The government constantly restates the importance of Article 4 in the National Security Law and clearly stipulates human rights shall be respected and protected while safeguarding national security, and that the rights and freedoms, including freedom of the press, which the residents of Hong Kong enjoy under the Basic Law and the provisions of the UN international covenants. However, we can see that "national security" permeates everything, being a "holistic concept" as if almost anything can be a potential danger.

But the "red lines" to be avoided remain vague. Journalists and the rest of society are unsure what is permissible and what might be considered a violation of national security. "In the interests of national security" becomes a catchphrase, and because national security is a holistic concept in the Chinese context, any aspect of society can endanger it. Also, something to be considered is the Hong Kong authorities appearing to be acting "over-zealously" in a bid to demonstrate their patriotic credentials, "It is the worst practice to be leftist in everything, to try to gain credit and to demonstrate loyalty to the left" commented a former Chinese People's Political Consultative Conference committee member (Lee 2024). A well-known local Hong Kong columnist stated that the "frontline bureaucrats" of Hong Kong were trained in the colonial era" and "only know how carry out orders from their superiors" (ibid.). A prominent blogger who has been both praised and criticised in mainland media, argued that Hong Kong's "excessive application" of the National Security Law was causing it to lose "its unique characteristics and "there were fears that the city had lost its attraction while being marginalized internationally" (Ma 2023). Hong Kong is thus experiencing a hybridity of forms of systems, resulting in a mixed discourse of control and freedoms that seem to be in conflict.

References

AFP. "New Hong Kong M+ Art Museum Will Not Show Ai Weiwei's Tiananmen Photo—Official". Agent France Press, March 29, 2021. https://hongkongfp.com/2021/03/29/new-hong-kong-m-art-museum-will-not-show-ai-weiweis-tiananmen-photo-official/

Chan, Bernard. "Art Censorship: Why the Hong Kong Government has no Business Playing Cultural Gatekeeper." *South China Morning Post,* March 26, 2021. https://www.scmp.com/comment/opinion/article/3126963/art-censorship-why-hong-kong-government-has-no-business-playing

Chan, Irene. "No Need for 'Fake News' Law as Long as Media Industry Practices Self-discipline, Hong Kong Leader John Lee Says." *Hong Kong Free Press,* April 13, 2024. https://hongkongfp.com/2024/04/23/no-need-for-fake-news-law-as-long-as-media-industry-practices-self-discipline-hong-kong-leader-john-lee-says

Chan, Johannes. "The Village of the Sheep Case (HKSAR v Lai Man-ling)." HKU Legal Scholarship Blog, 17 September, 2022. https://researchblog.law.hku.hk/2022/12/johannes-chan-village-of-sheep-case.html

Chau, Candice. "Explainer: Hong Kong's Sedition Law—A Colonial Relic Revived after Half a Century." *Hong Kong Free Press,* July 30, 2022a. https://hongkongfp.com/2022/07/30/explainer-hong-kongs-sedition-law-a-colonial-relic-revived-after-half-a-century/

Chau, Candice. "Renewal of Lease of Hong Kong Foreign Press Club a 'Huge Relief,' President Says, as Gov't Adds National Security Clause." *Hong Kong Free Press,* November 30, 2022b. https://hongkongfp.com/2022/11/30/renewal-of-lease-of-hong-kong-foreign-press-club-a-huge-relief-president-says-as-govt-adds-national-security-clause/

Chau, Candice. "Hong Kong Women's Group Cancels Rally Night Before demo; Police say 'Violent Groups' Sought to Attend." *Hong Kong Free* Press, March 4, 2023a. https://hongkongfp.com/2023/03/04/hong-kong-womens-group-cancels-rally-night-before-demo-police-say-violent-groups-sought-to-attend/

Chau, Candice. "Hong Kong Official Warns Against Harming Nat. Security on 'Special Occasion' as Tiananmen Crackdown Anniversary Nears." *Hong Kong Free Press*, May 29, 2023b. https://hongkongfp.com/2023/05/29/hong-kong-official-warns-against-harming-nat-security-on-special-occasion-as-tiananmen-crackdown-anniversary-nears/

Chau, Candice. "Film Censorship Law Does Not Apply to Gov't, Hong Kong Censor Says After Police Publicity Movie Shown Without Vetting." *Hong Kong Free Press*, June 26, 2023c. https://hongkongfp.com/2023/06/26/film-censorship-law-does-not-apply-to-govt-hong-kong-censor-says-after-police-publicity-movie-shown-without-vetting/

Chen, Zifei. "Censorship in Hong Kong has Led to 'War' on Libraries and Publishers." RFA Cantonese May 5, 2023. https://www.rfa.org/english/news/china/hong-kong-war-on-libraries-05052023142826.html

Cheng, Kris. "Hong Kong Activists Complain Police Failed to Display ID Numbers, as Security Chief says Uniform has 'No Room'." *Hong Kong Free Press*, June 21, 2019. https://hongkongfp.com/2019/06/21/hong-kong-activists-complain-police-failed-display-id-numbers-security-chief-says-uniform-no-room/

DoJ. In The District Court of the Hong Kong Special Administrative Region Criminal Case No 854 of 2021 - "Reasons for Verdict." Department of Justice, September 9, 2022a.

DoJ. In The District Court of the Hong Kong Special Administrative Region Criminal Case No 854 of 2021. "Reasons for Sentencing." Department of Justice, September 10, 2022b.

Gao, Feng. "Hong Kong Police Force Protesters to Wear Numbered Badges, March in Cordon." Radio Free Asia, March 27, 2023. https://www.rfa.org/english/news/china/protesters-badges-03272023124326.html

Hamlett, Tim. "Hong Kong's New Protest Regulations are Designed by Those Who Don't Like Protests." *Hong Kong Free Press,* March 31, 2023. https://hongkongfp.com/2023/03/31/hong-kongs-new-protest-regulations-are-designed-by-those-who-dont-like-protests/

HKFP. "Video: Over 180,000 Attend Hong Kong's Tiananmen Massacre Vigil, Organisers Say." *Hong Kong Free Press*, June 4, 2019. https://hongkongfp.com/2019/06/04/live-english-thousands-gather-hong-kong-candlelit-vigil-mark-30-years-since-tiananmen-massacre/

HKFP. "Explainer: Is it legal for people in Hong Kong to commemorate the Tiananmen crackdown?" *Hong Kong Free Press*, June 4, 2023. https://hongkongfp.com/2023/06/04/explainer-is-it-legal-for-hongkongers-to-commemorate-tiananmen-crackdown/

HKU Council. "HKU Council Statement on the Removal of a Statue from Campus." University of Hong Kong Council, December 21, 2021. https://www.hku.hk/press/press-releases/detail/23802.html

Ho, Kelly. "Hong Kong's John Lee Unable to Give Concrete Answer on Whether Mourning Tiananmen Crackdown is Legal." *Hong Kong Free Press*, May 30, 2023a. https://hongkongfp.com/2023/05/30/2023ahong-kongs-john-lee-unable-to-give-concrete-answer-on-whether-mourning-tiananmen-crackdown-is-legal/

Ho, Kelly. "Exclusive: Public Submit 50 Reports About Suspected 'Objectionable Content' at Hong Kong Gov't Libraries." *Hong Kong Free Press*, October 19, 2023b. https://hongkongfp.com/2023/10/19/exclusive-hongkongers-submit-50-reports-about-suspected-objectionable-content-at-public-libraries/

Huang, Lanlan, and Chen Qinging 2024 "GT Investigates: Hong Kong Journalists Association 'Fails to Represent HK Media'; Connection to Riots Raises Eyebrow." *Global Times,* July 1, 2024. https://www.globaltimes.cn/page/202407/1315203.shtml

Hui, Mary. "A Cultural Revolution 2.0 is Sweeping Through Hong Kong's Offices and Schools." *Quartz,* 22 July 2020. https://qz.com/1882496/cultural-revolution-2-0-political-repression-sweeps-hong-kong-workplaces

IFJ. "Lights Out Is this the End for Hong Kong Media? An IFJ Report on Press Freedom in Hong Kong.: International Federation of Journalists, February 2022. https://www.ifj.org/fileadmin/user_upload/IFJ_China_Report_Lights_Out_February_2022.pdf

Info.gov.hk. "Transcript of Remarks by CE at Media Session before ExCo (with video). November 8, 2022. https://www.info.gov.hk/gia/general/202211/08/P2022110800332.htm

Info.gov.hk. "HKSAR Government Strongly Disapproves of and Firmly Rejects Skewed Remarks by Foreign Countries in Name of So-called 'Media Freedom Coalition' Members Against Press Freedom in Hong Kong." December 29, 2023. https://www.info.gov.hk/gia/general/202312/29/P2023122900766.htm

Lai, Eric. "Hong Kong's Sedition Law Is Back." The Diplomat, September 3, 2021. https://thediplomat.com/2021/09/hong-kongs-sedition-law-is-back/

Lawson-Tancred, Joe. "A Controversial Film Had Its Title Censored During a Screening at Hong Kong's M+ Museum." Artnet.com, January 22, 2024. https://news.artnet.com/art-world/m-museum-censored-zhang-yuan-film-title-2421708

Lee, Jyh-An and Ching-Yi Liu. "Real-Name Registration Rules and the Fading Digital Anonymity in China." *Washington International Law Journal* 24, no. 1 (2016). https://digitalcommons.law.uw.edu/wilj/vol25/iss1/3/

Lee, James. "Nat. Security Trial for Tiananmen Crackdown Vigil Group Members to Begin November at Earliest." *Hong Kong Free Press*. February 19, 2024. https://hongkongfp.com/2024/02/19/nat-security-trial-for-tiananmen-crackdown-vigil-group-members-to-begin-november-at-earliest/

Leung, Hillary. "Hong Kong Gov't Department Told to 'Step Up' Efforts to Ensure Books Do Not Threaten National Security." *Hong Kong Free Press*, April 26, 2023. https://hongkongfp.com/2023/04/26/hong-kong-govt-department-told-to-step-up-effortsto-ensure-books-do-not-threaten-national-security/

Leung, Mimi, and Yojana Sharma. "Removing Campus Tiananmen Artworks 'Obliterates History'." *University World News*, January 5, 2020. https://www.universityworldnews.com/post.php?story=20220105094622287

Ma, Mary. "'Soft resistance' Blog Stirs Things Up." The Standard, July 24, 2023. https://www.thestandard.com.hk/section-news/section/17/254488/'Soft-resistance'-blog-stirsthings-up

News.gov.hk. "CE Addresses Public Gatherings Issue." *The Standard*, March 28, 2023. https://www.news.gov.hk/eng/2023/03/20230328/20230328_101326_683.html

OFNAA. Film Censorship Guidelines for Censors. Office for Film Newspaper and Article Administration, November 5, 2021. https://www.ofnaa.gov.hk/filemanager/ofnaa/en/content_1398/filmcensorship.pdf

Pang, Jessie. "Hong Kong Film-makers Say Censorship Law Spooks Investors, Actors." Reuters.com. June 28, 2023. https://www.reuters.com/world/china/hong-kong-film-makers-say-censorship-law-spooks-investors-actors-2023-06-28/

Smith, Adam, Charline Yim, and Marryum Kahloon. "The Crime of Sedition: At the Crossroads of Reform and Resurgence." The Trial Watch Program at Columbia Law School, Human Rights Institute, April 2022. https://hri.law.columbia.edu/sites/default/files/publications/sedition-report-april-2022.pdf

Smith, Michael. "Censorship Challenge Looms for Australian Head of New Asia Art Capital." CIMAM – International Committee for Museums and Collections of Modern Art. February 15, 2021. https://cimam.org/news-archive/censorship-challenge-looms-australian-head-new-asia-art-capital/

RTHK. "Radio Television Hong Kong "Authorities Must Stop Protests Being Hijacked: CE." March 28, 2023. https://news.rthk.hk/rthk/en/component/k2/1693894-20230328.htm/2023-03-28

The Standard. "Hong Kong Filmmakers Say Censorship Law Spooks Investors, Actors," *The Standard*, June 28, 2023. https://www.thestandard.com.hk/breaking-news-print/205343/Hong-Kong-filmmakers-say-censorship-law-spooks-investors,-actors%C2%A0

Tsui, Enid. "Hong Kong Movie Industry Body Baffled by Censors' Requirement for Film's Screening: 'How Can You Sell Tickets for a Film Without Disclosing Its Name?'. *South China Morning Post,* January 19, 2024. https://www.scmp.com/lifestyle/arts-culture/article/3249078/hong-kong-museum-has-rename-banned-chinese-film-order-screen-it

Wong, Brian. "Inquest into Death of Protester 'Raincoat Man' Begins in Hong Kong, but his Family can no Longer be Located." *South China Morning Post,* May 10, 2021. https://www.scmp.com/news/hong-kong/law-and-crime/article/3132934/inquest-death-protester-raincoat-man-begins-hong-kong

Wong, Silvia. "Hong Kong's Fresh Wave Film Festival Hit by Censorship." Screendaily.com, June 13, 2023. https://www.screendaily.com/news/hong-kongs-fresh-wave-film-festival-hit-by-censorship/5183044.article

Xi, Jinping. "Xi Jinping's Talks at the Beijing Forum on Literature and Art." chinacopyrightandmedia.wordpress.com. October 16, 2014. https://chinacopyrightandmedia.wordpress.com/2014/10/16/xi-jinpings-talks-at-the-beijing-forum-on-literature-and-art/

7

Hong Kong Democracy Activists in Self-Exile

"Most of Hong Kong's opposition are behind bars, have gone into self-exile, have quit politics or are banned" according to *Hong Kong Free Press* at the end of many of its articles about politics.

Hong Kong transformed from being a traditional shelter of mainland Chinese political exiles like Sun Yat-sen in the late Qing dynasty into a source of political fugitives itself after the anti-extradition movement and the imposition of the National Security Law. A number of local democracy activists, student leaders, and former legislators fled Hong Kong since 2020 into self-imposed exile, to escape imminent incarceration, or future prosecution. Local media estimates that more than 350 Hong Kong democracy activists have claimed asylum globally since 2018, while others have fled to safe havens such as Taiwan, which does not have an asylum law but could offer shelter (Marsh et al. 2020). They now form the basis of a what could be called a fledgling Hong Kong "Overseas Democracy Movement".

In this chapter, apart from analysing what is meant by "exile", or more appropriately, "self-exile", we will look at, briefly for comparative purposes, an overall picture of the Tiananmen exile movement after June Fourth 1989 and speculate whether the Hong Kong group could follow a

J. Eagleton, *Hong Kong's Second Return to China*,
https://doi.org/10.1007/978-3-031-84587-1_7

similar trajectory over time. This chapter will look at how some self-exiled Hongkongers first became involved in political activism, how they saw themselves vis-à-vis their homeland during their exile, the importance of their identity as Hongkongers, and relevance in their new homeland through selected media texts. How these activists continued their activism outside their homeland will also be discussed as well as their effects to harness the collectivity of the Hong Kong diaspora in those places.

Situational Background

Distrust of the Chinese Communist Party, moved by the happenings in Beijing in 1989, and fearful of possible changes to Hong Kong's systems after the 1997 handover, many Hong Kong people emigrated during the 1984 to 1997 period, seeking a foreign passport as an "insurance" policy. One parent would often stay behind (become an "astronaut") while other family members went abroad, to keep contact with Hong Kong and take a "wait and see" approach to life under Chinese rule. Many returned to Hong Kong when the status quo seemed to have been maintained. However, this changed after the introduction of the NSL, reforms to the education curriculum, and the electoral system (refer back to Chaps. 4 and 5).

A 2022 survey of recent arrivals to the United Kingdom found that "political factors" were the most significant influence on people's decision to leave Hong Kong, with more than 60 percent having no intention of returning in the foreseeable future (Tung 2024). Many did have overseas passports or a BNO (British National Overseas). Since 2019, Britain extended the BNO visa for those born before 1997, so BNO visa-holders could stay for five years and then become eligible for permanent residency, later extended to children of passport holders after 1997. Originally the BNO was a kind of British Nationality but without right of abode.[1] The new BNO conditions China says the UK has "repeatedly

[1] For types of British Nationality, see https://www.gov.uk/types-of-british-nationality; for information on the BNO visa, see https://www.gov.uk/british-national-overseas-bno-visa; visit Whatpassport.com—which gives the history of the BNO—https://www.whatpassport.com/countries/UnitedKingdom/Passport_and_Nationality/British_National_Overseas_(BNO)

manipulated the BNO issue under the pretext of the national security law in Hong Kong, and openly provided shelters for anti-China forces in Hong Kong, laying out in plain sight its hypocrisy and motive to disrupt Hong Kong" (Xinhua 2022). Many ordinary Hongkongers have taken up the offer; low-profile political activists may have also obtained a BNO passport as a "just in case" mechanism if they thought obtaining political asylum difficult.

Hong Kong political activists face difficult choices: stay in Hong Kong to face the potential risk being jailed like activist "icons" like Joshua Wong, Agnes Chow, and Jimmy Lai (two of whom are still currently in prison, Chow is in Canada), or flee to a democratic safe haven to exist in self-imposed exile far from the people and places that have been the source and inspiration of their activism. Edward Said stated of exile:

> Just beyond the frontier between "us" and the "outsider" is the perilous territory of not belonging: this is to where in a primitive time people were banished, and where in the modern era immense aggregates of humanity loiter as refugees and displaced persons. (2001, 177)

Said and others have long considered "exile" a central concept with which to deal with questions to do with distance from the homeland: displacement, disorientation (Harlem 2010), "hybrid" belongings or not belonging (Gust 2018) and identities. Said was silent on what those lingering in the zone of not belonging sometimes got up to: those in Lebanon, Iraq, or Jordan all paid heavy prices. Those in actual exile (a forcible removal from the homeland) also focus on the sadness, suffering, and loss involved in being away from family and friends without the possibility of a meeting. The experience of this displacement from the homeland, their likely alienation is in addition to what they see as what they needed to do: continue on with the political struggle started elsewhere, that had caused their exile. "Self-exile" could also be the same, if return is almost impossible for a number of reasons like potential prosecution or arrest like in Hong Kong.

Fleeing or Staying Away

There are Hongkongers who were only marginally involved in activism who flee and stay away from Hong Kong, because of uncertainty of how far over the "red line" they may have crossed given the lack of clarity of what are considered minor, serious, or grave criminal acts in the National Security Law. Take the case of Amity Chan below:

> Amity Chan watched the protests from afar as a student at the Maryland Institute College of Art in Baltimore. Not particularly politically active but angered by the scenes of police beating protesters, she created a "Lennon Wall" to give herself and other students a chance to show solidarity with the movement.
>
> I couldn't participate in person, so I used my own way to show support," she said.
>
> But there were consequences here, too. The worst was when a group of Chinese students surrounded her on campus as she handed out fliers for a protest in Washington. "They pushed me and said, 'Do you want to die?' I ran to campus security. I didn't get hit. But that experience made me feel very unsafe." (Snyder et al. 2024)

Furthermore, there is the extraterritoriality reach of the NSL and newly enacted Article 23 of the Basic Law. A Hong Kong student was arrested on her return to Hong Kong from studying in Japan for "seditious" postings on Facebook (Leung 2023). Chan is in the US waiting her asylum claim to be processed. Lack of name recognition as an activist like Chan (means little evidence like documents, photographs, or video) means it will be difficult for her to claim asylum. For asylum the UK, for example, as a Hongkonger, you must be outside the country and the person applying for asylum must demonstrate that they have a well-founded fear of persecution. In essence, this is the "credibility test" of an asylum claim.[2]

In addition to the inevitable feelings of isolation and displacement felt by those in exile, fleeing does not necessarily mean feelings of safety, and it was said in 2020 that "Western democracy doesn't guarantee safety"

---

[2] https://www.paragonlaw.co.uk/resources/hong-kong-nationals-asylum-in-the-uk

(Marsh et al. 2020); it is even more so in 2024. A number of the more prominent of the self-exiled activists, have had million-dollar bounties placed on their heads by the Hong Kong Government over alleged national security violations who should be treated according to Hong Kong's leader John Lee like "rats in the street", who "should be left alone at all costs, and who will be "pursued to the end of their days" (Cheng 2023). This kind of discourse "others" or employs the discourse of "eradication" along with other the notion that their cause has no merit due to their criminality.

Furthermore, the bounties may affect the exiles' ability to engage with members of the Chinese and Hong Kong diaspora, being a tactic to "rile up a mob mentality among pro-Beijing supporters" and to "pit people against people", which would serve to "exacerbate community tensions." Overseas organisations might also be put under pressure to question their links to activists which would threatens activists' support system outside Hong Kong (de Guzman 2023).[3]

The exiles abroad note constant surveillance, so they communicate on secure apps, and fear the slightest contact with people in Hong Kong could endanger them. Their families back in Hong Kong have been repeatedly taken in for questioning but not charged (Ho 2023). This family questioning is more about "sending a message" rather than being a regular law enforcement activity, since "If you are investigating money laundering or [organised] crimes, then you will not announce who you're going to interrogate to alert fugitives and wanted persons" (Hale 2023). This is also a technique frequently used in mainland China.

Then there is also the Qiaowu Policy (侨务) to be considered. Translated as "Overseas Chinese Affairs" or "Extra-Territorial Policies for the Overseas Chinese". This policy involves China's interactions with its diaspora; its main purpose being "to cultivate, influence, and manage ethnic Chinese as part of a global transnational project to rally support for its proponents" (To and Hua 2014).

[3]Two of the self-exiled run a current affairs commentary channel called "Tuesdayroad" on YouTube and a Patreon page, on which they monetise their content through advertisements and encourage supporters to sign up for paid subscriptions. (Wong 2024). The pair said the number of Hong Kong-based subscribers on YouTube had "dwindled to nearly zero" since police issued warrants for their arrest December 2023.

There have also been recent accusations of "secret police stations" around the globe, in place to control the actions of the overseas Chinese diaspora. Actions under this policy have caused a number of Chinese exiles (not Hongkongers) to have been persuaded or forcibly returned from Europe back to China (dos Santos 2022).[4]

There is also the exterritoriality effect of Hong Kong's National Security Law as well as the recently enacted local security law Article 23 (March 2024), extending even further the reach of the Law to places outside Hong Kong. Although, generally speaking, many Western countries have repealed extradition laws after the NSL, but these still impact on the self-exileds' global movements to some extent.

The Hong Kong government noted that even the US "abuses 'long-arm jurisdiction' and unilateral sanctions to target residents of other countries, adding that the US government's smears on the extraterritorial effect of Article 23 legislation are simply untenable" (News.gov.hk 2024). "If the legislation lacked extraterritoriality, it would amount to condoning activities threatening national security" the Hong Kong Government noted (Info.gov.hk 2023). Under the new Article 23 Security legislation, some of the exiles with bounties have had their passports cancelled (Wong 2024). The "authorities said the latest move was 'necessary' to combat and deter absconders who committed offences under the separate, Beijing-imposed national security law", whom the government described as still "colluding with external forces to protect their evil deeds" (ibid.). But the cancellations might not limit activists' ability to travel outside the UK if they hold BNO passports or other valid travel documents, but it might dissuade Hong Kong-residing supporters of activists from funding them as they can be charged with national security offences.

These exiled activists, mostly are still being activists abroad, practising what Chinese officials call "Long-distance resistance" (遠對抗), referring to any activism carried out by Hong Kong people beyond Hong Kong borders, "framing what was once normal political engagement as an imminent national security threat" (Kilpatrick 2023). Many of these

---

[4] "China has claimed the facilities are administrative hubs, set up to help Chinese expatriates with tasks like renewing their driver's licenses. China has also said the offices were a response to the Covid-19 pandemic, which had left many citizens locked down in other countries and locked out of China, unable to renew documentation" (dos Santos 2022).

self-exiled activists, according to Beijing, continue to oppose the government from their new bases abroad, beyond the reach of national security police. It was obvious to Beijing that the "opposition" would not simply "go quiet and go into hiding." On the contrary, they would "study the law thoroughly" and become "more and more sophisticated" in how they express dissent (Kilpatrick 2023). The National Security Laws' inability to neutralise critics abroad was considered a legal "loophole" waiting to be plugged. Writing those amendments to the city's Crimes Ordinance regarding seditious intent do not specify their extraterritoriality in all provisions, and it was argued that supplementary local legislation (Article 23) "could clarify that all provisions have extraterritorial effects."[5] These aspects would likely have an impact on the emotions and actions of Hong Kong activists living abroad.

There have been a group of Chinese activists who have experienced displacement and exile for over 40 years, and they could pose lessons for how Hong Kong's self-exiled by looking at the similarities and differences.

The Post-Tiananmen Chinese Overseas Democracy Movement

The Chinese Overseas Democracy Movement is a loose collection of individuals and organisations who have been trying to promote Chinese democracy from locations outside of China since June 1989 (Nathan 1993). After the crackdown on dissent in 1989, activists who had fled China could be summed up in the following paragraph:

> The activists and their Western supporters anticipated that millions of dollars would be donated by sympathetic individuals and foundations in the West. The exile appeared constantly in the news. They were lionized as symbols of the people's heroism. They were showered with book contracts and lecture invitations, and had to get agents. (Nathan 1993, 316)

[5] For FAQs about Article 23, see https://www.sb.gov.hk/eng/bl23/faq.html

Immediately post June Fourth 1989, there was universal condemnation by Western nations of what happened in Beijing; this was followed by economic and diplomatic sanctions against China. There was enormous sympathy for exiled activists and overseas Chinese students at large. There was the Pelosi Bill that protected the status of Chinese students and scholars in the US, and most-favoured nation trading privileges became linked to Human rights. However, over time, rivalry, competition, and corruption amongst various exile groups in the US, for example, saw splits in the movement.

Chen Jie, a noted scholar of the Tiananmen exile movement, on whose work this section is based (Chen 2014, 2016, 2018) attributed the rivalry and competition of the activists mainly to the beliefs formed and attitudes due to their early political education. The activists held an idealistic view of democracy, a system they had not experienced in their homeland. While overseas they were immersed in democracy, but the legacies of education in communist political culture, which tended to see matters in terms of black and white heavily influenced their youth. Thus, they saw the political world in a black-or-white fashion, unable to reconcile differing views in an open-minded manner.

The Soviet Union and Eastern Europe initially exerted a positive influence over China's slightly more liberal opening for a time, but the resultant social turmoil, and economic hardship in post-Soviet Russia and other Eastern European states scared China and the Chinese people out of enthusiasm for democracy. Second, when economic reform in China accelerated under Deng who replaced virulent ideology with economic promises after 1989, many new business activities emerged. By the late 1990s, the rapidly growing Chinese economy exerted an effect on Western nations, resulting in diminishing support for the Tiananmen exiles or the cause of Chinese democratisation at large.

Chapter 3 in Chen Jie's 2019 book *The Overseas Chinese Democracy Movement: Assessing China's Only Open Political Opposition* (Chen 2019) presents a more positive assessment of the movement by highlighting and analysing the trends which have emerged or strengthened from about the second decade of the twenty-first century, that reshaped the movement. These have been characterised by new and more diverse forms of activism, all the way from creating political parties (the author has identified eight of them) or NGOs, to human rights advocacy work and cultural or scholarly activities aimed at countering the growing assertiveness of the CCP's political narrative abroad. Many had also gone into business. Chen concludes that the longer the exile, the stronger the home country has become in the minds of the exiles, and the more difficult it is for any overseas opposition movement to remain relevant.

Many activists feel that efforts to promote democracy in China from abroad have been unsuccessful, and many have grown disconnected from the country where they grew up, the Tiananmen incident itself has been wiped from historical memory by censorship and propaganda, becoming the "The People's Republic of Amnesia" (to borrow the title of a 2015 book by Louisa Lim) on the impact of the Tiananmen crackdown on China since 1989. Many of those who did stay in China and tried to continue the struggle were neutralised with one former Tiananmen activist, Nobel Peace Prize laureate Liu Xiaobo, dying in custody in 2017.

Rowena He's case studies of a number of exiles in her book. *Tiananmen Exiles: Voices of the Struggle for Democracy in China* (2014) show the difficulties that the exiles had in adjusting to their new homeland language-wise, culturally, workwise and politically. The evolution of these student leaders' political philosophies from being critics of the Chinese Government to critics of US domestic and foreign policy is particularly interesting as later in the chapter will show, the involvement of Hong Kong exiles in their new homeland have been heavily involved in mobilising the Hong Kong diaspora through not only cultural links but links with issues in the new homeland in order to further their political causes. The Tiananmen exiles decades on from their original struggle still yearn a return to the land of their birth, some refusing to become naturalised citizens, seeing this as a betrayal of the homeland. He's book also follow the Tiananmen exiles through their continual search for identity over three decades; Hongkongers seem already sure of their identity (this will become apparent later), but fear it will disappear in the homeland after the National Security Law's implementation and the rise in dominance of the discourse of the "One Country" rather than the "Second System".

The Hong Kong Self-Exiled

Our perception of the world stems from our "habitus", that is, our history, which is influenced by our social and cultural environment as well as our historical context. It is a set of acquired patterns of thought and behaviour that determines actions. These patterns (or "dispositions") are carried over through social change and of course are realised in discourse. Given the reflexive reaction holding between social change and discourse change (Fairclough 1995, 96), the actors of that discourse (Goffman 1973), the Hong Kong self-exiled, may be regarded in some sense as spokespersons of this social change as they "battle for public opinion" vis-à-vis actors, Hong Kong public, the Hong Kong Government, and later the world, first when they were in the homeland and then when then in the place of exile—their location—their "field" has changed.

A field, according to Bourdieu (1991) is a setting in which agents and their social positions are located. The position of each particular agent in the field is a result of interaction between the specific rules of the field, the agent's habitus and the agent's capital (social, economic, cultural) in that particular "marketplace". Participants use this "symbolic capital" in the "linguistic marketplace" to negotiate a specific gain. During the 2019 protests, those involved in activism gained much capital with a large sector of the population (but not all); with the National Security Law in place, their linguistic and cultural capital "become obsolete and lose in value…with regards to acting structures" (Bourdieu 1991, 43ff) because what they could discuss was now officially illegal, specifically "liberate Hong Kong, revolution of our times". However, capital, has a certain value in this "marketplace of values" (Calhoun et al. 2003).

The activist's symbolic capital as "freedom fighters" has increased on the global stage, but even less than previously on decreased on the Beijing and Hong Kong Government stages. Fields interact with each other, and are hierarchical (with subordination to the larger field of power). Like Wodak's (2001) "fields of action", the field also includes textual and discursive elements that interact with the wider socio-political marketplace (of symbolic capital) and of intersecting discourses. These activists, now in self-exile, have a more diverse "fields of action" (such as government forums, the US Congress, the United Nations and so on)—for the Hong Kong audience back home, but also for the world. For example, when the—but the global spectacle—they seem to be drawn out for comment whenever the Hong Kong does something controversial—such as the recent Article 23 enactment and the cancellation of passports, which both occurred in 2024.

The self-exiles" habitus have been shaped by certain "foundation moments" regarding certain central events in Hong Kong's past have forged their political ideologies. This shows the importance of historical background and their relation to the "foundation moments" of Hong Kong politics pre-1919 and pre-NSL. For activists born just before or just after the handover in 1997, who have lived in relative freedom to speak their minds, have less ties to the mainland and less linkages to the "old democratic guard"—the latter who chiefly focused on changing China, overturning the verdict on June Fourth 1989 as well as the "one-party" system on the China mainland. The lack of democratic reform over time and the rise of "localism" (Kwong 2016; Lam 2018) because of frustration with the lack of progress using "traditional activism" ultimately lead to the "static" Occupy Central/Umbrella Movement and then to the "fluid" anti-extradition protests.

Carmen Lau has been a community organiser for the Hong Kong diaspora in the UK and work on Hongkongers civil society overseas. She co-organises Hong Kong March, an annual UK-wide Hong Kong cultural month, and Vote for Hong Kong 2024, a campaign aiming to mobilise Hongkongers to vote in the election. She is also currently serving on the Leadership Council of the World Liberty Congress.

Frances Hui is the policy and advocacy coordinator for the Committee for Freedom in Hong Kong Foundation and other groups (italics added):

> My story starts when I was 10 years old and I saw a documentary on TV about the Tiananmen Square Massacre. I saw soldiers shooting at unarmed citizens and driving tanks into the crowd. I saw students, covered in blood on makeshift stretchers, rows of bodies covered in sheets, and a man curled up on the sidewalk in the fetal position with his skull cracked open. It's shocking no matter how old you are, but especially as a 10-year-old. So, I went to the annual vigil on June 4th. *Hong Kong was the last place in China*

> *that could honor the victim.* It was my first experience seeing people freely gathered to express themselves. *And it left a profound impression on me about freedom of speech and freedom of assembly, both values that define Hong Kong yet cease to exist in mainland China.*
>
> Speech given at the 15th Annual Geneva Summit for Human Rights and Democracy, UN. Opening, Tuesday, May 16, (Hui 2023)

The fact that Hong Kong was the only place where the crackdown was commemorated was considered significant to Lau and others in her cohort. Hong Kong authorities often mentioned Hong Kong's "core values" of freedom of speech, of assembly and openness. The difference to mainland China was key to Lau. Seeing these freedoms being potentially compromised during the discussions about the proposed extradition law, she became active in the 2019 protest movement.

Finn Lau co-founded the groups Hong Kong Liberty and Stand with Hong Kong, which work to "liberate Hong Kong". For Lau it was a strong memory from his schooldays:

> It was 1999, two years after the handover, and a primary school teacher was telling students about Beijing's *now-breached promise* to keep Hong Kong's way of life unchanged for 50 years. Lau, then aged six, raised his hand to ask the teacher: "What happens after 50 years?" (Wong 2020)

Here, Lau's teacher had likely voiced her opinion that Hong Kong's way of life had changed and that promises had not been kept. Hong Kong had an unlikely hope: that its future would remain its past. We are not told if the teacher answered the young Lau's question. At six, he probably would not really comprehend a comprehensive answer. Note the significance of the young age of Hui and Lau in their political awakening.

Nathan Law is based in London. During 2014's Umbrella Movement, he was one of five representatives who took part in dialogue with the government about political reform. In 2016, Law, Joshua Wong, and others founded Demosistō, a pro-democracy political party, and ran for the Legislative Council election, where Law was elected the youngest ever legislative councillor. However, his seat was overturned in July 2017 following Beijing's constitutional reinterpretation, and Law was later jailed for his role in the Umbrella Movement.

> It was not until I learned about the story of the Tiananmen massacre in high school and the story of dissident human rights activist Liu Xiaobo that I had the idea that, well, maybe it's time for me as a young person to step up and to fight for something that I think is really important to Hong Kong people. So, when I was in college, I ran for the student union; I became the representative of it. Then the Umbrella Movement took place in my term so that I became the student leader and became a public figure. (De Groot 2022)

Again, learning about the Tiananmen crackdown and one Tiananmen protester remained behind in China, Liu Xiaobo, appealed to his youthful idealism and spurred him on to become active in civil society at a young age. Nathan Law could be said to be the most prominent and well-known of the Hong Kong exiles.

Huen Lam is the Senior Communications Associate of Hong Kong Democracy Council (HKDC), where she develops media campaigns, undertakes community building, and maintains political contacts at various levels.

> Lam had grown up in a Hong Kong where protests were not uncommon. She has vague memories of demonstrations in 2002 against initial efforts to limit speech through a national security law, an early effort to pass Article 23 and for protesters a rare success. In 2012, demonstrators rallied against curriculum changes that would promote "patriotic education." Lam attended university lectures to learn about the different points of view. In 2014, as the Umbrella protests called for universal suffrage, Lam was old enough to take part in the discussions. Her high school allowed students to skip class and made the auditorium available for debate. (Snyder et al. 2024)

Possibly the cumulative effect of protests before Lam was of a sufficient age to understand the reason for them eventually led her to become educated about them, and therefore wanting to become involved. Note that her high school allowed students to skip class and to make school premises available for students to discuss political topics. Note that the national security guidelines for teachers discussed in Chap. 5 prevent any discussion of political views at all within the school campus.

Topics of Voices in Exile

Interviews and videos of activists in self-exile were gleaned from various sources, both of prominent activists and others less. Where possible, direct quotes will be given; otherwise reported/indirect speech excerpt where a direct quote was not found. A number activists quoted had "bounties" on their heads and were accused of or had been accused or convicted of "inciting secession" or "collusion with foreign forces" under the National Security Law or the colonial ordnance of sedition; crime that can carry heavy sentences. The following themes were found, each represented by a number of examples.

Reaction to Bounties on Heads

Reaction to having bounties put on the heads of the self-exiled can be summed up as enabling them to become more determined to continue the struggle; this is taken as a sign that Beijing and Hong Kong consider them important:

> My response to the Chinese Communist regime's intimidation is short: I will never be silenced, I will never back down. – Joey Siu Nam (Chen 2023)

> Being hunted by China (Hong Kong)'s secret police, under a one-million-dollar bounty, is a lifelong honor. – Simon Cheng (Bloomberg 2023)

> They are, you know, giving me more reason to fight on … – Anna Kwok (Pomfret and Pang 2023)

> This calculated move seems to attach a price tag to my life as well as my unwavering quest for democracy – Finn Lau (DW Stories on Facebook)

Attitude to the Struggle

Perhaps "slow and steady" would achieve results as the image of "water dripping on a rock" was what Kwong used to describe her lobbying efforts. She is obviously seeing results which encourages her to continue her work.

> Kwong believes in the power of persistent lobbying, like "water dripping on a rock," noting that four years of effort by Hong Kong advocates have succeeded in deepening awareness and concern over Hong Kong in European political circles, and vowing to continue her activities despite the new legislation. – Glacier Kwong (Chen 2024)

> If those of us who are not dead or arrested continue to participate in the democratic movements of other countries and use democracy to fight back against Chinese invasion, infiltration and United Front activities, that will become the basis for the liberation of Hong Kong – Lo Tzu-wei (Chen 2024).

Lo Tzu-wei implies that those who are free are obligated to keep on with the struggle for democracy will eventually achieve something. It does not seem to be a fast task. He seems to follow the "water dripping on a rock" philosophy of eventual success; although this seems to be a rather utopian mindset.

Sense of Guilt: Failure/Family

"For us the younger politicians, we got into politics because we saw hope that Hong Kong might have a chance to be a democratic society one day. But within a year, the government's attitude had changed"; "Moving to a new country or settling in a new country is one thing, but I think the bigger challenge is that we face a failure, and we need time to recover". – Carmen Lau (Lau 2022)

Carmen Lau acknowledges failure of the protest movement with the introduction of the National Security Law; that what is needed now is a time of thinking strategically about future plans before proceeding to physical action. Glacier Kwong below feels guilt as her leaving Hong Kong has repercussions for her family left behind. She acknowledges harassment, which could involve family members being questioned by police, being followed, or threats from unnamed sources.

"The biggest pressure I've faced over the years is worrying about the impact my choices might have on the people close to me", "I chose this path to help advocate for Hong Kong, but my friends and family didn't choose it. They've been dragged into it, and have faced quite a bit of harassment." – Glacier Kwong (Chen 2024)

Some of those in exile like Lo Tzu-wei choose to cut ties with their families to avoid them being harassed by police or others.

> He is prepared to consider cutting off all contact with his family, for their own protection. – Lo Tzu-wei (Chen 2024)

> "I keep asking myself what I'm going to do here in England, an elected politician [from Hong Kong]." "It's a question I hardly dare to answer, because I feel as if I have let down the people who voted for me by leaving." – Yau Man-chun (Yam and Wang 2022)

Yau Man-chun feels guilt that as an elected official that he had fled Hong Kong, leaving behind those who could not flee. He feels cut off from his work and lost in England, yet to find his role in his new homeland. The following is another typical expression of leaving those who are paying the penalty for what Lam is avoiding by fleeing Hong Kong.

> There's a huge need in the Hong Kong community," "I always felt like Hong Kong was my home, but it doesn't really hit until you leave. "There's a sense of longing." "I was dealing with anxiety about the future and guilt of leaving," she said. "I have friends who are in jail who I won't be able to see anymore"—Huen Lam (Snyder et al. 2024).

The Need to Preserve Hong Kong Culture

It is clear that culture and the preservation of Hong Kong's identity is a major issue for those in exile. Getting rid of the Hong Kong identity means adopting another one that fits in more deeply with mainland China's norms and ideology as well as erasing the events of the recent past with a different, official narrative. The first two quotes below reflect this view. This topic will be dealt with more fully later in the chapter.

> It's clear that the government is trying to erase protest memory by banning the movies and arts. As we are now living overseas, it's crucial for us to preserve them, as well as our culture and identity. These are our weapons to fight against the authoritarianism. – Nathan Law (Lau 2022)

> He has put culture high on the list of the community's priorities. After all, observers say, China's ruling Communist party would like nothing more than for Hong Kong's democrats in exile to forsake their identity and dissolve into innocuous English exile – Nathan Law (Lau 2022)

About Unity

Unity of the Hong Kong exile is "not a given" according to Nathan Law. Many Hongkongers have moved to Britain after the introduction of the National Security Law under the BNO passport and visa scheme, not just activists in self-imposed exile. "Talk of politics" is not common as opening up about your views to a strange of unknown political allegiance could result in awkwardness ore retaliation.

> Hong Kongers is wary of each other because of potential clashes over political allegiance. The fact that someone has come to Britain does not necessarily mean that they are in the prodemocracy camp, since the new British BNO visa is not a refugee scheme, which means that there's no political assessment on applicants. For many who've arrived, the most pressing concerns focus on integration and the practicalities of life. Indeed, many of the new arrivals who try to engage one another by joining groups on Facebook and WhatsApp are quick to realize that any talk of politics would be the exception, not the norm. – Nathan Law (Lau 2022).
>
> "When we meet up, we only talk about which restaurants to go to, where to do shopping or look for a nice flat. No one feels safe enough to share political thoughts with strangers who've just known each other," said Carol, a recent migrant who works in the tech industry. "There's a lot of mutual suspicion." (Lau 2022)

Although activists in Britain continue in their advocacy and work with the Hong Kong diaspora in Hong Kong, care is needed not to have infiltration into the course. Because of the Qiuwu policy mentioned earlier, there is a fear or forcible extraction back to Hong Kong or the Mainland.

The Self-Exiled as Political Activists Abroad

"Activism by exiles of various ideological and religious strands has been a salient mover and shaper of political life in the modern world, if not since ancient times" (Shain 1988, 387). Sun Yat-sen once declared that "Huaqiao [overseas Chinese] are the mother of revolution" due to the fact that his campaign was carried out and supported by overseas Chinese communities under the himself, a long-term exile. This saying, in various forms, serves to use it as an "umbilical cord" connecting the Chinese diaspora with its motherland, in particular as regards to politics (Huang 2011).

"The fight for Hong Kong's democratic freedoms is so hamstrung at home" that most activists agree it must also happen from abroad (Marsh et al. 2020). This involves lobbying, rallying, and keeping the ties with Hong Kong Cantonese culture together in community.

The movement is unable to directly compel the political regime of the SAR to change. In particular, due to the revised electoral law, any external support for domestic opposition is futile to tip the balance of election results, although the exiles can call for boycott of elections as they did with the Legislative Council elections in December 2021 in which they were roundly condemned by the Hong Kong Government. On the other hand, capitalising on the international uproar over the events of 2019–2020, the exiles have exerted clear impact on the host states' Hong Kong policy through intense lobbying activities.

In the realm of civic politics, the exiles have been making broader and potentially more enduring impact. Here individual activists and a multitude of organisations play diverse niche roles in continuing their activism. By engaging with the media, international NGOs (such as *Hong Kong Watch* based in Britain) and staging various awareness-raising events, the exiles have proactively mounted information and publicity campaigns to maintain the international memory of what has happened in their homeland and kept the international community informed of the incidents of repression as they unfold.

Reviving a distinct Hong Kong cultural sphere will likely sustain the democracy movement, but also provide an "educational window" for the host societies. The increasing integration with the cities of the Greater Bay Area (Macau, Zhuhai, and Shenzhen) and the increasing migration of people mass inflow of mainlanders fill the gaps created by mass departure of professionals from Hong Kong.

Building a Hong Kong Community Overseas

Building a Hong Kong community overseas seems to be one of the most prominent projects of the exiles (and ordinary Hongkongers abroad as well), not only to keep their traditional culture alive, but to stop from being the ideology of the freedoms promised to them in the Basic Law, the NSL, and the UN covenants, but in effect diluted and compromised by the NSL in practice open in the new homeland.

Hongkongers have organised protests in Manchester, Bristol, and Birmingham to show support for jailed pro-democracy supporters back home. New groups have been formed teaching "Hong Kong-style Cantonese" and screening (made and banned in Hong Kong) documentaries about the 2019 protests. A news presenter who used to work for Hong Kong's largest broadcaster set up a YouTube channel with Cantonese news about Britain (Lau 2022). The British government also offered funds to campaigners providing assistance and counselling services to recent migrants from Hong Kong.

In the UK, Carmen Lau decided to "package" Hong Kong's political issues in the form of a cultural festival, not just lobby for government change at the ballot box which may bore voters. By being more "leisure-focused and cultural, so local people and non-Hong Kongers would welcome it more (Loi and Chen 2023); "We want to highlight this Hong Kong identity in a number of different ways, and we want to be recognized as Hong Kongers in the international community and by the people of different countries" (ibid.). More importantly this double-pronged approach is to "remember who they are" and why they are doing it. "Everything we do is to go home". "If we can't forge an identity for ourselves that is distinct from a Chinese or an Asian identity, then everything we do will have been in vain" (ibid.).

A common means of these activists is to link Hong Kong's issues with direct relevance to local issues in the new homeland. Ted Hui, a former lawmaker now in Australia is trying to make loss of Hong Kong's promised freedoms an issue for Australian politicians. "Hong Kong isn't a big issue in Australian politics, while China policy and trade are very important to Australians"; "They are also very concerned about regional security and China's soft-power infiltration." Hui said he is trying to show Australians how the struggle of the Hong Kong people for freedom and democracy is closely bound up with Australia's China policy. [We want] to show people the true nature of the Chinese Communist Party through the lens of Hong Kong's situation (Loi and Chen 2023).

In Taiwan, Sky Fung, secretary-general of the Taiwan-based exile group Hong Kong Outlanders, there has been a similar need to link the suppression of freedom and democracy in Hong Kong with the potential loss of Taiwan's democratic way of life, should China try to block or invade the Island who it sees as its territory (Loi and Chen 2023). "There has been a long process of conversion here since 2019, when Hong Kong's local politics gradually shifted people's focus to

Taiwan's domestic politics,"

"Our organization doesn't just explain what happened in Hong Kong in the past, but has shifted into focusing on Taiwan's policies as they relate to Hong Kong." This is likely a wise strategy to keep pace with the changing situation in the new homeland to keep relevant by showing connections.

Two interesting case studies, one in the United States and one in the United Kingdom, the two major locations where there are large populations of Hongkongers that reflect on what the activists see as the need to keep a consistent Hong Kong identity in the diaspora to influence and impact the host society, and hopefully have some influence on the situation in their homeland.

We The Hongkongers

"We The Hongkongers" (https://www.wethehongkongers.org - all the following quotations come from this website) is an initiative devoted to

Hongkonger identity and Hong Kong culture, set up by Frances Hui, one of the exiled. It is "committed to strengthening the Hongkonger identity and promoting the Hong Kong culture among the communities in the U.S." The group's website stresses the importance of coordination between locals in the US and resident Hongkongers, and acknowledges how passes of congressional acts in the US and sanctions have helped raise the profile of issues important to Hong Kong, particularly since 2019. In the background section on the group's website, the US Constitution is invoked:

> The clause "We The People" is also known as the name of the White House petition platform, which is a right guaranteed by the First Amendment. It became an agent to empower the voice of the American public to demand change from the government. In addition, the platform "We The People" provides an opportunity for like-minded people to form communities and to discuss ways to make changes on certain issues.

The connection between the contents of the US Constitution is obviously being made by juxtaposing "We The people" and "We The Hongkongers"; note the capitalisation of "The" in both phrases (it is not written that way in the US Constitution). The "The" in "We The Hongkongers" indicate a *specific group* of Hongkongers—the Hong Kong diaspora in the United States.

> *We The Hongkongers*" is all about the same concept. We hope to follow the footsteps of the framers to safeguard the dignity and freedom of Hongkongers. On the pathway to pursue democracy for our city and freedom for our people, it is essential for us to sustain the identity of Hongkongers by forming a community and promoting the culture of the city both inside and out of the land.

This is invoking the discourse of the founding of the US state and the prominent role that "freedom" and "liberty" had played in its history. In the first ten years after the Hong Kong handover, 1960s civil rights discourse was constantly invoked by those in the democratic camp. At that time, democrats focused on the "tenacity" of the democratic struggle, and the long distance from the "democratic dream" promised to them. Posters on the "Lennon Walls" of Occupy Central/Umbrella Movement and the 2019 anti-extradition law also invoked 1960s American civil right discourse (Martin Luther King's "dream" and Rosa Parks bus action were all seen as equivalent to Hongkongers' struggle at the time.[6]

Wanting specific recognition in the US, the group came up with a "Write In" campaign for the 2020 US Census.[7] On the census form there were around four categories of Asians, one of which was "Chinese". There was also the category of "other Asian" with a question above it "What is your race?" Hongkongers were encouraged to write in "Hongkonger" given that was not an available option to select:

> If we have the official number on record, the representation of our community would be strengthened and it will benefit: policymakers to make relevant decisions and proposals Hong Kong-related congressional advocacy the Hongkonger community to show our social significance to the U.S. society.

Unfortunately, this campaign was unsuccessful and "Hongkonger" did not end up as a category in the released census data:

> Today, we regret to learn that the U.S. Census Bureau has failed to reflect distinct data of Hongkongers in the newly released 2020 Census Data of "Detailed Demographic and Housing Characteristics File A," despite concerted efforts from the Hong Kong community to distinguish our identity.

Despite "Among the 41 race groups in the Asian category, 18 of them are newly admitted and are available on the decennial report for the first time. Yet Hongkongers or any specific statistics representing the Hong Kong population in the U.S. continue to be missing and counted towards the

[6] This was noted in the author's unpublished PhD thesis: "'The Ultimate Aim': Discourse of Democratization in Post-handover Hong Kong", Department of Linguistics, Macquarie University, Sydney, 2012.

[7] https://www.wethehongkongers.org/2020census

Chinese group," noting that "Hong Kong heritage in America Hong Kong heritage in America can be traced back to 1965 as Hong Kong migrants settled in the U.S. after the passage of the Immigration and Nationality Act."

> We sincerely encourage the Census Bureau to conduct research and consultation with experts and stakeholders on the history of cultural heritage and the significance of Hongkongers as they proceed in understanding the demographic of this nation. We The Hongkongers will continue its mission to promote the distinct identity and culture of Hongkongers in the U.S., as well as to amplify the interest of our Hong Kong community.

This could be seen as a reaction against becoming part of a "monolithic" identity of being "Chinese" subsumed over an overarching Chinese identity where China mainland would likely be invoked, rather than more specifically a "Hongkonger" (italics added) with its own unique culture:

> As the repressive rule of the Chinese Communist Party intensifies its effort in forcing Hong Kong people and other ethnic communities into *adopting the Chinese identity*, it has become increasingly important for Hongkongers to assert our identity free *from any political and false representation*. In order to promote racial diversity across the nation, the U.S. should make an effort to *recognize the cultural heritage of Hongkongers and provide an accurate picture of the demographic*, as the American people rely on the data to better understand the communities among us.—Frances Hui, Executive Director of We The Hongkongers

By asserting identity "free from any political and false representation", Frances Hui is saying to the Hong Kong Government and to the Beijing Governments, that they are first and foremost "Hongkongers" and as such, have their own views of what is best for them. And by being recognised as a large bloc of voting residents in the US, with the potential to have an effect on the ballot box, issues relevant to the Hong Kong community would able to be heard. This is also the case in Britain, with BNO passport holders who number in the hundreds of thousands.

Still Performing Democratic Acts

Although Hongkongers could be considered "fully British" as BNO passport holders, those who have moved to the UK under the scheme are able to vote unlike other migrants (those with just a BNO visa cannot vote). It is estimated that approximately 140,000 BNO Hongkongers will be eligible to vote in the July 2024 British general election. Since politics is the reason why Hong Kong activists and ordinary people moved to the UK post 2019, it is interesting to see how they react and respond to it. Hong Kong has never been a "full", rather it has been a limited one of sorts. The Umbrella Movement, mass demonstrations, widespread arrests, and further limiting of democratic rights under the National Security Law in 2020 had its origins in campaigns for full, rather than the existing partial voting rights from the time of the handover in 1997. The 2024 British election might be the first "full" election for some.

"Being a pro-democracy activist is increasingly self-isolating and marginalised. We've found it harder and harder to get in touch with the mass public to tell them that they are relevant to bringing democracy back to our society" said Simon Cheng, a former British consulate staffer in Hong Kong who was granted asylum in the UK in 2020 (Quach 2023). However, with a sizable Hong Kong diaspora in Britain, it makes sense for activists mobilise Hongkongers residing in Britain to register to vote or to help to canvass votes. Thus, "The UK is where the Hong Kong diaspora can truly participate in local politics, unlike other countries where Hong Kongers cannot easily take an active part on the political scene" (Cheng 2024).

The organisation "Hongkongers in Britain" was founded by self-exiled Simon Cheng and is part of a collective of Hong Kong-related civil society groups that launched the "Vote for Hong Kong 2024" campaign (https://www.vote4hk.uk) especially focusing on voting in marginal seats with a high Hongkonger population. Voting in the British election had a two-fold action of integrating into the new homeland and pursuing advocacy of their rights and interests, which would be dealing and negotiating with the Hong Kong government about its security law and getting better conditions for their residency in Britain, thus Hongkongers in Britain were urged to vote:

> Voting is everyone's civic duty in a democracy. Additionally, participating in the democratic process is an indispensable part for recently arrived Hongkongers to integrate into British society and safeguard their rights and interests. (https://vote4hk.uk)

> We implore everyone to cast their votes, even without a preferred candidate. While a single vote may seem trivial, collectively, they send a powerful message. By voting, Hongkongers will ensure that British politicians will take note of their collective demands and uphold their rights. (https://vote4hk.uk)

There are some issues that affect the Hongkonger vote specifically. Many worry about the worsening situation in Hong Kong and about family who still live there. They want assurance that a future government will commit to the BNO scheme. Conservatives say they will maintain the BNO visa scheme, while the Liberal Democrats' manifesto pledges to close gaps in the BNO visa scheme and to extend integration funding for Hongkongers. Labour's manifesto also expresses support for Hongkongers in the UK.[8]

> All political parties in the UK should take note of this significant new cohort of voters from Hong Kong who have never before voted in a General Election. Voter registration is high among this cohort and we urge all parties to listen to the needs of Hong Kongers in the UK and back these with clear policies. (Hong Kong Watch 2024)

Sam Goodman, Hong Kong Watch's Director of Policy and Advocacy noted: "At the time of writing (22 November 2023) this research there were at least two ministers who stand to lose their jobs if they do not gain the support of the Hong Kong BNO community at the next election" because of a large concentration of Hongkongers in these electorates. If parties offer a solid policy platform for new arrivals from Hong Kong, they would likely help parties pick up key target seats across the UK" (Hong Kong Watch 2023).

---

[8] https://ukandeu.ac.uk/general-election-2024-what-are-hong-kong-bno-voters-looking-for/ "There are also very specific changes which Hong Kongers would like to see from a prospective government. These are first, action on the Mandatory Provident Fund, the Hong Kong contributory pension scheme which currently cannot be accessed by Hong Kongers living in the UK."

"By voting, Hongkongers will ensure that British politicians will take note of their collective demands and uphold their rights." Hongkongers will perform various roles in the election, some will simply be voters, other will be lobbying for certain Hong Kong issues to be put on the agenda, and others will devote their time to working for a particular candidate. This might have a downside for the UK Hong Kong community; there is little appetite for global adventurism in modern UK—which has many problems of its own.

For Richard Wong, 25, who moved to Britain from Hong Kong in 2022, it "feels strange" taking part in a free election, exercising exactly rights that he once fought for, knowing that people back home in Hong Kong cannot do so. They can vote, but the choices are now more limited to those who are vetted by committee to be "patriots" (John 2024).

> Back in Hong Kong we tried so hard to get democracy and then lost it. And I moved here, and we are actually *practicing democracy, but in a very different context*," said Wong, who has been knocking on doors as a volunteer for an opposition Labour party candidate in next month's UK general election.
>
> "I still have friends spending their time in prison and I'm … doing this at the other end of the world."
>
> I know the power of votes. I think if we have that power we should utilise it," said Carmen Lau, a campaign coordinator for Vote for Hong Kong 2024, a group rallying Hong Kongers in the UK to participate in the British election. (John 2024)

While eager to have the "power to vote" many are still worried that they will be targeted by pro-Beijing or other groups for their actions. Lau noted at cultural events many attendees wore masks and avoided cameras because they were afraid repercussions for their family back in Hong Kong but still emphasize that the "right to vote is "precious" (John 2024).

Perhaps this involvement of those exiled and other Hongkongers who left Hong Kong because they disagreed with the changes brought about by the National Security, will serve to integrate both groups so that there is a synergistic effect on their lobbying and advocacy work as well as maintaining Hong Kong culture. In addition, seeing how elections work in a full democracy will better prepare Hongkongers to understand the reality of democracy on the ground rather than theoretically which they often had to do in the homeland.

Conclusion: Thinking of Home While Away

How Hong Kong's overseas democracy movement will develop is hard to predict at this point.

They are likely, for example, to remain active in British (and to a lesser extent in US) politics as the UK Hong Kong diaspora is of a significant size and likely to grow bigger and thus will be able to have an effect on politics in that place. Integrating Hong Kong issues and making them relevant with issues in the new homeland (wherever that is) is probably crucial in maintaining interest in their cause. Or this may have the unintended consequence of actually generating general opposition to it.

This group will likely continue to work on building up and maintaining Cantonese culture while away to counteract the mainlandisation of society and its culture back home as well as telling their story of the Hong Kong of 2019 since the official narrative of that time differs from that of those now in exile. Their focus might increasingly be on the Hong Kong diaspora who as a mass group can lobby for actions against the Hong Kong Government that will hopefully make society better in their homeland.

A major potential challenge lies not in "internal disunity" as factional tension and endemic infighting among the ranks of dissidents and democracy organisations been shown in the post-Tiananmen exiles (Shain 1988) because there is no overarching single collective of Hongkongers in exile. There seems to be a number of different organisations that have separate and complementary purposes. However, the effect of bounties, the "Qiuwu Policy", and Hong Kong's various security laws with their extraterritorial reach will necessitate the exiles to be vigilant about safety for themselves and their loved ones back home.

The second potential major challenge is that there is no guarantee of persistent international or Western focus on Hong Kong, which depend on the dynamics of the broader geopolitical environment and self-interests of the host states, which are vital conditioning factors for all cases of exile movements. These are beyond the control of the activists themselves. Like the Tiananmen exiles, the Hong Kong exiles also long for their homeland, knowing full well that they cannot return anytime soon, feeling guilt for those left behind serving prison sentences, and for their families who might suffer harassment because of their "fugitive" family member overseas.

In the next and final chapter of the book, the future of Hong Kong is discussed in terms of how the past is talked about in the present, and so into the future. It is also about how the Hong Kong people are supposed to tell "good stories of Hong Kong".

References

Bloomberg. "Hong Kong Expands Bounties in Hunt for Democracy Activists." December 14, 2023. https://www.bloomberg.com/news/articles/2023-12-14/hong-kong-expands-use-of-bounties-tohunt-democracy-activists

Bourdieu, Pierre. *Language and Symbolic Power*. Edited and introduced by John B. Thompson; translated by Gino Raymond & Matthew Adamson. Cambridge: Polity Press, 1991.

Calhoun, Craig, Edward LiPuma, Moishe Postone, eds. *Bourdieu: Critical Perspectives*. Cambridge, UK: Polity Press, 2003.

Chen, Jie. "The Overseas Chinese Democracy Movement after Thirty Years: New Trends at Low Tide." *Asian Survey* 54, no. 3 (2014): 445–470.

Chen, Jie. "The Chinese Political Dissidents in Exile: Struggle for a Sustainable and Relevant Movement." *Open Journal of Political Science* 6 (2016): 53–66.

Chen, Jie. "The Chinese Political Opposition in Exile: A Chequered Development." *Europe-Asia Studies* 70, no. 1 (2018): 108–129.

Chen, Jie. *The Overseas Chinese Democracy Movement: Assessing China's Only Open Political Opposition.* Edward Elgar Publishing, 2019.

Chen, Nian. "Hong Kong Activists in Exile Remain Defiant in Face of Bounties." Voice of America News, July 14, 2023. https://www.voanews.com/a/hong-kong-activists-in-exile-remaindefiant-in-face-of-bounties/7400571.html

Chen, Zifei. "Interviews: 'If I Take a Step Back, How Will Hong Kong be Free?" Radio Free Asia, February 14, 2024. https://www.rfa.org/english/news/china/law-impact-02142024132804.html

Cheng, Kris. "Hong Kongers Embrace Political Activism in Their New Home." *The Hong Konger*, June 26, 2024. https://hongkonger.world/2024/06/26/hong-kongers-embrace-political-activism-in-their-newhome/

Cheng, Mandy. "Treat Hong Kong's 8 Wanted Democrats Like 'Street Rats' Who Should be 'Avoided at All Costs,' Leader John Lee Says." *Hong Kong Free Press*, July 11, 2023. https://hongkongfp.com/2023/07/11/treat-hong-kongs-8-wanted-democrats-like-street-rats-whoshould-be-avoided-at-all-costs-leader-john-lee-says/

De Groot, Kristen. "Hong Kong Activist Nathan Law Continues the Fight." *Penn Today*, November 29, 2022. https://penntoday.upenn.edu/news/hong-kong-activist-nathan-law-continues-fight

De Guzman, Chad. "Hong Kong's Million-Dollar Bounties Are About More Than Arresting 8 Activists." *Time*, July 2, 2023. https://time.com/6292047/hong-kong-activists-arrest-warrantsbounties/

dos Santos, Nina. "Exclusive: China Operating over 100 police Stations Across the world with the Help of Some Host Nations, Report Claims." CNN, December 4, 2022. https://edition.cnn.com/2022/12/04/world/china-overseas-police-stations-intl-cmd/index.html

Fairclough, Norman. *Media Discourse*. London; New York: E. Arnold, 1995.

Goffman, Erving. *The Presentation of Self in Everyday Life*. New York: Overlook Press, 1973.

Gust, Onni. "The Perilous Territory of Not Belonging': Exile and Empire in Sir James Mackintosh's Letters from Early Nineteenth-century Bombay." *History Workshop Journal*, 86 (Autumn 2018): 22–43.

Hale, Erin. "Hong Kong Targets Exiles' Loved Ones as Crackdown Turns to Old CCP Playbook." *Al Aljazeera*, August 4, 2023. https://www.aljazeera.com/news/2023/8/4/hong-kong-uses-china-playbook-as-crackdown-turnsto-dissidents-loved-ones

Harlem, Andrew. "Exile as a Dissociative State: When a Self is "Lost in Transit." *Psychoanalytic Psychology* 27, no. 4 (2010): 460–474.

He, Rowena. *Tiananmen Exiles: Voices of the Struggle for Democracy in China*. New York: Palgrave Macmillan, 2014.

Ho, Kelly. "Hong Kong National Security Police Issue HK$1 Million Bounty Each for 8 Self Exiled Activists." *Hong Kong Free Press*, July 3, 2023. https://hongkongfp.com/2023/07/03/breaking-hong-kong-national-security-police-issue-hk1million-bounty-each-for-8-self-exiled-activists/

Hong Kong Watch. First-time and Floating: How 140,000 Hong Kongers Could Swing Seats at the Next UK General Election. Hong Kong Watch.

November 11, 2023. https://www.hongkongwatch.org/all-posts/2023/11/22/first-time-and-floating-how-140000-hong-kongers-could-swing-seats-at-the-next-uk-general-election

Hong Kong Watch. "UK General Election to Take Place on 4 July 2024—BNOs can Register to Vote." Hong Kong Watch, June 11, 2024. https://www.hongkongwatch.org/all-posts/2024/6/11/uk-general-election-to-take-place-on-4-july-2024-bnos-can-register-to-vote

Huang, Jianli. "Umbilical Ties: The Framing of the Overseas Chinese as the Mother of the Revolution." *Frontiers of History in China* 6, no. 2 (June 2011):183–228.

Hui, Francis. "Glory to Hong Kong with Frances Hui." Geneva Summit for Human Rights and Democracy, May 16, 2023.https://genevasummit.org/speech/china-3-frances-h/

Info.gov.hk. "The Jurisdiction of Hong Kong National Security Law Accords with International Norms and Double-standard Criticisms are for an Ulterior Motive." Hong Kong Government, July 6, 2023. https://www.info.gov.hk/gia/general/202307/06/P2023070600680.htm

John, Alun. "Hong Kongers Embrace Politics in UK, But Some Still Fear Beijing." Reuters, June 21, 2024. https://www.reuters.com/world/hong-kongers-embrace-politics-uk-some-still-fear-beijing-2024-06-21/

Kilpatrick, Ryan Ho. "Long-distance Resistance." China Media Project, August 8, 2023. https://chinamediaproject.org/the_ccp_dictionary/long-distance-resistance/

Kwong, Ying-ho. "The Growth of "Localism" in Hong Kong, A New Path for the Democracy Movement?" *China Perspectives.* (September 1 2016): 63–68

Lam, Wai-man. "Changing Political Activism: Before and After the Umbrella Movement." In: Fong, Brian and Tai-lok Lui, eds., *Hong Kong 20 Years after the Handover. Studies in the Political Economy of Public Policy*. Cham: Palgrave Macmillan, 2018.

Lau, Stuart. "From Lantau to Ealing: Hong Kong's Homesick Exiles in Britain Greet the Year of the Tiger." Politico, February 1, 2022. https://www.politico.eu/article/hong-kong-unitedkingdom-exile-visa-year-of-the-tiger-celebration/

Leung, Hillary. "Hong Kong Student Who Made 'seditious' Online Posts in Japan Jailed for 2 Months." *Hong Kong Free Press,* November 3, 2023. https://hongkongfp.com/2023/11/03/hongkong-student-who-made-seditious-online-posts-in-japan-jailed-for-2-months

Lim, Louisa. *The People's Republic of Amnesia: Tiananmen Revisited.* Oxford University Press, 2015.

Loi, Amelia, and Chen, Zifei. "Interviews: Hong Kongers Overseas Keep Alive Their Struggle for Freedom and Democracy." Radio Free Asia, June 19, 2023.

Marsh, Jenni, James Griffiths, Angela Dewan, and Sara Faidell. "The Exiles and the Inmates: The Heart-wrenching Hand Dealt to Hong Kong's Democracy Activists." CNN, December 20, 2020. https://edition.cnn.com/2020/12/17/asia/hong-kong-exiles-and-inmates-dst-hnkintl/index.html

Nathan, Andrew. J. "Historical Perspectives on Chinese Democracy: The Overseas Democracy Movement Today." In Edward S Krebs, Roger Jeans, Parks Coble, Marilyn M. Levine, *Roads Not Taken: The Struggle of Opposition Parties in Twentieth-Century China.* Routledge, 1993.

News.gov.hk. "Criticism of Article 23 Rejected." Hong Kong Government, February 29, 2024. https://www.news.gov.hk/eng/2024/02/20240229/20240229_222451_415.html

Pomfret, James, and Jessie Pang. "Wanted Hong Kong Activist Fears for Safety, Hopes for US Asylum." Reuters, July 13, 2023 https://www.reuters.com/world/china/wanted-hong-kong-activist-fears-safety-hopes-us-asylum-

Quach, Georgina. "Hongkongers Make a Splash in UK Politics." *The Financial Times,* November 10, 2023. https://www.ft.com/content/90477190-32c1-4ca5-9ca3-6604e6f3ff62

Said, Edward W. *Reflections on Exile and Other Literary and Cultural Essays.* London: Granta, 2001.

Shain, Yossi. "Who is a Political Exile? Defining a Field of Study for Political Science." *International Migration* 26, no. 4 (October 1988): 387–400.

Snyder, Jim, Amelia Loi, and Gemunu Amarasinghe. "Five Years After a Summer of Protest, Hong Kong Exiles are Still Rebuilding Their Lives." *Radio Free Asia,* June 7, 2024. https://www.rfa.org/english/news/special/hongkong-exciles/index.html

To, James, Jiann Hua. *Qiaowu, Extra-Territorial Policies for the Overseas Chinese.* Brill, 2014.

Tung, Cheryl. "Hong Kong Asylum-seekers in the UK Face fear and Uncertainty." Radio Free Asia, January 9, 2024. https://www.rfa.org/english/news/china/uk-01092024122549.html

Wodak, Ruth. "The Discourse-historical Approach." In Ruth Wodak and Michael Meyer, Methods of Critical Discourse Analysis (pp. 63–94). London: Sage, 2001.

Wong, Natalie. "What Will be Impact of Hong Kong Passport Cancellations on 6 Fugitives?" *South China Morning Post,* June 13, 2024. https://www.scmp.com/news/hong-kong/politics/article/3266394/what-will-be-impact-hongkong-cancelling-passports-6-fugitives

Wong, Rachel. "Wanted Hong Kong activist Finn Lau—Behind the Faceless 'Laam Chau' Persona—Says He Will seize Any 'Chance of Survival and Give Back'." *Hong Kong Free Press,* October 25, 2020. https://hongkongfp.com/2020/10/25/wanted-hong-kong-activist-finn-laubehind-the-faceless-laam-caau-persona-says-he-will-seize-any-chance-of-survival-and-giveback/
Xinhua. "Britain's Repeated Manipulation of BNO Scheme Will Backfire: Commissioner's Office of Chinese foreign ministry in HKSAR." Xinhua, February 25, 2022.
Yam, Chun, and Wang Bo Jing. "'Leaving Hong Kong was Worse than Dying': Pro-democracy Politicians in Exile." Radio Free Asia, January 5, 2022. https://www.rfa.org/english/news/china/exile-01052022135350.html

8

The Future of One Country, Two Systems

No one can predict the future, only possible trends. Before 1997 there was a prediction of the "death of Hong Kong" (Kraar and McGowan 1995) prior to the signing of the Sino-British Joint Declaration (Richburg 2018; Wu 2018). This predicted "death" referred to the loss of what many saw made Hong Kong different from China, such as freedom of the press, the rule of law, and an independent judiciary. Nothing much happened after midnight on 30 June 1997 – life seemed to go on as much as before, with democrats fighting for the early universal suffrage promised in the Basic Law, while the Hong Kong establishment and Beijing sought delay. The "death metaphor" was resurrected with the introduction of the National Security Law in 2020. Hong Kong was now experiencing a "slow death", a "lonesome death", or the end of Hong Kong "as we know it", or the death of the rule of law" (Tai 2020). It could also be "just entering a new phase of struggle" (Bland 2020), a story about the city's "rise and fall" (Overhalt 2019) or alternately a stabilisation of the "One Country, Two Systems". On the other hand, Hong Kong's "dead end" would only be due to "those who want Hong Kong to be separated from the motherland" (Zhang 2021). Whatever the metaphor, Hong Kong will undoubtably continue exist.

J. Eagleton, *Hong Kong's Second Return to China*,
https://doi.org/10.1007/978-3-031-84587-1_8

Hong Kong has always been obsessed by dates, and speculations about its future. This chapter will deal the issue of how the Hong Kong story was once told, how it is being told now, and how it is likely to be told in the future. It will look at how the Hong Kong story is told in the museum, in Chinese histography, and in recently published historical chronicles. The discussion will also bring in themes and theories that have arisen from other chapters of the book as well as the language strategies and techniques used to justify and legitimise changes in present-day Hong Kong.

Background

To recap, in the late 1970s, with the 99-year lease over the New Territories of Hong Kong due to expire in 1997, London approached Beijing to negotiate about the colony's future, hoping to secure a future for Hong Kong's economic, and social systems unless an accord was reached with China. Eventually, Beijing agreed in the Sino-British Joint Declaration (1984), and later, the Basic Law (1990) that Hong Kong's systems would remain unchanged for 50 years after its return to Chinese sovereignty on July 1st, 1997, under a policy known as "One Country, Two Systems". The result was a 13-year-long discussion, from 1984 to July 1st, 1997 of what Hong Kong would be like in the future.

This desired future was thus the preservation of the (then) present Hong Kong; in other words, a Hong Kong that wanted its present to be its future – with one legal expert called the Sino-British Joint Declaration a "snapshot of 1984",[1] but with the removal of the colonial ruler. After

[1] This meant that the Joint Declaration was a "snapshot" of 1984: "…transport system, legal system, financial system, taxation system. There were 12 large areas - basic policies - which will never change. And the whole idea was what we call a snapshot, a 1984 snapshot. Take out your Kodak camera; take a picture of Hong Kong in 1984 and you can say that is what will not change for at least 50 years. That was the bargain struck." This was said by Alan Hoo, Chairman of the Basic Law Institute and Member of the CPPCC National Committee, In a speech entitled "The Roadmap towards Universal Suffrage in Hong Kong", speech given at the Hong Kong Democratic Foundation luncheon on 10 April 2008. The full speech used to be available on the Foundation's website, but now the Foundation no longer exists and the website has been removed. The author attended this speech and had made notes on it.

1997, many were looking towards a future where the universal suffrage promised in the Basic Law would finally be realised. With the introduction of the National Security Law, many uncertainties about the future and this promise have come into play. Global criticism about the recent changes in Hong Kong has seen the need for the authorities to state that there are still "good stories" to be told about Hong Kong.

Telling Good Stories About Hong Kong

Delivering his first Policy Address in 2022, Chief Executive John Lee said, that as an externally oriented economy, Hong Kong must look for opportunities beyond the city and "be adept at telling the world good stories about itself, which would allow the city to shine" (Hong Kong Gov. 2022; news.gov.hk 2022).

> With an intricate and volatile international political environment, certain external forces have been deliberately spearing our country and distorting the situation in Hong Kong.
>
> We have to present the true picture of Hong Kong to the world and promote our strengths, achievements and opportunities, and that the city is a good place where people can make their dreams come true. (Hamlett 2022)[2]

Lee is saying that other countries were not telling the "truth" about Hong Kong's current reality. According to Lee, the foreign media focused on telling bad stories about Hong Kong giving outsiders an unfair impression of the city. They were "badmouthing" Hong Kong and the National Security Law (Wong 2023), and "those who unfairly criticise Hong Kong must be put in their place" (SCMP 2023).

The true picture seemed given by the Hong Kong and Central People's Governments, with "good stories" revolving around trade and integration

[2] Hong Kong's new Chief Executive John Lee had his first Legislative Council Q&A on 6 July 2022. He described Hong Kong as a *junzi* (君子, gentleman) among *xiaoren* (小人, nasty people) in the world and said Hong Kong could not leave its achievements to be discovered by chance; it had to be "upfront and explicit" in promoting itself (Han 2022).

with China's "belt and road" initiative while stating that the rights and freedoms of Hong Kong residents "are better protected in a safer and more orderly environment" with the NSL in place (CMAB 2023, 2). But as one columnist opined: "But Hong Kong's problem with the world is not so much a shortage of good stories as a surplus of bad ones" listing incidents such as "delayed prosecutions," "lack of jury trials", and "weaponization of bad laws" as "bad stories" (Hamlett 2022).

Officials want journalists to tell "good" stories about the city, which is a misrepresentation of what journalism entails. Journalists do not set out to write "good" stories or "bad" stories per se, they write about what is "newsworthy". What is considered "newsworthy" relates to five news values: timeliness, proximity, conflict and controversy, human interest, and relevance. That the sun rises in the east every day is not news, but if it does not rise, that would certainly be news. It is also not the role of journalists to promote places or policies, that is the role of government information services departments, as this comes into conflict with ethical values such as accuracy, independence, and impartiality (Ethical Journalism Network n.d.). A story shedding light on a problem is not necessarily a "bad" story. A good many stories in the media deal with the future implications of present actions.

Thinking About the Future

The thinker Slavoj Zizek (1989, 274–275) tells us that the future is the "supreme object of ideology" and that the future is "without form, shape or color: it demands yet exceeds all figuration". Consequently, Zizek sees discourse about the future as a necessary site for conceptualising and examining language as a "virtual space" and as "action and event"; this "virtual space" is an ideal place for such things as metaphor to take root. Competing representations of the future are presented to the public and there is a process through which a particular future is privileged over other futures.

Beijing seems to be privileging a future where Hong Kong is increasingly assimilated into the mainland despite promising a high degree of autonomy as part of the "One Country, Two Systems" framework; others in Hong Kong wants a future that maintains this high degree of autonomy. The Extradition Bill of 2019, which led to massive protests, was seen by a broad section of the community as the ultimate "tipping point" in Hong Kong's full integration into China.

The future conceptualised for Hong Kong does not lie with the average person on the street, however. Hongkongers have never had a real say in the development of their systems as the negotiations in the 1980s over the future handover attest. The "virtual space" for contesting the future seems to be narrowing to one uttered to by Beijing (the "one country"). The public's choices in responses to previous consultation papers were often limited in scope.[3] The future of the "second system" as a real "second system" with a promised "high degree of autonomy" is delegitimised. Thus, the discourse of Hong Kong's future is a clash of diametrically opposite futures, which of course is based on the past.

As noted by Jaworski et al. (2003a, 2003b, 2004), a significant amount of news items refers to future events. The media basically constructs "reality" for the public and postulates about situations that may never happen. Neiger (2007) examined the "discourse of the future" as used by the Israeli press. The discourse of the future not only gives a framework for how to think about future change, it also impacts on how people deal with it (Ibid.). Neiger found that the "discourse of the future" involved four various possible futures: predictable future, informed assessment, speculative assessment and conjectured future. The conjectured future has a "very high level of speculation" as such discourse has cultural and political importance because "it provides fertile ground for releasing trial balloons, magnifying threats, creating solidarity, and justifying acts of government" (p. 310), involving "worst-case scenarios", and "what would have happened if…" which relate to the cultural and political norms of the place.

The potential for a "worst-case scenario" is used by various institutional bodies to assess possible risk (Candlin and Crichton 2011, 4) by the presence of a known "deficit", which has the possibility of worsening. Hongkongers were told to "take it" or take the dire consequences of not

[3] A Green Paper on political reform had a three-month public consultation period in 2007; in 2024, there was barely four weeks consultation over the proposed Article 23 legislation.

accepting the Sino-British Joint Declaration as constructed. They were told to accept a certain course to ensure Hong Kong's "stability and prosperity" would continue, playing also on constant cultural fears about the past (and so this has continued into the present and thus the future). In thinking about the future, of course, we must also think about history. We will return to the "actual future" later on in this chapter. The next section looks at how the past has been envisioned (or rather "re-envisioned) around 1997 onwards to fit in with the present reigning ideology of "One Country, Two Systems".

Telling the (Past) Hong Kong Story in the Present

While past events cannot be changed, they can be interpreted differently multiple times by different actors. Revisioning history can be positive when previously unheard voices are given voice in the historical narrative as in the history of women and minorities. Take Napoleon Bonaparte, for example has been subject to many contrasting historical interpretations ever since his meteoric rise from a Corsican artillery officer to the Emperor of French, controlling for a time, large parts of Europe (see https://reviews.history.ac.uk/review/1707).

Hong Kong has often been depicted being "a barren rock and no more than a tiny fishing village upon it" (Lim 2022, 38). Ever since the time of British arrival, Hong Kong was depicted as the "Pearl of the Orient", a prosperous cosmopolitan city. Since the Hong Kong Special Administrative Region was established in 1997, the government has positioned the city as "Asia's World City", attributing its success to the rule of law and the free market to Hong Kong's identity as a British colony (Patton 1997),[4]

[4] On the night of the handover in 1997, two stories of Hong Kong were told. For Britain, it was an honourable exit leaving behind a flourishing economic city with "British values" – the rule of law, "clean and light-handed government" as well as the "values of a free society". For China, it heralded the end of over a century of humiliation and a confirmation of its rise after the "decade of chaos" known as the Cultural Revolution. Jiang's speech can be found at: http://th.china-embassy.gov.cn/eng/ztbd/AboutChina/HKMacau/200306/t20030626_1433053.htm; last governor Chris Patton's speech can be found at: https://www.americanrhetoric.com/speeches/chrispattenhongkonghandoverceremony.htm

with the help of the hardworking Chinese. Museum-telling of the Hong Kong story entered a new phase after 1997.

There have been many obvious attempts to increase national feelings towards China since 1997. There was the patriotism debate by pro-Beijing elements about the need to elect "patriotic" politicians in the 2021 elections, being the most recent example. The visits to Hong Kong of China's first man in space, Deng Xiaoping's daughters, and the Chinese Olympic team in earlier years also served this function. This is rather ironic since, while Hong Kong needs to become "more Chinese" the mainland is increasingly putting on a more "international" front (Brooker 2023). It is in this context that museum as identity construction came into its own. In the first few years of the HKSAR years new museums have opened, the Museum of Coastal Defence (August 2000) and the Heritage Museum (December 2000). The Hong Kong Museum of History was established in July 1975, but moved to new, modern premises in 1998.

On 18 October 2020, many Hongkongers queued for hours to pay a visit to the Museum of History, the last day before the permanent exhibition "The Hong Kong Story" closed for an extensive two-year renovation. There were fears that the new displays might censor or exclude politically sensitive events such as the city's colonial history and its relationship with China, although plans for the exhibition revamp were made a few years prior to 2019 when the political atmosphere was less tense.[5]

The Hong Kong Story

What kind of Hong Kong story did the old exhibition tell? The original exhibition could be faulted for not presenting history in a comprehensive and Hong-Kong-oriented way. Instead, it infused the display with the ideological narrative of "Hong Kong culture equates to Chinese culture" (Lai 2020). The author, studying both the Chinese and English texts of displays in the exhibition in preparation for a conference presentation in 2004, discovered that most of the texts largely corresponded in both

[5] A visual archive of images from the "old" version of the museum's "Hong Kong Story" can be found at https://hongkongfp.com/hkfp-visual-archive-the-history-museums-hong-kong-story/.

languages, but with subtle and pragmatic differences.[6] Hongkongers and mainland Chinese, possessing certain inculcated values and lived/separated histories, would read the text in certain ways that the non-Chinese viewer would not, ways that appealed to their sense of Chineseness. Simply put, the theme was that Hong Kong had always been a part of China and that it never has been really separated from it.

As a non-Chinese visitor, it seemed that the exhibition's constructors wanted to tell those reading the English text, that ultimately the city was never really "British". The sense was that the colonial past was only marginal to Hong Kong's history, while events in China were never marginal in Hong Kong. Indeed, it is remarkable how little the activities of the colonial administration and other foreigners in Hong Kong were shown in the old exhibition (colonial governors' portraits were placed in an obscure location). The word "colony" was seldom used in the exhibition. The past, or at least to its fullest extent, had disappeared.

The Hong Kong Story focused on the past rather than the relatively modern era. Four of the eight galleries featured the history of Hong Kong before British administration, in comparison with only one gallery focused on post-war history: Galleries 1–4: The Natural Environment, Prehistoric Hong Kong, *The Dynasties: from the Han to the Qing, and Folk Culture in Hong Kong*. The emphasis was that Hong Kong is in the Lingnan region: "Hong Kong is situated at the eastern end of the Pearl River Delta region on the South China Seaboard. Archaeological evidence reveals that Hong Kong has a long history, *like the rest of China*." (Gallery 1: The Natural Environment" – English text, italics added). This is done through the display of certain archaeological artefacts, for example a *dou*, a Chinese vessel unearthed in Hong Kong, and the finding of antiquities from the Ming and Qing dynasties for example. Hong Kong folk tales, such as the myth of the half-man-half-fish creature "Lo-Tings", and so on.

Gallery Five: The Opium Wars and the Cessation of Hong Kong. In Chinese history, the Opium War was the start of its "Century of

[6] I have unpublished notes from that presentation. The presentation was "The Hong Kong Story: Just Who Is It For?" Paper given at the Midwest Modern Language Association Conference, St. Louis, Missouri, November 2004.

Humiliation". The conflict was caused by the expansion of British imperialism, Britain's dumping of opium on China and the subsequently bullying of the nation by gunboat diplomacy. In short, Britain was the wrongdoer and the Hong Kong people were the victims. "The Hong Kong Story" embraced this theme by showing a large statue of Commissioner Lin Zexu to commend his destruction of British opium at Humen. There are multiple causes of the Opium War, for example the different perceptions of free trade and property rights between the Chinese and the British.

Gallery 6: Birth and Early Growth of the City and The Japanese Occupation; This section also showed developments in Hong Kong's political structure, law, people's livelihood, industry and education. Dr. Sun Yat-sen's revolutionary activities in Hong Kong and the role the territory played in the modern history of China:

> Whenever China encountered any natural disasters or foreign threats, local Chinese were eager to contribute by raising funds. The Hong Kong people even launched strikes and protests to show their patriotism and anti-foreign feelings when China was attacked by foreign countries. (author's translation of the Chinese text)

In the Chinese, the second sentence was somewhat different: "The Hong Kong people even launched strikes and protests to voice their support when China was attacked by foreign countries." "Show their patriotism and anti-foreign feelings" is entirely missing from the Chinese, which seems strange. Perhaps it is specifically for the non-Chinese museum-goer to know how sensitive the Chinese were to events on the mainland.

There was only one gallery, *Gallery 8: Modern Metropolis and the Return of China*, depicting the post-war period, the most influential time in the development of the city, and even that gallery focused more on people's daily lives and the economy. There was little or no information on historically significant events: the struggles between the Chinese Communists and the Nationalists in Hong Kong, the 1956 riots, drives by different governors for democratisation, the reaction to the 1989 Tiananmen Square protests and the subsequent mass migration from Hong Kong.

The portraits of governors were not in a prominent spot, rather they were displayed in a corner. Even the 1967 leftist riots, dubbed a "post-war watershed" (Cheung 2009) was only mentioned in a brief video clip. Events stopped at the handover.

Dr Joseph Ting Sun-pao, former museum director commented on the exhibition: "We are, after all, Chinese. That's why 'The Hong Kong Story' is told by the Hong Kong Chinese." From this remark, we realise that "The Hong Kong Story" was not given from a Hong Kong perspective, but from a general Chinese one (Lai 2020). Dimarche et al.'s 2017 article "One Museum, Two Stories: Place Identity at the Hong Kong Museum of History" illustrates that while the displays have been "developed for mainlanders" – as said by one exhibition goer, (p. 298), all visitors had to follow this "master" narrative.

According to the Museum of History's website about the revamp of "The Hong Kong Story," research into ten aspects has been completed, including "Hong Kong People's lives from the 19th to the middle of the 20th century", "The districts of Tsuen Wan, Kwai Chung and Tsing Yi", "History of Hong Kong Football after WWII", "The Ancient History and Culture of Hong Kong from an Archaeological Perspective", and "Hong Kong Portuguese Soldiers and Civilians in the Second World War".[7] There seems to be no explicit political message as far as one can tell from these topics, although no conclusions can be drawn before the exhibition reopens. Perhaps it will be question of absence, about what is omitted. The exhibition was slated to open at the end of 2024 (private communication with the museum), but at time of this book's publication, no opening date has still not been set.

While the new "Hong Kong Story" exhibition has not yet opened, more museums have been planned, but with even more of a China focus, post NSL. The Palace Museum opened in July 2022, providing "a platform for the visitors to appreciate China's 5,000-year history and raise cultural confidence and national pride" (Tong 2022), while the museum has the responsibility "to facilitate Hong Kong people's national identity" (Gittings 2022). It was controversial as it was established without any

[7] See https://hk.history.museum/en/web/mh/exhibition/hksrenovation.html

public consultation.[8] In Chief Executive John Lee's 2023 Policy address, the government plans to set up a museum to showcase the development and achievements of China, covering areas such as its history, politics, economic development, and culture. The existing Hong Kong Museum of Coastal Defence will be converted into the Hong Kong Museum of the War of Resistance and Coastal Defence in 2024. "It will focus on the history of the War of Resistance [against Japan] to cultivate a stronger sense of national esteem and patriotism" (The Standard 2023).

Sensitive events like June Fourth, 1989 that have had a significant bearing on Hong Kong's political development, tend to be hidden as in the new M+ Museum of Visual Culture with the removal of artworks as discussed in Chap. 5. The Hong Kong Story is also being told in a new English version of the multi-volumed publication: *The Hong Kong Chronicles*.

The Hong Kong Chronicles

The first English-language volume of the *Hong Kong Chronicles*, namely "Overview & Chronology" were published by the Hong Kong Chronicles Institute on July 27, 2022, to great fanfare with Hong Kong Government, Central Government officials and other notable figures in attendance. The volume consists of around 360,000 words and nearly 800 pages.[9] This is a long-term publishing project which will ultimately consist of 54 volumes with 25 million words in 10 content categories, namely Overview, Chronology, Nature, Economy, Culture, Society, Politics, Notable People, Appendices and Special Topics, covering over 7000 years. The publication of the entire (Chinese) series is scheduled for completion by 2027. The entire English series is scheduled for completion by 2032.

[8] Chief Executive Lam had proposed a Hong Kong version of the original Palace Museum in Beijing after a trip to that city in late 2016. She did not consult the public and without Legislative Council's approval as it had a 3.5 billion Hong Kong dollars by the Hong Kong Jockey Club Charities Trust. There were complaints about lack of transparency, Lam defended the project, saying it would be "embarrassing" if a public consultation resulted in opposition (Tong 2022).

[9] The *Overview & Chronology* can be found (as well as other related information about the project) at https://hkchronicles.org.hk/en/firstBook.php

Chief Executive John Lee praised former Chief Executive Tung Chee-hwa for "spearheading the project, says the English volume is opportunity to tell the 'success story of Hong Kong'" (Cheung 2021). Beijing's top official in Hong Kong, Luo Huining, director of the Liaison Office of the Central People's Government in Hong Kong, was one of the honorary patrons of the project. Chief Executive John Lee said of the project:

> In addition to knowing the story of Hong Kong, reading the Hong Kong Chronicles will also enhance our understanding, and appreciation of the nation we are all so proud to be part of. That includes not only the history we share, but the future we can look forward to.
> help in, our nation's progress and development. (news.gov.hk 2022)

We can again see the continuance of emphasising Hong Kong's connections with China. Given that this publication has been endorsed by government authorities we might be expected a more positive treatment or at least a "state-sanctioned" version of certain events; let us look briefly at the functions of traditional Chinese historiography.

Historiography was a supremely important part of the Chinese classical tradition. It was ultimately interdisciplinary and linked with traditional philosophy and morality. The importance attached to the study and writing of Chinese history can to a great extent be attributed to Confucianism, thus humanism, reverence for the past, emphasis on moral education, and concern with order and harmony. History in China was written by scholars either in office, out of office, or in retirement. officials. Sinologist Etienne Balasz once noted that Chinese historiography as "written by officials for officials" (Balasz 1964, 135). What this meant, was that history writing reflected the concerns of the present dynasty. The Confucian emphasis on "rule by virtue" meant that an emperor had not only to base his right to rule through family or conquest, but on morals and virtue (the "Mandate of Heaven").

The major concern of the historian was writing the history of previous dynasties or of previous rulers was done to enhance the prestige of the current ruler and his family for future generations to come, was therefore a major concern of the historian. The major works of history were sponsored or commissioned by the rulers themselves. The *Chronicles* follows in this tradition. It is also part of a Chinese traditional form of preserving history known as "local chronicles". The following is an excerpt from the Forward: "Preservation of Our History Through Hong Kong Chronicles" (p. xvii) to the *English Chronicles* written by first Chief Executive of Hong Kong Tung Chee-hwa (italics added):[10]

> It is said that "A mighty tree grows from its roots just as a great river flows from its source." As part of human civilisation and of Chinese tradition, we in Hong Kong have long aspired to *trace our roots and preserve our history.*
>
> Since ancient times, our ancestors have lived and thrived on the land of Hong Kong, leaving behind traces of their lives and of an evolution spanning thousands of years. However, for over 200 years since the compilation of *Chronicles of Xin'an County* in 1819, no other Chinese local chronicles with reference to Hong Kong had been published.
>
> ...
>
> Local Chronicles have the important functions of preserving history, providing reference for policymaking and *educating the people.* Through the compilation of local chronicles, it serves to seek out and promotes stories of people, their socio-economic development, and way of life as well as political structure. It plays an important role of cultural significance in *driving the future by reflecting on the past.*

We can see from the above the traditional values applied to this new publication. We are told that in the above publication, that "The book series [the Chronicles] is of profound historical significance and cultural value as an *accurate, objective, systematic and comprehensive* record of 7,000 years of Hong Kong's transformation" (italics added).[11] But can facts be neutral? What is the use of facts without context or interpretation? that "humblest narrative is always more than a chronological series of events" (Ricoeur 1980, 177; McCullagh 1987). There is a variety of ways in which historians have given their chronological accounts of the

[10] Tung is a former Vice Chairman, National Committee of the Chinese People's Political Consultative Conference and also Honourary Chairman, Our Hong Kong Foundation.

[11] This first volume of "Overview & Chronology: A Record of 7,000 Years of Social Transformation" can be found at https://hkchronicles.org.hk/en/overviewchronology.php

past, their basic narratives, a meaning as a whole. We are given some "general rules of the chronicle" which frames our reading of the text in a particular ideological way.

General Rules of the Hong Kong Chronicles

This section of the *Hong Kong Chronicles* says that the publication is not a government project as in the mainland; however, the publication is initiated and compiled by the non-profit. Our Hong Kong Foundation "with support from the Chinese Central Government and the HKSAR government, community-wide participants and academic authorship".[12] However, Our Hong Kong Foundation is seen as a pro-government government organisation. Arguably, it is still funded by officially approved channels.

The Overview

The first part of the publication is an *Overview* – which "gives an overall account of Hong Kong's history, providing readers with an all-round impression of the structural cohesion underlying the different components of the book series" (p. vxiii):

(1) Superior geographic location and natural environment
(2) A highly open economic system
(3) Migration and the growth of an immigrant city
(4) British colonial rule
(5) Hong Kong's unique position in modern Chinese history
(6) From "long-term view" to "One Country, Two Systems"
(7) A place of cultural diversity

[12] Given the establishment by Tung Chee-hwa, a vice-chairman of the Chinese People's Political Consultative Conference (CPPCC), Our Hong Kong Foundation may have political views biased towards the Chinese Communist Party and the Hong Kong government, as suggested by some media.

A selection of Topics 4, 5, and 6 will be briefly analysed as the discourses of history have been particularly contested during Hong Kong as an HKSAR are contained in these sections. The *Overview* and *Chronicles* conclude in the year 2017; it is unclear why this particular year was chosen. The *Overview* being more long form as compared to the following *Chronicles* has the potential to show certain connotations on certain events and situations.

Topic 4: British Colonial Rule

Topic headings for this section include the cessation of Hong Kong Island, the annexation of Kowloon, the New Territories lease, Hong Kong's system of government, development of the rule of law, and the concept of direct and indirect rule. Two things are highlighted, the use of "colony" and "colonial" and the "rule of law" that figure large in Hong Kong discourse and politics. The term "colony" as a noun seems not to be used to describe the status of Hong Kong in the *Chronicles*, only the adjective "colonial". This of course, is what is told in newly published school textbooks on Hong Kong's history as mentioned in Chap. 5 of this book.

According to the *Overview*, Hong Kong is "Based on a culture of respect and compliance with the rule of law. The rule of law has played a critical role in facilitating law and order in Hong Kong and in the broad development of Hong Kong and as a core value highly prized by the people of Hong Kong" (p. 25). As a long-held core value of Hong Kong that is repeated often in Hong Kong discourse as has already been shown in this book. The narrative of a law-abiding location and a peaceful society is reiterated here, insinuating that violence is largely the exception, not the norm in the community, due to the influence of outside actors/agitators.

The Riots in Kowloon and Tsuen Wan

The 1950s and 1960s were a particular time of much political contention on the mainland. This part on British colonial rule avoids discussing some important points, particularly about the Chinese Communist

Party's involvement in the riots of the 1950s and 1960s in Hong Kong. For example, the book mentions that "The first major post-war social conflict" was the Double Tenth Riots that took place in Kowloon and Tsuen Wan on 10 October 1956. However, there was one earlier, on 1 March in 1952 which is missing in the *Chronicles* (Cheng 2023). The Double Tenth Riots was instigated by supporters of the Kuomintang (KMT), and the 1 March riot was incited by the Chinese Communist Party ("leftists") so this might be the reason for the omission.

The book says of the riots instigated by the KMT that the trigger for the riots in Kowloon and Tsuen Wan had "These riots were deemed politically motivated as pro-Kuomintang unions and triad groups took part in provoking the protests" (p. 27) and there was obvious and provocative involvement by pro-KMT trade unions and triad organisations. It says people who fled to Hong Kong were having trouble making a living, and there was huge public dissatisfaction with the current situation. It blames these people and pro-KMT figures who had suffered political and economic defeat, for this social unrest: "These social challenges, combined with the political frustration and economic hardship amongst the pro-KMT groups, were the root causes of the riots" (p. 27).

The 1967 Riots

The riots in Hong Kong in 1967 were actually the result of an extension of the Cultural Revolution [1966–1976] in mainland China to Hong Kong.

> In 1967, given the persistent social conflict against the backdrop of the Cultural Revolution in the Mainland Hong Kong endured its longest and largest social unrest in the post-war colonial period. It was generally known as the 1967 Hong Kong Riots and sometimes also called the Anti-British Colonial Rule movement by the leftists. (p. 28)

But the book describes them as "At the time, many leftist groups believed in fighting colonial rule and resisting heavily armed police" (p. 28) and then being negatively labelled as a result of a propaganda campaign by the Hong Kong government. "The public, largely disagreed and resented their tactics leaving the leftists with a tainted reputation for long time afterwards" (p. 28). This is a completely different political approach than was used to assess the Double Tenth riots. If the riots launched by the Kuomintang in 1956 had "obvious political overtones"' did the riots instigated by the Communist Party in 1967 ("leftists") have no political overtones? The book's condemnation of the KMT and its sympathy for the CCP is relatively obvious. The section on the 1967 riots ends with the following passage:

> At the time, many leftist groups believed in fighting colonial rule and resisting heavily armed police. The public, however, largely disagreed with their tactics, leaving the leftists with a tainted reputation for a long time afterwards. The Hong Kong government seized the opportunity to strengthen its publicity campaign for greater public support. (p. 28)

This passage is somewhat sympathetic in tone, implying that the wrong tactics caused public disapproval, rather than the cause itself. There was a controversy on how the Cultural Revolution was depicted on the Hong Kong police website in 2015, with certain activities by leftists were downplayed (Eagleton 2022, 212–215).

Topic 5: Hong Kong's Unique Position in Modern Chinese History

The heading of this section serves to indicate that Hong Kong has a prominent and significant role in important Chinese historical events such as Hong Kong and Hundred Days Reform; Hong Kong the 1911 Revolution; the seaman's strike and the Canton-Hong Kong strike; and Hong Kong and the War of Resistance against Japan. The introductory paragraph to this section focuses on Hong Kong as a patriotic outpost despite being outside the national fold:

> Hong Kong, a Chinese territory once under foreign colonial rule, is a place where Chinese and Foreign cultures collide and intermingle. Under unique political circumstances, combined with its geographic location and *sense of patriotism towards* the Mainland, Hong Kong has played an important role

> in the development of modern China. Hong Kong was at the forefront of Chinese contemporary history through its involvement in a series of historical events, including the Hundred Day's Reform. 1911 Revolution, Labour Movement, War of Resistance against Japanese Aggression and the decades of national reform and opening up. (p. 30)

It is interesting that the 1911 Revolution is mentioned here when it was depicted in videos to "sell" the NSL to the public (Chap. 3). In that video, and in other videos discussed in that chapter, the word "revolution" was always taken as a political act with violence. However, obviously, as indicated here, the 1911 Revolution was a righteous patriotic one, and one step towards ridding China of autocratic imperial rule.

Over and over again, Hong Kong was seen as the "birthplace" of crucial happenings related to the Mainland because of its "open status" and as a colony. Hong Kong was home to several key figures of the Hundred Days' Reform, such as Hung Jen-kan who picked up "In 1859 Hung Jen-kan, left Hong Kong for Tianjing ......on politics, he emphasized *the rule of law* and the importance of public sentiment" – these ideas being "influenced by his life experiences, especially from the time, he spent in Hong Kong." And "Although unrealized, his ideas of saving the nation and its people through the adoption of Western learning were inspirational for the thinkers after the Opium War" (p. 31).

In addition, "Hong Kong was the birthplace of Sun Yat-sen's revolutionary ideas." Where he formed groups, sought funds and "promoting a revolutionary agenda and plan for an armed rebellion", choosing also to "to complete my studies in Hong Kong given a new school with an English curriculum and more freedom to promote a revolution" ...on 20 February 1923, in his speech at The University of Hong Kong, Sun Yat-sen reiterated that his political philosophy had indeed originated in Hong Kong (p. 32).

During the War of Resistance against Japan, Hong Kong too was an important hub of supplies and served as a centre of the Anti-Japanese National Salvation Movement."

Topic 6: From "Long-term View" to "One Country, Two Systems"

This section deals with Hong Kong's return to China. The introduction to the section uses (ironically) its "special status" of being a British colony of helping Chinese Communist Officials to plan revolution (italics added):

> The Chinese Communist Party's policy and guiding principles towards Hong Kong were shaped by many years of experience, Party leaders Zhou Enlai (周恩来) and Deng Xiaoping (鄧小平) visited Hong Kong in their early years, *taking advantage of its special status to carry out revolutionary work*. The party's top leader Mao Zedong (毛澤東) began making plans for the future of Hong Kong during the Chinese Civil War. After the founding of the People's republic of China, Mao Zedong and Zhou Enlai summarized their policy as "*taking a long-term view and making full use of Hong Kong" to ensure its political stability and economic prosperity*. (p. 37)

Even in the early days of the People's Republic of China, the central authorities were focused on ensuring Hong Kong's prosperity and thus its stability.

Decades later and with the implementation of the "One Country, Two Systems", Hong Kong has "witness complex changes in the internal and external environment" (p. 44). "The stalling economic reform, exacerbated by two financial crises, has made it difficult for young people to move up the socioeconomic ladder…History learning and civic education in Hong Kong had had little impact on a generation of young people, leading to a weak sense of national identity and cultural belonging." Thus, the "One Country, Two Systems" had "run against turbulence as a result". This is why the April 2012 curriculum reform for Moral and National Education was ultimately unsuccessful, probably providing a catalyst for the Occupy Central Movement of 2014.

The Occupy Central Movement of 2014, it was always modified in the *Overview* and the *Chronology* section by the word "illegal". In the following, implying:

> The protests ended after 79 days following a police operation on 15 December. On the same day a spokesperson of the Liaison Office of the Central People's Government in the HKSAR said that the illegal protests had harmed the rule of law, social order and vital interests of Hong Kong, causing much *tangible and latent harm*. The Chinese government also reiterated its support for the HKSAR government to implement political reform, including on the issue of universal suffrage in accordance with the Basic Law, and approach the illegal protests according to the laws of Hong Kong. *It was also noted that only by holding lawmakers accountable could Hong Kong safeguard its core values, stability and prosperity*. (p. 49)

In its evaluation of the "One Country, Two Systems" that has been in place since the [1997] handover, the *Chronicles* says that the model is based on the Chinese constitution and Hong Kong's Basic Law. It identifies a broad social consensus for the principle as the key to its implementation. The protest movements of recent years were seen as violating the Basic Law. But it does not say why these protests arose in the first place, which many saw as being due to the delay by the Chinese Central Government and the Hong Kong authorities repeatedly delaying the promised universal suffrage since the 1997 handover and its definition of universal suffrage in its 31 August White Paper from the National People's Congress Standing Committee. The book seems blame the protests on situations post 1997 for Hong Kong people's lack of feelings of identification with the Mainland despite earlier identification prior to 1997. Could this be because the more "autonomy" afforded to the Hong Kong people be abused by certain individuals?

The Chronology

A chronology is "a historical account of events arranged in order of time usually without analysis or interpretation" (*Merriam-Webster Dictionary*). These are short, fairly basic entries, and a few are selected for analysis here. Earliest dynasties are written in a general way reflecting the lack of specific historical detail and then from 1841 to 1st July 2017. Most of these are pretty straightforward, but let us look at some dates that could possibly be either contested or disputed in some way.

The Chronology starts off Neolithic or New Stone Age at 5000 BC–4000 BC: "Traces of human activity in Hong Kong from this period has been found…." (p. 69). These are quite longish and general entries. "Hong Kong" as such did not exist, but other places are equated to Hong Kong as it is today, "present day" places in Hong Kong. For example, Feng Tili, in 1521 of "Wudu (present-day Hong Kong) in Dongguan passed a provincial civil service examination…"; in 1567–1572, Tang Hung-lun "of Dabu (present-day Tai Po) offered himself as a ransom for his father…" (p. 73). In 25 – 220 AD "Hong Kong remained under the administration of Panyu County of Nanhai Prefecture". Perhaps it would be more accurate to say the "area now occupied by Hong Kong". In this latter example, it is not a matter of a name change. These wordings are similar to the old version of texts in early topics in the Hong Kong Museum of History's "The Hong Kong Story".

In more modern times, the date of June Fourth 1989 remains controversial in its depiction. The following is the *Chronology's* example (italics added for all the following examples):

> 04 June 1989
>
> Following the *June Fourth Incident* in Beijing, more than 200,000 people in Hong Kong took part in a sit-in at Happy Valley Racecourse organised by the Hong Kong Alliance in support of Patriotic Democratic Movement of China. The Alliance organized a six-hour march on Hong Kong Island with 1 million participants. (p. 483)

"Incident" seems "neutral" on the surface, but it is still a term of perhaps appeasement, and thus not neutral in practice. In October 2022, Activist Chow Hang-tung was barred from saying "Tiananmen massacre" in a national security trial with a special appointed national security judge urging her to use "proper terminology" (Chau 2022). The prosecution's barrister suggested using the term "June Fourth incident" instead. The magistrate stated "we are not putting anything [political] in the court," then asking the activist to use "proper terminology in [a] neutral form." The activist replied: "I do protest to the term Tiananmen incident, what is a massacre cannot be downgraded to an incident, this is not a neutral term" (Ibid.). The prosecution also objected, the magistrates' subsequent banning of Chow's use of "the killing" for June Fourth in regards to some information before the court. “Then how do I describe it? That some people died on that day?” Chow asked, after the magistrate agreed with Cheung and asked the barrister not to say “the killing” (Chau 2022).

> 01 Jul 2003
> A march organised by the Civil Human Rights Front in protest of the proposed legislation with respect to Article 23 of the Basic Law took place in the afternoon. It started from Victoria Park and ended at the Central Government Offices with a turnout of 500,000 and 350,000 people according to estimates by the organiser and police respectively. (p. 606)

This entry states what happened in “bare bones” style. However, every year on July 1st, till 2020 a march was organised by the Civil Human Rights Front, with police permission, often which a huge turnout that had significant media coverage. None of the marches after 2003 were mentioned in the *Chronology*. Many scholars took part in compiling the *Chronicles*, but it is unclear what was the definite criterion for inclusion in the volume. Next, we will look the “facts” given about the Occupy Central/Umbrella Movement in 2014. Any reference to the civil disobedience campaign devised by legal academic Benny Tai. Any reference to “Occupy Central” was prefaced with the word “illegal” (italics added).

> 28 Sep 2014
> Benny Tai Yiu-tin.......announced the beginning of the *illegal Occupy Central sit-in Campaign*. Police officers began closing of the Central Government Offices in the morning; protesters occupied several major traffic sections, including Harcourt Road, in the afternoon. The police attempted to disperse crowds of protesters with tear gas and pepper spray in the evening; protesters had spread to Causeway Bay and Mong Kok by nightfall. (p. 689)

In the following, the spokesman’s words are reported speech rather than a direct quotation, taking that Occupy Central was a movement against the rule of law. The official designation of the protest is thus given.

> 28 Sep 2014
> A spokesman of the Hong Kong and Macao Office of the State Council in a statement condemned the Occupy Central movement, denouncing

> *any illegal acts poised to undermine* the rule of law and stability in Hong Kong. The spokesman reiterated the legitimacy of the National People's Congress Standing Committee's Decision on 31 August. (p. 790)

The legitimacy of the decision by this mainland official body is paramount for meaning of the Occupy Central as an illegal activity. Even "facts" can be made ideological through the use of modifying adjectives:

> 14 Jan 2015
> The HKSAR government released its 2015 Policy Address titled *Uphold the Rule of Law, Seize the Opportunity, Make the Right Choices.* It condemned *irrational concepts,* including that of *a Hong Kong promoted* in *Undergrad* (a publication of HKU Students' Union) and by student leaders of the *illegal* Occupy Central movement. (p. 693)

We are just told that the concepts contained within the student publication were "irrational", with Hong Kong being promoted apparently not aligned with the official narrative promoted by the authorities. The "irrational concepts" implies that the students were "irrational" and that they should "make the right choices". Hong Kong readers (residents) knowledgeable about the affairs of the time, might make this inference.

> 28 Mar 2016
> The Hong Kong National Party – an advocate of separatism and local independence – was established. On 24 September 2018, it was officially declared an illegal organisation and banned from operation by the Secretary on the grounds of national security and public safety. (p. 703)
> Oct 2016
> At the inaugural meeting of the 16th Legislative Council…invalidated the oath of office taken by councillors-elect…for *alteration with political statements and slogans insulting Chinese sovereignty.* Twelve other members also altered the oath of office with political remarks of varying degrees. (p. 707)

Quotations by officials about something that has "happened", becomes a "fact". This gives the utterance meaning as discourse "gatekeepers" with the right to speak on Hong Kong issues), (italics added):

> 05 Mar 2017
>
> *Premier of the State Council Li Keqiang*... in his annual government work report pledged the continual implementation of "One Country, Two Systems" in Hong Kong, stressing that "the notion of Hong Kong independence will lead nowhere." He also highlighted the role of Hong Kong and Macao in the Guangdong-Hong Kong-Macao Greater Bay Area with respect to national economic development. (p. 711)
>
> 27 Mar 2017
>
> Organisers of the illegal Occupy Central movement in 2014... [*many names are mentioned*] were arrested and charged with conspiracy to commit public nuisance, inciting others to commit public nuisance *and inciting others to incite public nuisance*. (p. 712)

"Inciting others to commit public nuisance and inciting others to incite public nuisance" seems like it would be a typographic error but it is not. "Inciting others to incite others" is to encourage someone to do or feel something unpleasant or violent:

History is written and rewritten to relate to the prevailing dominant ideology, either subtly or more overtly. While generally reasonably "factual" in most respects, omissions and choice of words can still give as a false picture of the period (particularly "chronicles" in their minimum of detail limit elaboration). Official records and government documentation that have been stored for future reference can be referred to and "factchecked". However, for this storage to be secure for future generations, an archive law is needed. Hong Kong has no such law.

Keeping the Historical Record: Hong Kong Archives

Hong Kong has a Code on Access to Information, but this is of limited value since there is no archive law in the city (Li n.d.).[13] An archives law "requires a government to create and maintain full and accurate records

[13] There was a sub-committee in May 2013 to look at relevant laws in overseas locations, a report of recommendations in March 2014 by the Ombudsman and a public consultation paper in 2018, but still there is no archive law. See the Law Reform Commission of Hong Kong (https://www.hkreform.gov.hk/en/projects/accesstoinfo.htm)

as evidence of their functions and activities", it also being and "the basis for public accountability and a storage space for society's collective memory" (Ibid.). If a member of the public requested records or information held by the government through the Code on Access to Information,[14] officials could find an "excuse" to withhold the requested records or information, if they consider that disclosure would embarrass the administration. In countries where there is an archives law, the authorities have the legal obligation to account for why they cannot produce records upon public request and would be libel to prosecution having lost, destroyed, or failed to create and keep records. Without such a law, destruction of documents by officials would likely escape punishment. Destruction of records by Independent Commission Against Corruption (ICAC) seem to be rather arbitrary (ibid.) and the premature destruction of Falun Gong records by the Immigration Department (Gentle 2007) are examples of such acts. The National Security Law could also be invoked to withhold documents on the grounds that certain documents endanger national security, given the wide scope of the NSL. Even narratives of events in the recent present could be altered over time and archives are useful to consult to see how issues have been viewed over time. This will be also looked at in the next section.

The Recent Present

On 16 June 2019, the Chief Executive Carrie Lam's response to the "public procession" held on that day was as follows. She had "clearly heard the views expressed in a peaceful and rational manner. She acknowledged that this embodied the spirit of Hong Kong as a civilised, free, open, and pluralistic society that values mutual respect, harmony and diversity", and also that:

> She admitted that the deficiencies in the Government's work had led to substantial controversies and disputes in society, causing disappointment

[14] "A department may refuse to disclose information, or may refuse to confirm or deny the existence of information" in certain situations subject to a "harm or prejudice test" (see https://www.access.gov.hk/en/home/index.html)

> and grief among the people. The Chief Executive apologised to the people of Hong Kong for this and pledged to adopt a most sincere and humble attitude to accept criticisms and make improvements in serving the public. (info.gov.hk 2019)

On May 2, 2023, Chief Executive Lee responded to a reporter's question about how post-protest Hong Kong was set to see local elections, he rebuked her "It is not the 2019 protests. It is the black violence. It's the attempt to make Hong Kong independent, and the attempt to cause disaster to Hong Kong society as a whole" (Grundy 2023). Subsequently, "black violence", "black clad violence", and other similar phrases were used by the authorities to depict the protests of 2019 in an attempt to normalise, through repetition, a certain perspective to the events of 2019. There are few references to the wider causes of the protests (the anti-extradition law is barely mentioned), just that they were violent. Changing the narrative of a particular incident also serves to emphasise the official story of events. The following is one such shifting narrative of a major political event in 2019 (Hamlett 2021).

The Yuen Long MTR Station Incident: A Case Study of a Shifting Narrative

The Yuen Long MTR station events of July 21, 2019 was described in the *South China Morning Post* on July 22, 2019 as follows:

> At least 45 people were injured in unprecedented late-night violence at a Hong Kong railway station on Sunday, as a rampaging mob of men in white T-shirts attacked black-clad protesters and passengers indiscriminately. No police officer was in sight as dozens of men, who witnesses suggested were triad members, stormed into Yuen Long MTR. (Lam, Mok, and Lum 2019)

This seems a straightforward account of the incident. The Hong Kong Police were soon accused of colluding with the attackers and were criticised for arriving at the scene 39 minutes after being contacted. Few arrests were made, and uniformed officers were spotted walking away from the station as emergency calls were ignored and nearby police stations shut their gates. The following is the "flow" of the narrative over time.

Police: "some people attacked commuters at the platforms of the Yuen Long MTR Station and train compartments, resulting in multiple injuries" (Early morning 22 July). The viciousness of the attack seems to be underplayed. The attackers were given a general designation of just "some people".

Hong Kong Government: "Some people congregated at the platforms of the MTR station and train compartments, attacking commuters. It led to confrontations and injuries" (Early morning 22 July). This was similar to the police report above; again, the viciousness of the attack is not mentioned.

Government Press Conference, 22 July: "At a press conference the following morning, reporters fired questions about the police handling of the Yuen Long incident at Chief Executive Carrie Lam, Secretary for Security John Lee and the then-police commissioner Stephen Lo. Lam described the attacks as "shocking" and said the whole city was "furious" at such an "unscrupulous disregard of the law. Lo also hit out at allegations of collusion, saying police were in "opposition to all violators of the law".

Media Briefing on July 26, Chief Secretary for Administration Matthew Cheung said: "Thugs arbitrarily attacked unarmed citizens in Yuen Long MTR station – such behaviour is outrageous".

Cheung also admitted there was a "gap" between the police handling of the incident and people's expectations, adding that he was "absolutely willing" to apologise to the public over the controversy.

Police press conference on 26 July 2019, Anthony Tsang (acting commander of the New Territories North region) said police had not sent officers to Yuen Long on the night of the attack because they deemed it was of "lower risk" than the skirmishes on the Hong Kong Island. Tsang said police did their utmost to deal with the incident, but admitted the operation was "slightly worse" than what the public had expected.

In an interview with the Sing Tao newspaper published on 18 November 2019: former police chief Stephen Lo retired from his role amid criticism of the force's behaviour during the citywide pro-democracy movement. Lo, was defensive over claims that police deliberately ignored emergency calls. He said many people had dialled 999 while police manpower was concentrated on Hong Kong Island. He said there were "incidents" in Yuen Long and police had tried its best to adjust its manpower. "We are very saddened, for we could not stop the incident causing injuries in time," he said.

East Week Magazine, 24 November 2019. New police chief Chris Tang. His account was different from previous accounts. Tang claimed the scene had gotten "bigger and bigger" as a lawmaker had brought a group of black-shirted people to the area.

Pro-democracy lawmaker Lam Cheuk-ting stood accused by pro-Beijing groups and newspapers of leading protesters to Yuen Long and "stirring up" confrontations between the white-clad men and protesters. They claimed it eventually led to a "fight" between the two sides. Tang said the force had immediately sent riot police to the scene but, under "complicated circumstances," the performance of the force was very different from what citizens may expect.

iCable News, 30 December: Former Police Public Relations Branch chief superintendent Kong Wing-cheung blamed protesters for the Yuen Long attacks a month later. In an interview with, Kong said people should take a "broader view" and claimed the attacks were caused by "a group people leading protesters to Yuen Long." He later said such remarks were his "personal observation" rather than a conclusion from any police investigation.

Ming Pao 16 March 2020: The new police chief stated that the Yuen Long attacks were "complicated," claiming that the whole incident involved "many parts". He said some "thugs" had assaulted people in the afternoon, while other "thugs" – coming from outside to Yuen Long – sprayed water from a fire hose.

At a Yuen Long District Council meeting on May 12, 2020 Tang repeated a similar narrative by saying police would investigate violence from both the "white-clad thugs" and "black-clad thugs." He added there was room for improvement in terms of the police handling of the July 21 attacks, but said it was "too early" to make an apology.

The Independent Police Complaints Council (IPCC) published a report in May 2020 on police behaviour during the protest, and mentioned the Yuen Long incident. In the report, police said the public were "misled" into seeing the Yuen Long attacks as a "one-sided indiscriminate terrorist attack". The force said the incident was in fact "started off as a gang fight involving a sizeable number of participants from both sides" (IPCC 2020, 85 10.68).[15]

On 26 August 2020: police arrested 13 more men – including Democratic Party legislator Lam Cheuk-ting who was injured in the attacks on suspicion of rioting inside the Yuen Long MTR station. Lam and six others were charged and granted bail a day after. Senior Superintendent Chan Tin-chu of the New Territories North headquarters' crime squad said at a media briefing following the arrests that the public had been "misled" by "one-sided live streams" into viewing the incident as an "indiscriminate attack" (BBC 2020). Referring to a widely circulated video that showed a riot police officer touching the shoulder of an alleged assistant, Chan said: "The act of pushing them was an order for them to leave. But it was distorted by ill-intended people who slandered the force as colluding with the triads."

These remarks stirred controversy, with critics accusing police of attempting to "alter history and erase facts", In reply, police chief Chris Tang rejected the claims a day later: "Police have no intention to rewrite history, because history will pass a fair judgement [on the incident] (Ho 2020).

"The history of Yuen Long is of a tacit 'live and let live' approach to rural criminality which has persisted for decades", in a reference to the area being well-known for triad activity (Hamlett 2021). This is one major example of the changing of stories, post 2019.

Hard Resistance Gone, Soft, and Long-Distance Resistance Remains

> With no more opposition to vote for, protests to attend, or openly critical media to consume, Hongkongers have been learning to find subtle, roundabout ways in their daily lives to assert their own autonomy and hold onto

[15] The IPCC said police showed "inadequacies" in collecting and collating actionable intelligence in a timely manner to enable timely action regarding the attacks. But the IPCC, which lacks investigation powers, cleared the force of misconduct over the incident. A summary of the report can be found at https://www.ipcc.gov.hk/doc/en/pr/pr_20200515_e.pdf

their beliefs — even as they are forced to hide them. The response from the government is unequivocal: no act of disobedience is too small to ignore. *No resistance is too soft to break*. (italics added) (Kilpatrick 2023)

From this paragraph we can see that even "subtle, roundabout ways" of Hongkongers voicing displeasure about the situation was frowned upon.

On 15 April 2021 Luo Hui-ning, then director of the China's Liaison Office in Hong Kong at the opening of National Education Day, referred to the protests of 2019 as "criminal acts" (硬對抗), in the official English translation, but often translated more accurately as "hard resistance" elsewhere.[16] This had largely been crushed with the introduction of the NSL. Despite the "restoration of stability" in 2020, Luo still feared radical thinking by people, and that the so-called "non-criminal acts" (軟對抗) in the official English version, often translated more accurately as "soft resistance" elsewhere, would still be employed. The characters "對抗" can also be translated as "confrontation" (for links to both English and Chinese versions of the speech, see endnote 16):

> 凡破壞國家安全的，屬"硬對抗"，就依法打擊；屬 "軟對抗"，就依法規管。
>
> *My translation*: Anyone who undermines national security will be condemned in accordance with the law if it is a "hard resistance"; if it is a "soft resistance" it will be regulated in accordance with the law.
>
> *Official Translation*: All "criminal acts" undermining national security must be brought to justice, while "non-criminal acts" must be regulated.

"Soft resistance" (or "non-criminal acts") was used to refer to the following actions: is the accusation at people who sprayed water at police during the traditional New Year's water festival (Mok 2023); Cathay Pacific cabin crew who mocked a mainland passenger's poor English (Wang 2023); and local residents who chose to withdraw from a voluntary organ donation scheme ahead of its integration with mainland

[16] National Education Day speech given by Luo Huining: "Reinforce Foundations of National Security Safeguard Peace and Prosperity of Hong Kong" – Speech was given in Chinese: http://big5.locpg.gov.cn/jsdt/2021-04/15/c_1211111436.htm; an English translation can be found at http://big5.locpg.gov.cn/2021-04/15/c_1211111452.htm

registries (Tse 2023)[17] as well playing the song "Glory to Hong Kong" (that some call Hong Kong's "unofficial anthem") being played in lieu of the actual National Anthem at sporting events.

"Soft resistance" could be seen to be associated with attempts to express dissatisfaction with the government. Therefore, this term seems to target *attitudes* deemed unacceptable. "Soft resistance" then is a kind of "catch-all phrase" for behaviour that is not necessarily illegal but behaviour that the Hong Kong authorities would prefer not to occur. Pro-establishment commentator Lau Siu-kai (seen in Chap. 3's NSL videos) sees soft resistance as "disseminating disinformation, creating panic, maliciously attacking the SAR government and the central authorities and distorting the Basic Law" (HKFP 2023). "Those were the major causes of unrest in Hong Kong in recent years.... but they belonged to the 'ideological realm' which as 'difficult to be fully addressed by the law'" (ibid.). Inciting blank votes at an election could also be an example of soft resistance.

Secretary of Security Chris Tang refuted claims that describing various acts as soft resistance were an attempt "to control the citizens' thoughts." Tang said that this "soft resistance" could "radicalize people", and they would need to be counteract the "wrong view of history, China, or whatever" (HKFP 2023). This brings us back to what the authorities see as the need to "tell good stories of Hong Kong", which are the ones being told by the Beijing and Hong Kong governments. As a result, "It is, therefore, necessary for the special administrative region authorities to continue to crack down on *latent subversives* by leveraging the power of the NSL" (italics added) (Tu 2023).

Despite the strength of the NSL, "latent subversives" still exist. "Hard confrontation" and "soft resistance" are two sides of the same coin in mainland thinking. Like "hard resistance", "soft resistance" is also against the Constitution, the Basic Law, and the NSL, but it is more covert. For example, "subversive activities are carried out in the pretext of human rights, freedom, democracy, and people's livelihoods, and are "fundamentally deceptive" and "must not be taken lightly".

[17] Hong Kong has an opt-in organ donation registry. The government had made a controversial proposal to allow the transfer of organs across the border with mainland China.

In a 27 July 2023 editorial in the *Ming Pao Daily*, Zhang said he had predicted that after NSL "that the opposition would not simply "go quiet and go into hiding". On the contrary, they would "study the law thoroughly" and become "more and more sophisticated" in how they express dissent (Kilpatrick 2023). Zhang's solution seems to be the creation of a social, political, and educational environment in which the NSL itself is rarely used since critical thoughts about "changing the way the power structure in Hong Kong is formed" can be "neutralized" before they can turn into competing schools of thought and potential political action. This relates to Gramsci's concept of hegemony of power, in which "what is "correct behaviour" is inculcated into the populace, so they, in effect, "police" themselves. This takes time to achieve.

Despite the introduction of Hong Kong's National Security Law on June 30, 2020, a local security law (Article 23 of the Basic Law) was still required to fill in "gaps" in the NSL. The "gaps were to prohibit any act of treason, secession, sedition, subversion against the Central People's Government, or theft of state secrets, to prohibit foreign political organisations or bodies from conducting political activities in the HKSAR, and to prohibit political organisations or bodies of the HKSAR from establishing ties with foreign political organisations or bodies. The draft bill had a public consultation of one month in February 2025 and passed the Legislative Council in March 2024. There have already been the first arrests in connection with "seditious intention" under this law related to Facebook posts on Tiananmen deemed to incite "hatred" against Beijing (Se and Ye 2024).

Conclusion: Past, Present, and the Future

On 1 July 1997 Hong Kong became a Special Administrative Region of China (SAR) and the first example of the One Country, Two Systems principle.[18] This principle was to build a new political order that embod-

[18] Other "autonomous regions" exist in China – these areas have large non-Han or ethnic minority populations. There are five autonomous regions: Tibet, Guangxi, Xinjiang, Inner Mongolia, and Ningxia. China describes these regions as "autonomous" but unlike Hong Kong, which has separate legal, administrative, and judicial systems from the rest of the country, these regions have little legal ability to govern themselves.

ies a new hegemony of beliefs and ideology (Loh 2010, 234). The almost 27-year ideological framework requires an acceptance that the SAR is subordinate to Beijing, and that a "high degree of autonomy" does not mean full autonomy and that those who share the values of the new political order of the "One Country" are ones that will best defend the beliefs and ideology of the new political order. As ideology also "rationalizes" social interests; "rationalizing" something is to imply that there is something not quite right about an ideology or potential course of action (Eagleton 1991, 51). For example, there are constant arguments that Hong Kong needs certain things like an "executive-led system" and functional constituencies in order to remain an international financial hub and "Asia's world city".

In 2020 Hong Kong needed a new rhetoric of legitimisation and justification to show why the National Security Law was necessary and why the resultant changes were compatible with Hong Kong's existing systems and its core values of rule of law, freedom of speech, publication and assembly. The linguistic strategies employed in the "second return" of Hong Kong after the introduction of the National Security Law involve several aspects and serves several functions.

Employing a "discourse of instability" – the Hong Kong collocates (my term) of "stability and prosperity" were used as justification for keeping the status quo, had long-been used for delaying political reform, the promise of universal suffrage, for implementing the National Security law and for changes in the electoral system. This has been evident in slogans used to promote the NSL and any other changes since 2020.

The strategic use of vagueness and ambiguity – has long been used way before the National Security Law, in preparations for Hong Kong's future (inserting "elections" in the Sino-British Joint Declaration), and phrases in the Basic Law ("actual situation" and "gradual and orderly progress") without firm definitions used as confidence builders and to put off decision-making in the future), thereby authoritative language gatekeepers had the right frame the language to have particular desired meaning. Even the governance framework of "One, Country, Two Systems" were developed "pragmatically" by "crossing the river by feeling the stones". As far as the National Security Law is concerned, the lack of clarity about what constitutes an offence under the Law, meant that the "red lines" of crossing it were unclear, resulting in self-censorship, the closing down of various media organisations, and disbanding of many civil society organs.

Changing the Narrative – the tone of official discourse makes it seem that the protest movement of 2019 was "almost a colour revolution" (a term that also used in official Mainland discourse) and was simply violence for the sake of violence; the recontextualising of the recent past (the Yuen Long incident is a notable example) to fit the "official" version of events as well as the finessing of Hong Kong's past in the museum attests to this fact.

Using established concepts or institutions keep their names but change their definition – Hayek (1944) said it best about the effective way to make people accept certain new values "is to persuade them that they are really the same as those they have always held, but which were not properly understood or recognized before", the most efficient technique to this end is to use the old words but change their meaning." For example, saying, or at least implying that the election of 2021 was more democratic than before despite fewer directly elected seats and so on.

Hong Kong's present has seen a global spotlight directed at the city, and while Hong Kong has always had a high level of speculation about its future, a future that has always been decided by outsiders not its citizens. In 2021 the authorities stated:

> Violence has all but disappeared. Advocacy of "Hong Kong independence" has subsided. Stability has been restored. This means that you can move about without fearing for your personal safety. It means, too, that you are free to express your views openly, while being respectful of the rights of others and not undermining national security. (Cheung 2021)

No one can predict a place's future with any certainty, let alone a place like Hong Kong. The National Security law is still undergoing a "settling in" process, and Article 23 has been drafted, consulted, and implemented. While "hard" resistance seems to have been stamped out, but according to the authorities, "soft" and "long-distance" resistance remains. It remains to be seen what the future will bring.

References

Balasz, Etienne. *Chinese Civilization and Bureaucracy; Variations on a Theme*. Translated by H.M. Wright and edited by Arthur F. Wright. New Haven: Yale University Press, 1964.

Bland, Ben. *Hong Kong is not Dead, Just Entering a New Phase of Struggle*. The Lowy Institute, August 12, 2020. https://www.lowyinstitute.org/publications/hong-kong-not-dead-just-entering-new-phase-struggle

Brooker, Mathew. "Hong Kong's New Normal Isn't Fooling Anyone." *Bloomberg.com*, March 9, 2023. https://www.bloomberg.com/graphics/2023-opinion-how-livable-are-cities-three-years-after-start-of-covid/hong-kong.html

Candlin, Christopher N., and Jonathan Crichton (Eds) *Discourses of Deficit*. Basingstoke: Palgrave Macmillan, 2011.

CMAB. "Report of the Hong Kong Special Administrative Region for the United Nations Human Rights Council Universal Periodic Review." The Constitutional and Mainland Affairs Bureau, December 2023, page 2. https://www.cmab.gov.hk/doc/en/documents/policy_responsibilities/the_rights_of_the_individuals/human/UPR_HKSAR_4th_report_E.pdf

Chau, Candice. "Hong Kong Court Bars Activist Chow Hang-tung from Saying 'Tiananmen Massacre' in National Security Trial." *Hong Kong Free Press*, October 26, 2022. https://hongkongfp.com/2022/10/26/hong-kong-court-bars-activist-chow-hang-tung-from-saying-tiananmen-massacre-in-national-security-trial/

Cheng, Sun. "Interview: Hong Kong Chronicles is CCP's Bid to Rewrite City's History. Radio Free Asia, August 1, 2023. https://www.rfa.org/english/news/china/hongkong-history-08012022151908.html

Cheung, Gary. *Hong Kong's Watershed: The 1967 Riots*. Hong Kong: Hong Kong University Press, 2009.

Cheung, Kin-chung. "CS' "Letter to Hong Kong" (English only)." April 11, 2021. https://www.info.gov.hk/gia/general/202104/11/P2021040900747p.htm

Dimache, Alexandru, Amare Wondirad, and Elizabeth Agyeiwaah. "One Museum, Two Stories: Place Identity at the Hong Kong Museum of History." *Tourism Management* 63 (2017): 287–301.

Donny Mok. "2 Hong Kong Men Held Over Disorderly Conduct After Allegedly Soaking Hong Kong Police Officers with Water Gun at Songkran Festival." *South China Morning Post*, April 13, 2023. https://www.scmp.com/news/hong-kong/law-and-crime/article/3216857/2-hong-kong-men-held-over-disorderly-conduct-after-allegedly-soaking-hong-kong-police-officers-water

Eagleton, Jennifer. *Discursive Change in Hong Kong Sociopolitical Dynamics, Metaphor, and One Country, Two Systems.* Lanham, Maryland: Rowman and Littlefield, 2022.

Eagleton, Terry. *Ideology: An Introduction.* London; New York: Verso, 1991.

Ethical Journalism Network. "Ethics 101: The Five Core Values of Journalism." Ethical Journalism Network, n.d. https://ethicaljournalismnetwork.org/5-core-values-of-journalism

Gentle, Nick. "Premature Destruction of Falun Gong Records by the Immigration Department. South China Morning Post, March 9, 2007. https://www.scmp.com/article/584312/judge-queries-destruction-falun-gong-files

Gittings, John. "Hong Kong's New Museums: Tradition and Challenge." SOAS China Institute, November 16, 2022. https://blogs.soas.ac.uk/china-institute/2022/11/16/hong-kongs-new-museums-tradition-andchallenge/.

Grundy, Tom. "Hong Kong's John Lee Chides Reporter for Referring to 2019 'Protests' Instead of 'the Black Violence'." *Hong Kong Free Press.* May 3, 2023. https://hongkongfp.com/2023/05/03/hong-kongs-john-lee-chides-reporter-for-referring-to-2019-protests-instead-of-the-black-violence/

Hamlett, Tim. "You Want 'Good' Hong Kong Stories? Do Something About the Bad Ones." *Hong Kong Free Press*, August 27, 2022. https://hongkongfp.com/2022/08/27/you-want-good-hong-kong-stories-do-something-about-the-bad-ones/

Hamlett, Tim. "Can You Trust these People to Record Hong Kong's History? The Rewriting of the Yuen Long Narrative Speaks Volumes." *Hong Kong Free Press*, January 8, 2021. https://hongkongfp.com/2021/01/08/can-you-trust-these-people-to-record-hong-kongs-history-the-rewriting-of-the-yuen-long-narrative-speaks-volumes/

Han, Yong Hong. The Hong Kong story according to John Lee amid criticisms from the West. https://www.thinkchina.sg/politics/hong-kong-story-according-john-lee-amid-criticisms-west 8 July 2022 By Translated by Candice Chan, Grace Chong.

Hayek, Friedrich A. von *The Road to Serfdom.* (1944) https://ctheory.sitehost.iu.edu/img/Hayek_The_Road_to_Serfdom.pdf

HKFP. "Explainer: What is 'Soft Resistance'? Hong Kong Officials Vow to Take a Hard Line Against It, but Provide No Definition." *Hong Kong Free Press*, August 5, 2023. https://hongkongfp.com/2023/08/05/explainer-what-is-soft-resistance-hong-kong-officials-vow-to-take-a-hard-line-against-it-but-provide-no-definition/

Ho, Kelly. "Yuen Long Attacks: Hong Kong Lawmaker Granted Bail as Police Chief Denies Trying to Rewrite History." *Hong Kong Free Press*, August 28, 2020. https://hongkongfp.com/2020/08/28/yuen-long-attacks-hong-kong-lawmaker-granted-bail-as-police-chief-denies-trying-to-rewrite-history

Hong Kong Gov. "Tell Good Stories About Hong Kong" (a section of the 2022 Policy Address), October 19, 2022. https://www.policyaddress.gov.hk/2022/en/p143.html

Info.gov.hk June 16, 2019 Government response to public procession https://www.info.gov.hk/gia/general/201906/16/P2019061600803p.htm

IPCC. "Thematic Study Report Independent Police Complaints Council" – Press Release." Independent Police Complaints Council, May 15, 2020. https://www.ipcc.gov.hk/doc/en/pr/pr_20200515_e.pdf

Jaworski, Adam, Richard Fitzgerald, and Deborah Morris. "Certainty and Speculation in News Reporting of the Future: The Execution of Timothy McVeigh." *Discourse Studies* 5, no. 1 (2003a): 33–49.

Jaworski, Adam, Richard Fitzgerald, Deborah Morris, and Galinsky, D. (2003b). "Beyond Regency: The Discourse of the Future in BBC Radio News." *Belgian Journal of English Language and Literature*. New Series I (2003): 61–72.

Jaworski, Adam, Richard Fitzgerald, and Deborah Morris. "Radio leaks – Presenting and Contesting Leaks in Radio News Broadcasts." *Journalism* 5, no. 2 (2004): 183–202.

Kilpatrick, Ryan Ho. "Soft Resistance." The China Media Project, May 26, 2023. https://chinamediaproject.org/the_ccp_dictionary/soft-resistance/

Kraar, Louis and Joe McGowan. "The Death of Hong Kong." *Fortune*, June 26, 1995. https://money.cnn.com/magazines/fortune/fortune_archive/1995/06/26/203948/.

Lai, Geoffrey. "History Museum was Far from Perfect, But It Now Faces a Gov't-sanctioned Revamp." *Hong Kong Free Press*, October 18, 2020. https://hongkongfp.com/2020/10/18/history-museums-hong-kong-story-was-far-from-perfect-but-it-now-faces-a-govt-sanctioned-rewrite

Lam, Jeffie, Danny Mok, and Alvin Lum, Alvin. "At Least 45 Injured as Rod-wielding Mob Dressed in White Rampages through Yuen Long MTR Station, Beating Screaming Protesters." *South China Morning Post*, July 22, 2019. https://www.scmp.com/news/hong-kong/law-and-crime/article/3019524/least-10-injured-baton-wielding-mob-suspected-triad

Li, Simon (Hong Kong Public Records Concern Group). "Without Archives Law, Code on Access to Information is Useless." LC Paper No. CB (2)1541/09-10(01); Written Submission on the Management of Public Records, n.d. https://www.legco.gov.hk/yr09-10/chinese/panels/ca/papers/ca0517cb2-1541-1-ec.pdf

Lim, Louisa. *Indelible City – Dispossession a Defiance in Hong Kong*. Melbourne: Text Publishing Company, 2022.

Loh, Christine. *Underground Front: The Chinese Communist Party in Hong Kong*. Hong Kong: Hong Kong University Press, 2010.

McCullagh, C. Behan. "The Truth of Historical Narratives." *History and Theory* 26, no. 4 (1987): 30–46.

Neiger, Motti. "Media Oracles: The Political Import and Cultural Significance of News Referring to the future. *Journalism: Theory, Practice & Criticism* 8, no. 3 (2007): 326–338.

News.gov.hk. "Strategies to Tell HK's Good Stories." October 19, 2022. https://www.news.gov.hk/eng/2022/10/20221019/20221019_093105_345.html

Overhalt, William H. "The Rise and Fall of "One Country, Two Systems." Harvard Kennedy School, Ash Center for Democratic Governance and Innovation, December 2019. https://ash.harvard.edu/wp-content/uploads/2024/02/overholt_hong_kong_paper_final.pdf

Patton, Christopher (1997). "Hong Kong Handover Ceremony Address." delivered June 30, 1997, Tamar, Hong Kong. https://www.americanrhetoric.com/speeches/chrispattenhongkonghandoverceremony.htm

Ricoeur, Paul. "Narrative Time." *Critical Inquiry* 7, no. 1 (Autumn, 1980): 169–190.

Richburg, Keith. "It Took a While but the Death of Hong Kong has Arrived." October 9, 2018. https://www.keithrichburg.com/keith-richburg-expelling-foreign-correspondent-marks-beginning-hong-kongs-demise/

SCMP. "Those Who Unfairly Criticise Hong Kong Must Be Put in Their Place." *South China Morning Post,* December 6, 2023. https://www.scmp.com/comment/opinion/article/3243988/those-who-unfairly-criticise-hong-kong-must-be-put-their-place

Se, Kenji Kawase, and Peggy Ye "Hong Kong Makes First Known Arrests under Article 23 Security Law." Asia.nikkei.com, May 28, 2024. https://asia.nikkei.com/Spotlight/Hong-Kong-security-law/Hong-Kong-makes-first-known-arrests-under-Article-23-security-law

Tai, Benny. "The Death of Hong Kong's Rule of Law." November 29, 2020. https://www.promarket.org/2020/11/29/hong-kong-rule-of-law-authoritarian-national-security-law/.

The Standard. "(Policy Address 2023) New Offices and Museums to Step up Game in Patriotic Education." *The Standard*, October 25, 2023. https://www.thestandard.com.hk/breaking-news/section/4/209611/(Policy-Address-2023)-New-offices-and-museums-to-step-up-game-in-patriotic-education

Tong, Trevor. "Hong Kong Palace Museum Opens with Treasures Loaned from Beijing." The China Project, July 14, 2022. https://thechinaproject.com/2022/07/14/hong-kong-palace-museum-opens-with-treasures-loaned-from-beijing/

Tse, Hans. Hong Kong police charge 2 men with property damage over alleged disruption of organ donation register." *Hong Kong Free Press*, November 9, 2023. https://hongkongfp.com/2023/11/09/hong-kong-police-charge-2-men-with-property-damage-over-alleged-disruption-of-organ-donation-register/

Tu, Haiming. "Vigilance Against 'soft resistance' Warranted." *China Daily*, Hong Kong edition. August 18, 2023. https://www.chinadailyhk.com/hk/article/346362

Wang, Wallis. "Cathay Fires Three Cabin Crew over Mocking of Non-English Speakers." *South China Morning Post*, May 24, 2023. https://www.thestandard.com.hk/section-news/section/11/252732/Cathay-fires-three-cabin-crew-over-mocking-of-non-English-speakers/.

Wong, Natalie. "Hong Kong's John Lee Rebuts 'Badmouthing' of National Security Law, Stresses Criminal Intent Key When Determining Guilt." *South China Morning Post*, June 29, 2023. https://www.scmp.com/news/hong-kong/politics/article/3225807/hong-kongs-john-lee-rebuts-badmouthing-national-security-law-stresses-criminal-intent-key-when

Wu, Alice. "Hong Kong Isn't Dead (Yet), But It Has Lost Its Edge. *South China Morning Post*, November 5, 2018. https://www.scmp.com/comment/insight-opinion/hong-kong/article/2171449/hong-kong-isnt-dead-yet-it-has-lost-its-edge

Zhang, Zoey. "Is Hong Kong Really a 'Cursed' City?" *Global Times*. April 16, 2021. https://www.globaltimes.cn/page/202104/1221251.shtml

Zizek, Slavoj. *The Sublime Object of Ideology*. London; New York: Verso, 1989.

Index[1]

[1] Note: Page numbers followed by 'n' refer to notes.

J. Eagleton, *Hong Kong's Second Return to China*,
https://doi.org/10.1007/978-3-031-84587-1

The manufacturer's authorised representative in the EU is Springer Nature Customer Service Centre GmbH, Europaplatz 3, 69115 Heidelberg, Germany. If you have any concerns regarding our products, please contact ProductSafety@springernature.com

Printed and bound by CPI Group (UK) Ltd, Croydon, CR0 4YY
30/09/2026
02225595-0008